Economic Sanctions and American Diplomacy

Economic Sanctions and American Diplomacy

Edited by Richard N. Haass

A COUNCIL ON FOREIGN RELATIONS BOOK

The Council on Foreign Relations, Inc., a nonprofit, nonpartisan national membership organization founded in 1921, is dedicated to promoting understanding of international affairs through the free and civil exchange of ideas. The Council's members are dedicated to the belief that America's peace and prosperity are firmly linked to that of the world. From this flows the mission of the Council: to foster America's understanding of its fellow members of the international community, near and far, their peoples, cultures, histories, hopes, quarrels, and ambitions; and thus to serve, protect, and advance America's own global interests through study and debate, private and public.

From time to time books, monographs, and reports written by members of the Council's research staff or others are published as a "Council on Foreign Relations Book." Any work bearing that designation is, in the judgment of the Committee on Studies of the Council's Board of Directors, a responsible treatment of a significant international topic.

Council on Foreign Relations Books are distributed by Brookings Institution Press (1-800-275-1447). For further information on Council publications, please write the Council on Foreign Relations, 58 East 68th Street, New York, NY 10021, or call the Director of Communications at (212) 434-9400. Or visit our web site at www.foreignrelations.org.

Library of Congress Cataloging-in-Publication Data

Economic sanctions and American diplomacy / edited by Richard N. Haass.
   p.   cm.
   Includes bibliographical references and index.
   ISBN 0-87609-212-1
   1. Economic sanctions.   2. Economic sanctions, American.
   3. United States—Foreign relations—1993.   I. Haass, Richard.
KZ6373.E28   1998
327.1'17—DC21   98-23408
                                                   CIP

Contents

Foreword

WHILE ECONOMIC sanctions have long been a mainstay of U.S. diplomacy, now that the Cold War is over they play a more central role. U.S. policymakers frequently turn to sanctions as a policy response to international crises and rogue states. Accordingly, in April 1996 the Council on Foreign Relations undertook a study of economic sanctions as a tool of American foreign policy under the leadership of Richard N. Haass, now Director of Foreign Policy Studies at the Brookings Institution (and previously Director of National Security Programs at the Council). The study group, consisting of members drawn from universities, government, and the private sector, discussed each of the chapters included in this volume. Their deliberations helped shape the book.

The purpose of *Economic Sanctions and American Diplomacy* is to provide a detailed analysis of the use of economic sanctions in the post–Cold War era. Eight case studies were selected to illuminate the wide range of sanctions currently employed by the United States. The chapters examine China, Cuba, Haiti, Iran, Iraq, Libya, Pakistan, and the former Yugoslavia as target countries. Each chapter analyzes the voice of domestic constituencies in shaping U.S. sanctions policy; the legal authority invoked to implement sanctions; the impact of U.S. sanctions on American allies; and the characteristics of target states that make them more or less vulnerable to sanctions. Each case study offers conclusions about whether sanctions "worked" against the target, as well as their consequences for the United States, its allies, and the world system. The result is a volume that is instructive in every sense: It contributes to what we know of this increasingly important foreign policy instrument, and it makes clear how we can better use economic sanctions in the future.

Gary C. Hufbauer
Maurice R. Greenberg Chair, Director of Studies
Council on Foreign Relations

Acknowledgments

A LL BOOKS, even those authored by a single individual, are in reality collaborative efforts. This book, however, is more collective a product than most.

To begin with, there are the seven authors of the eight case studies, Patrick Clawson, Dennis Kux, Eric D. K. Melby, Susan Kaufman Purcell, Gideon Rose, Robert Ross, and Stephen Stedman.

For obvious reasons, I am beholden to them. In turn, we are beholden to the other members of the Council on Foreign Relations study group that participated in this project. Members of the study group included Dan Bob, Holly Burkhalter, Andrew Carpendale, Richard Clarke, David Cortright, Chester A. Crocker, Lori F. Damrosch, Timothy Deal, Terry Deibel, Marynell Devaughn, Frederick Downey, Kimberly Elliott, Pamela S. Falk, Robert Fauver, Joseph Fromm, Joseph Gavin, H. P. Goldfield, David Goldwyn, Morton Halperin, Adonis Hoffman, Kenneth Juster, Abraham Katz, Jonathan Kirshner, Ian O. Lesser, John H. Lichtblau, George Lopez, Michael Mastanduno, Robert Maxim, James Nathan, R. Richard Newcomb, Daniel O'Flaherty, Ann Pickard, Ernest Preeg, Arthur Ross, Susan C. Schwab, John Stremlau, Raymond Tanter, Enzo Viscusi, Sidney Weintraub, Edwin D. Williamson, Serena Lynn Wilson, and Andrew Winner. They not only met but critiqued draft cases, both verbally at the meetings and in written comments provided to the authors. Others who took the time to make comments included Daniel Poneman, Bruce Riedel, and Bernard Aronson.

Mary Richards is to be recognized and praised for providing the administrative support for this undertaking. Such support ranged from organizing the meetings to making sure that people had drafts to read beforehand. Together with Kari Rogers, she labored mightily to ready the final manuscript. This project would never have been completed without their efforts.

This project also would never have seen the light of day without support of a different kind from two other sources. The first is Arthur Ross, whose intellectual curiosity about the issue was matched by his generosity. The second is the Smith Richardson Foundation. In particular, I want to thank Marin Strmecki for his unflagging interest.

For the record, I also want to acknowledge Les Gelb who, as President of the Council on Foreign Relations, merits an award for his enduring commitment to this project and his patience. I began it while at the Council and completed it after moving to Brookings. I only hope that the result was worth waiting for.

Richard N. Haass

Contributors

Richard N. Haass is Director of Foreign Policy Studies at the Brookings Institution. From 1989 to1993 he was Special Assistant to President George Bush and Senior Director for Near East and South Asian Affairs on the staff of the National Security Council. He also was Director of National Security Programs and a Senior Fellow of the Council on Foreign Relations, and is the author of several books, including *The Reluctant Sheriff: The United States after the Cold War* (1997).

Patrick Clawson is Director for Research at the Washington Institute for Near East Policy. Previously he served as Senior Research Professor at the Institute for National Strategic Studies of the National Defense University, where he was editor of *Strategic Assessment*. He is also Senior Editor of *Middle East Quarterly*, a position he assumed in 1993 after four years as Editor of *Orbis*. From 1981 to 1992, Clawson was a Senior Economist for four years each at the Foreign Policy Research Institute, the World Bank, and the International Monetary Fund.

Susan Kaufman Purcell is Vice President of the Americas Society and Council of the Americas in New York City. Between 1981 and 1988 she was a Senior Fellow and Director of the Latin American Project at the Council on Foreign Relations. She was also a member of the U.S. State Department's Policy Planning Staff, with responsibility for Latin America and the Caribbean, between 1980 and 1981. Dr. Purcell is also author or editor of several books on Latin America, including *Mexico Under Zedillo* (1998).

Dennis Kux served in the Foreign Service from 1955 to 1994. From 1986 to 1990, he was U.S. Ambassador to the Ivory Coast. He also served as Deputy Assistant Secretary, Bureau of Intelligence and Research, from 1981 to 1984 and as Deputy Director of Management Operations from 1984 to 1986. In addition, he worked as the Senior Political Officer for India from 1972 to 1974 and as Country Director for India, Nepal, and Sri Lanka from 1974 to 1977. His overseas assignments included Pakistan, India, Germany, and Turkey.

Eric D. K. Melby is a Senior Fellow at the Forum for International Policy. From 1987 to 1993 he handled trade and economic issues on the National Security Council staff. He has also served in the Department of State, the Agency for International Development, the International Energy Agency, and the Peace Corps.

Gideon Rose is Deputy Director of National Security Studies and Olin Fellow at the Council on Foreign Relations. He served as Associate Director of Near East and South Asian Affairs on the National Security Council staff in 1994 to 1995.

Robert S. Ross is Professor of Political Science at Boston College and Research Associate at the John King Fairbank Center for East Asian Research, Harvard University. His most recent books include *Negotiating Cooperation: U.S.-China Relations, 1969-1989* (1995) and *Great Wall and Empty Fortress: China's Search for Security* (1997).

Stephen John Stedman is Senior Research Scholar at the Center for International Security and Arms Control at Stanford University. Previously he was Associate Professor at the Johns Hopkins University School of Advanced International Studies. In 1995, Stedman was a consultant for the United Nations on peacekeeping in civil wars and on problems of weapons proliferation in Africa.

Introduction

RICHARD N. HAASS

T HE WIDESPREAD use of economic sanctions constitutes one of the great paradoxes of contemporary American foreign policy. Sanctions are frequently criticized, even derided. "Sanctions don't work" is an oft-heard refrain. At the same time, economic sanctions are fast becoming the policy tool of choice for the United States in the post–Cold War world.

The evidence of the latter contention is widespread. The United States now maintains economic sanctions against literally dozens of countries. One recent study listed no less than 35 countries that had been targeted by new American sanctions from 1993 to 1996 alone.[1] What is critical, however, is not just the frequency with which economic sanctions are used but their importance. Increasingly, sanctions define or dominate a number of significant relationships and policies.

Sanctions—predominantly economic but also political and military penalties aimed at a state or other entities to alter political and/or military behavior—are employed for a wide range of purposes. Indeed, sanctions are now used by the United States to discourage the proliferation of weapons of mass destruction and ballistic missiles, promote human rights, end support for terrorism, thwart drug trafficking, discourage armed aggression, protect the environment, and replace governments. In any of these areas, the tactical purpose of a given sanction can be to deter, coerce, signal, and/or punish.

Excluded by this definition are sanctions introduced solely for the purpose of ensuring market access or compliance with trade arrangements. Such sanctions are different in several important ways: They are reactions to economic policy and behavior; they are meant to change economic policy or behavior; and they are introduced pursuant to an existing set of rules that govern or at least guide trade. The purpose of this study by contrast is to examine the use of economic sanctions for noneconomic purposes where there is little or no agreed legal or political framework.[2]

Actual sanctions range across the economic, military, and political spectrums. At various times, sanctions have taken the form of arms embargoes, foreign assistance reductions and cut-offs, export and import limitations, asset blockages and freezes, tariff increases, import quota decreases, revocation of most-favored-nation (MFN) trade status, votes in international organizations, withdrawal of diplomatic relations, visa denials, cancellation of air links, and prohibitions on credit, financing, and investment.

The legal bases for sanctions also have multiplied. A number of sanctions are implemented by the president or his designated representative exercising powers that exist in omnibus federal statutes. U.S. sanctions against individual countries also are codified in public laws passed by Congress and signed by the president; introduced through executive orders introduced by the president alone; and taken pursuant to resolutions of the United Nations Security Council.[3] Sanctions are even increasingly the result of measures passed at the state and municipal levels throughout the United States.[4]

What explains the popularity of sanctions? There is no single cause. There are, however, a number of inspirations and explanations. Sanctions can offer what appears to be a proportional response to a challenge in which the interests at stake are judged to be less than vital. In addition, sanctions are a form of expression, a way to communicate official displeasure with a certain behavior or action. They thus satisfy a domestic political need to do something and can serve to reinforce a commitment to a behavioral norm, such as respect for human rights or opposition to proliferation. In principle, such message-sending has the potential to affect the behavior of uninvolved but observant third parties, possibly deterring them from taking some action for fear of being penalized.

American reluctance to use military force is another motivation—particularly in those instances in which U.S. interests are not deemed sufficiently important to justify casualties and high financial costs. Sanctions provide a visible and less expensive alternative to military intervention at the same time they provide an alternative to doing nothing or limiting the U.S. reaction to rhetoric. Such sentiment captures the conditional support lent to economic sanctions by America's Catholic bishops: "Sanctions can offer a nonmilitary alternative to the terrible options of war or indifference when confronted with aggression or injustice."[5] In this sense, sanctions constitute not simply a form of expression but an action, one that appears to involve less risk and cost (be it human, financial, or moral) than using military force.

The great frequency with which sanctions are used is also a result of the increased strength of single-issue constituencies in American politics. Small, organized, focused groups can have an impact far beyond their actual strength, especially (and as is often the case) when no equally focused countervailing force exists. Many vocal constituencies argue that sanctions contributed to the achievement of U.S. policy aims in the past—for example, in helping to bring about an end to communism in the Soviet Union or apartheid in South Africa—and can do so again in different contexts.

The growth of congressional power also helps explain the prevalence of economic sanctions. The Constitution divided the foreign affairs power between Congress and the executive, and over the past quarter century there has been a shift in the pendulum toward Congress. Thus sanctions are introduced regularly by members of Congress—often at the behest of single or special interest groups—through legislation or as amendments to legislation.

The greater reach of media is another factor. The so-called CNN effect can increase the visibility throughout the United States of problems in another country and stimulate a desire on the part of Americans to respond. Sanctions offer a popular and seemingly cost-free way of so doing.

Despite these changes, sanctions are nothing new to the United States. The American Revolution was in part a revolt against British sanctions. Indeed, sanctions occupy an important if not always distinguished place in U.S. history. Sanctions helped trigger the War of 1812, weakened the Confederacy a half century later, and were levied against Spain during the Spanish-American War of 1898.

Sanctions were also an important tool of American statecraft during the Cold War. At times, the target was the behavior of the Soviet Union and its allies. Prominent among such efforts were the linking of most-favored-nation trade status to Soviet emigration practices and the embargo introduced against Cuba soon after the Communist takeover. But the United States also resorted to sanctions against other countries to settle what were viewed as illegal expropriations, to destabilize unfriendly governments, or to penalize foreign countries for their use of military force beyond their borders.[6] In the 1970s and 1980s, sanctions also were commonly employed to further U.S. nonproliferation and human rights objectives.[7]

Sanctions also have been a tool for others throughout the twentieth century. In the 1930s, the League of Nations undermined much of what promise and legitimacy it had with its failure to implement meaningful sanctions against Italy in response to Mussolini's aggression in Abyssinia. Sanctions were the central instrument relied on by the United Kingdom and the international community in the aftermath of Rhodesia's unilateral declaration of independence in 1965. Economic sanctions—the so-called Arab Boycott—were a central element of the Arab world's rejection of Israel.[8]

Much of the scholarship that focuses on these and other early experiences tends to be relatively harsh in its judgments of the effectiveness of sanctions. By contrast, many advocates of sanctions cite the high-profile South Africa case as evidence that sanctions can work.[9] To be sure, sanctions may have contributed to change in that instance. But the rapidity of change within South Africa cannot be connected to any meaningful ratcheting up of sanctions, which suggests that factors other than sanctions mattered as much or more. Moreover, even if sanctions did contribute to political change in South Africa, it is not obvious that all of the specific sanctions did so or did so equally or that they did not have undesirable side effects—for example, in retarding the emergence of a large middle class—along the way.

The South African case highlights a crucial problem for those who study sanctions. It is often impossible to isolate the effect of sanctions as distinct from the many other domestic and international factors at work in a given situation. It is similarly difficult to distinguish between the effect of one sanction and another. Still, it is necessary to try to measure the impact of sanctions—the frequency of their use demands it—even as one acknowledges the difficulty.

The purpose of this volume is to explore the growing importance of economic sanctions as a tool of American foreign policy. No other country uses economic sanctions so frequently—and no other country possesses America's power and influence. The goal is to derive insights and lessons drawn from recent American use of economic sanctions and to suggest guidelines for when and how sanctions should be used by the United States in the future. In so doing, an effort will be made to avoid broad generalizations about whether sanctions "work." (The most influential study thus far published on the subject concludes that economic sanctions have worked to some extent about one-third of the time.)[10] As is the case with most any other policy tool, the answer to the question "Do sanctions work?" must necessarily be "It depends." The goal of this volume is to determine just what it is that the impact of economic sanctions most depends on and to make policy-relevant recommendations based on these conclusions.

When assessing the impact of sanctions, it is important to avoid being more demanding of sanctions than of the alternatives. As David

Baldwin has usefully pointed out, any judgment of the utility of sanctions should not be made in isolation but compared to what could have been expected from using other policy tools, including private and public diplomacy, covert action, and military intervention. Thus, what is required is not just a weighing of the costs and benefits of a particular sanction but a comparison of the likely costs and benefits that would result from doing something else or nothing at all.[11]

One priority of this study is to highlight precisely what determines the effectiveness of sanctions, be it the scale of the goals, political and economic characteristics of the target, the nature and severity of the sanctions themselves, the degree of multilateral support, the source of any legal foundation, the duration the sanction was in place, the availability of military enforcement, or something altogether different. Case studies also will endeavor to demonstrate what particular sanctions accomplished—and what costs were experienced by all involved in the process.

Such analysis is not intended to be an end in itself. A second priority of this study is to generate guidelines for the future use of economic sanctions by the United States. In addition, a related aim will be to identify those reforms necessary to increase the ability of the executive branch and Congress to make intelligent decisions about the use of sanctions and to implement such decisions more efficiently.

The decision to focus analysis on a relatively recent period—one can fairly date the end of the Cold War to 1989—reflects the widespread use of sanctions in this period and the changed context.[12] The end of the Cold War and the demise of the Soviet Union altered international relations in basic ways. In many cases sanctions can now be introduced without Russian opposition, be it political (where a Russian veto in the Security Council is by no means automatic); economic (Russia has less of a commitment to relationships that would lead it to provide aid and thereby offset any penalty imposed on one of its allies); or military (Russia is less likely than was the Soviet Union to block any Western or U.S. attempt to enforce a trade-related sanction). In this sense at least, the end of the Cold War should make sanctions an instrument of greater potential impact.

The focus on the contemporary era reflects one other factor, namely, changes in the structure of international society. There is a greater number of states and nonstate actors as well as an increase in the volume of world trade and economic activity more generally. At least in theory, this greater degree of globalization (and the somewhat reduced centrality of the nation-state) ought to have an adverse impact overall on the effectiveness of sanctions. A target state now has many more potential suppliers and markets—and a would-be sanctioner has many more entities to enlist before sanctions are likely to be effective.

To help provide a basis for judgments and recommendations, this study draws heavily on eight cases: China, Cuba, Haiti, Iran, Iraq, Libya, Pakistan, and the former Yugoslavia. These eight cases are among the most prominent examples of sanctions used by the United States in the post–Cold War world. They are also quite different from one another in important aspects, something that is necessary if general propositions are to emerge.

China is a case where the United States introduced sanctions in part because of proliferation-related activity. In addition, sanctions were introduced for human rights reasons following the June 1989 suppression of dissent in Tiananmen Square. The case is useful in adding to what we know about the utility of sanctions in promoting U.S. interests in both these areas—and, perhaps more important, to the utility of introducing sanctions against a major country with whom the United States has a broad range of important or even vital interests.

Cuba is the case in which sanctions have been in effect for the longest period. It is also a case in which the United States stands alone, where Congress and public opinion have played a major role, and where (similarly now to Iran and Libya) U.S. law (the Helms-Burton legislation) would sanction not just Cuba but those countries, firms, and individuals who choose not to comply with U.S. sanctions. It also highlights one of the basic foreign policy questions of our era, namely, whether economic sanctions and policies of denial are more likely to promote desired political and economic changes in a society than policies of constructive, conditional engagement in which political and economic incentives (including the removal of sanctions) also are used to bring about desired reform.

Haiti demonstrates the phenomenon of unintended consequences, in this case, the torrent of refugees who headed for Florida. Haiti, though, is an important case for another reason. It highlights what can be the blunt nature of the sanctions tool. Political leaders and other elites often are able to shield themselves from the worst effects of broad sanctions, something most of the population is unable to do. Haiti also highlights the potential for sanctions to be designed so as to narrow their impact on select individuals or groups in a society.

Iran represents a unilateral, congressionally driven approach to sanctions by the United States. Washington has not been able to persuade most other nations that Iran's behavior, including its support for terrorism, subversion, and opposition to the Middle East peace process, warrants sharp economic penalties. As a result, the effects of sanctions on Iran are less clear-cut, although there have been consequences for U.S. relations with several of its traditional friends in Europe.

Iraq presents an almost archetypical case of "ideal" sanctions. Iraq's 1990 invasion and occupation of Kuwait constituted a clear-cut violation of a widely held international norm. Sanctions were introduced with full U.N. Security Council backing. Iraq's economy was highly dependent on the ability to sell oil. The sanctions were comprehensive and enforced militarily. Still, sanctions proved unable to persuade Saddam Hussein to vacate Kuwait, even when the alternative was war with the United States and a powerful international coalition. This is not the same as saying the sanctions failed completely, however, especially as regards those additional sanctions levied against Iraq in the aftermath of Desert Storm. Sanctions against Iraq have had multiple effects, and the case shows how sanctions can work in some ways even if they do not achieve their stated or maximum objectives.

Libya is one more case of sanctions introduced against an authoritarian, rogue state in the Middle East. Various sanctions were introduced at various times in response to a number of Libyan actions, including support for terrorism, development of chemical weapons, and subversion of its neighbors. In addition, strong evidence of Libyan complicity in the destruction of Pan Am Flight 103 over Lockerbie, Scotland, in 1988 led to additional sanctions. Like those directed toward Iraq, at least some of the sanctions enjoy broad international support. Like those directed toward Iran, though, some are solely American, introduced as a result of congressional initiative, and are causing significant problems for U.S. relations with several of its principal allies who are unwilling to further isolate Libya economically or politically.

Pakistan is a case in which sanctions have been introduced by the United States through legislation as a result of Pakistan's efforts to develop a nuclear weapons capability. Stemming such proliferation is a major goal of American foreign policy. This case offers insights into the utility of sanctions for this purpose—but also into the importance of weighing particular sanctions against the alternatives and how sanctions can adversely affect U.S. interests in a country beyond the policy concerns that prompted their use in the first place.

The former Yugoslavia, like Iraq, is a case in which economic and military sanctions were introduced with broad and formal international support. It offers insight into the potential and limits of sanctions as a coercive tool and as an adjunct to diplomacy and conflict resolution. Just as important, this case is also noteworthy for the phenomenon of unintended consequences, namely, that sanctions—specifically, the arms embargo that hurt Bosnia far more than either Croatia or Serbia— often have effects not anticipated and not necessarily desired by the United States.

Notes

1. *A Catalog of New U.S. Unilateral Economic Sanctions for Foreign Policy Purposes 1993–96* (Washington, DC: National Association of Manufacturers, 1997).

2. Also excluded from this study are general export controls, measures put in place by the U.S. government (often in association with others) to slow or disrupt the efforts of target states to acquire or develop technologies involving selected conventional armaments, chemical, biological and nuclear weapons, and/or advanced delivery systems. Such controls are not linked to altering or punishing particular behavior but are intended to further the foreign policy objective or norm of discouraging the proliferation of potentially destabilizing technologies and weapon systems.

3. See report of the President's Export Council, prepared with the assistance of Don Zarin and Meha Shah, *U.S. Unilateral Economic Sanctions: A Review of Existing Sanctions and Their Impacts on U.S. Economic Interests with Recommendations for Policy and Process Improvement*, Appendix I, Survey of U.S. Unilateral Economic Sanctions (Washington, DC: The President's Export Council, January 11, 1997).

4. See Paul Blustein, "Thinking Globally, Punishing Locally," *Washington Post*, May 16, 1997, pp. G1–2.

5. National Conference of Catholic Bishops, "The Harvest of Justice Is Sown in Peace: A Reflection of the National Conference of Bishops on the Tenth Anniversary of *The Challenge to Peace*" (Washington, DC: United States Catholic Conference, 1994).

6. See, for example, Sidney Weintraub (ed.), *Economic Coercion and U.S. Foreign Policy: Implications of Case Studies from the Johnson Administration* (Boulder, CO: Westview, 1982).

7. For basic background, see Erin Day, *Economic Sanctions Imposed by the United States Against Specific Countries: 1979 Through 1992* (Washington, DC: Congressional Research Service, 1992).

8. For background, see Margaret P. Doxey, *Economic Sanctions and International Enforcement* (London: Oxford University Press, 1971); Donald L. Losman, *International Economic Sanctions: The Cases of Cuba, Israel and Rhodesia* (Albuquerque, NM: University of New Mexico Press, 1979); Johan Galtung, "On the Effects of International Economic Sanctions: With Examples from the Case of Rhodesia," *World Politics* 19 (April 1967),

pp. 378–416; and Robin Renwick, *Economic Sanctions* (Cambridge, MA: Harvard University Center for International Affairs, 1981).

9. See, for example, Jennifer Davis, "Squeezing Apartheid," *Bulletin of the Atomic Scientists* 49, no. 9 (November 1993), pp. 16–19. For books that place the effects of sanctions on South Africa in a larger perspective, see Patti Waldmeir, *Anatomy of a Miracle: The End of Apartheid and the Birth of a New South Africa* (New York: W.W. Norton, 1997), and Allister Sparks, *Tomorrow Is Another Country: The Inside Story of South Africa's Road to Change* (New York: Hill & Wang, 1995).

10. Gary Clyde Hufbauer, Jeffrey J. Schott, and Kimberly Ann Elliott, *Economic Sanctions Reconsidered: History and Current Policy,* (Washington, DC: Institute for International Economics, 1990, 2nd ed.). This relatively positive assessment is itself hotly disputed on grounds that the authors were overly generous in judging what constitutes "success" and in not properly disaggregating the effects of sanctions from the impact of the threat or use of military force. See Robert A. Pape, "Why Economic Sanctions Still Do Not Work," *International Security* 22, no. 2 (Fall 1997), pp. 90–136. On this general question also see Makio Miyagawa, *Do Economic Sanctions Work?* (New York: St. Martin's Press, 1992); Lisa L. Martin, *Coercive Cooperation: Explaining Multilateral Economic Sanctions* (Princeton, NJ: Princeton University Press, 1992); and David Leyton-Brown (ed.), *The Utility of International Economic Sanctions* (New York: St. Martin's Press, 1987).

11. David A. Baldwin, *Economic Statecraft* (Princeton, NJ: Princeton University Press, 1985). For a similar theme, see Otto Wolff von Amerongen, "Economic Sanctions as a Foreign Policy Tool," *International Security* 5, no. 2 (Fall 1980), pp. 159–167.

12. For assessments of recent experience with sanctions, see David Cortright and George A. Lopez (eds.), *Economic Sanctions: Panacea or Peacebuilding in a Post–Cold War World?* (Boulder, CO: Westview, 1995); Elizabeth S. Rogers, "Economic Sanctions and Internal Conflict," in Michael E. Brown (ed.), *The International Dimensions of Internal Conflict* (Cambridge, MA: Center for Science and International Affairs, 1996), pp. 411–34; "Sanctions: Do They Work?" *Bulletin of the Atomic Scientists* 49, no. 9 (November 1993), pp. 14–49; John Stremlau, *Sharpening International Sanctions: Toward a Stronger Role for the United Nations* (New York: Carnegie Corporation, 1996); and Lisa L. Martin and Jeffrey Laurenti, *The United Nations and Economic Sanctions: Improving Regime Effectiveness* (New York: United Nations Association of the United States of America, 1997). Also see the Hufbauer et. al. volume cited in note 10 above.

1

China

ROBERT S. ROSS

T HE THREAT and application of economic sanctions have been central elements of Washington's effort to change Chinese domestic and international behavior. The United States has employed two distinct forms of sanctions in two distinct policy areas. To change China's human rights practices, the United States has threatened to terminate China's most-favored-nation (MFN) trading status and effectively end China's access to the U.S. market. To change China's proliferation policies, Washington has threatened and at times applied sanctions restricting Chinese access to advanced technologies. The outcome has been different in each area. The threat to suspend China's MFN status has had little impact on the country's treatment of dissidents. But U.S. policy has influenced Chinese policies in both areas and particularly in the realm of proliferation.

This chapter argues that sanctions are best understood as a form of traditional retaliation—one country threatens to retaliate against another country by adopting policy intended to hurt the interests of the other country if it does not satisfy a demand. As in any attempt to use sanctions to influence behavior, the explanation for the effectiveness of U.S. China policy is the combination of the cost of the sanction on Chinese interests compared to the costs to China of compromise and the credibility of the United States to carry out its threat to harm Chinese interests, a function of the cost to the United States of imposing the sanction and the importance of the interests involved.[1]

U.S. policy has been successful in shaping Chinese proliferation policy because Chinese leaders believed that the United States had the will to affect their interests by employing the "carrot" as well as the "stick"

10

against Chinese behavior, and the costs to China of compromise were nominal. The threat of ending China's MFN status to change its human rights practices has failed because Chinese leaders understood that Washington lacked the will to endure the costs of imposing sanctions. The exception has been when American partisan politics has combined with deep policy divisions to enhance U.S. credibility. Chinese leaders have understood that American presidents have been willing to sacrifice U.S.-China cooperation to avoid the domestic political costs associated with partisan charges of foreign policy "weakness." In these circumstances, Chinese leaders have compromised. Alternatively, when Chinese leaders believed that there would be a positive outcome from compromise—that is, not merely avoidance of sanctions but actual benefit—they have been willing to release dissidents.

The Threat of Sanctions and China's Human Rights Policy

In June 1989 human rights became the focus of U.S. attention toward China. Americans in their living rooms watched television coverage of the Beijing democracy movement and the Chinese government's violent response. Horrified Americans demanded that Washington's China policy reflect American values and their repulsion at the brutality of Chinese leaders. From June 1989 through May 1994, when President Clinton "delinked" trade and human rights, the United States threatened that unless China showed greater respect for human rights, it would withdraw that nation's MFN trading status, effectively pricing its goods out of the American market. U.S. focus was primarily on the fate of jailed Chinese dissidents. Human rights organizations tracked the fate of Chinese democracy activists, and their reports informed American understanding of the trend in Chinese politics. These organizations and their supporters demanded that Beijing release dissidents and allow them freedom of speech and movement.

The threat of suspension of China's MFN status formally derives from the Jackson-Vanik amendment to the 1974 Trade Act. The amendment was formally aimed at pressuring Communist countries to allow free immigration, in particular of Jews from the Soviet Union, but after June 1989 it was applied against China's human rights abuses. The amendment, as interpreted by Congress, requires the president to certify annually that the target country has fulfilled U.S. human rights expectations before that country's MFN status can be renewed. Each year between 1989 and 1994 China faced the threat of sanctions should it not satisfy U.S. demands to improve its human rights policies, primarily defined as treatment of dissidents. Thus it is important to note that the U.S.-China case is a study of the effectiveness of the *threat* of sanctions rather than a study of their application. Except for sanctions imposed in the weeks immediately following the Beijing massacre, most of which were lifted subsequently, the United States never has actually reacted to China's human rights violations with economic sanctions.

The source of the sanction threat has varied since 1989. The Bush administration opposed linkage of human rights with China's MFN status. Nonetheless, Congress threatened to apply sanctions by itself. It could overrule the president by voting to suspend MFN with enough votes to override the president's expected veto. In contrast, the Clinton administration adopted the threat of suspending MFN as its own method to pressure China to change its human rights policies. In May 1993 it issued a list of seven demands that China would have to satisfy before the president would renew MFN status.[2]

Advocates of sanctions argued that the United States had sufficient leverage to use MFN to compel Chinese leaders to accommodate U.S. demands. Indeed, economic sanctions seemed to be a powerful instrument. China's economic development plan depended on the acquisition of foreign currency to purchase the high technology China needed to become a global economic power and a modern military power. According to U.S. government statistics, in 1995 the United States was China's largest export market, attracting 32 percent of all Chinese exports. In contrast, in 1995 China's market attracted only 2 percent of total U.S. exports.[3] Moreover, Guangdong and Fujian provinces have been dependent on exports of textiles and other inexpensive consumer goods. Loss of the U.S. market would lead to significant unemployment and potentially significant political and social instability in this important region. A trade war also would enhance Chinese international isolation. It would lead to a deterioration in Sino-Japanese economic and political relations and inhibit many Southeast Asian countries from developing cooperative relations with China. The effect would be an overall deterioration of China's strategic environment and diversion of scarce financial resources from economic modernization to the defense budget.

Thus, from 1989 to 1994, Chinese leaders contended with a concerted U.S. effort to coerce them to change their domestic policies toward political opposition. The following discussion of U.S.-China conflict over human rights during both the Bush and Clinton administrations reveals that China consistently and successfully called America's bluff. During both administrations, despite considerable U.S. bluster and threats,

China paid no economic price for its intransigence—Washington neither affected Chinese policy nor did it follow through on its threat to impose sanctions. Ultimately, President Clinton's May 1994 decision to delink trade from human rights acknowledged policy failure. In subsequent years, despite White House opposition, members of Congress tried to mobilize enough support to link MFN with human rights. But through 1997 they failed to amass enough votes to pass the legislation, so the president did not have to exercise his veto.

The Bush Administration and Human Rights in China

The dynamics of U.S.-China negotiations changed during the period between 1989 and 1994. There were three distinct periods. In each period, a combination of international and domestic factors created a characteristic negotiating dynamic. The period in which the United States possessed the most internationally derived leverage over China was in the year immediately following the June 4, 1989, Beijing massacre. Universal horror at Chinese repression isolated the People's Republic from the major powers, and the collapse of the Warsaw Pact had ended the dynamics of the strategic triangle, vastly reducing China's immediate importance in U.S. security. Moreover, domestic politics in the United States pressured the White House to adopt retaliatory measures. In this context, the threat to suspend China's MFN status was more credible and the potential ramifications for China's relationships with other political and economic powers were more costly than at any other time since 1989. Nonetheless, the threat to suspend MFN failed to elicit Chinese compliance with U.S. demands.

In the aftermath of the June crackdown, the Bush administration suspended diplomatic exchanges at and above the assistant secretary level; all military exchanges, including ongoing technology and arms transfers; and U.S. support for assistance to China from international financial institutions. In addition, there was the possibility that the United States would suspend MFN the following June if China did not soften its policies. Nonetheless, for the six months following the June massacre, Chinese leaders stonewalled Bush administration efforts to elicit Chinese compromise, including two visits to Beijing by National Security Adviser Brent Scowcroft and Deputy Secretary of State Lawrence Eagleburger, insisting that it was up to the United States to break the U.S.-China deadlock. Only in January 1990 did it concede to open negotiations to restore the Fulbright Program and release minor participants in the June demonstrations. But Fang Lizhi, a leading

Chinese dissident who had sought refuge in the U.S. Embassy to avoid arrest, remained unable to leave China, student leaders of the democracy movement remained in jail, and China continued to jam Voice of America broadcasts. Only after President Bush announced his intention to renew MFN did Beijing allow Fang Lizhi to leave the country.

During the next year, China remained intransigent. It commenced the trials of the June 1989 democracy activists and handed down long prison terms for other democracy activists. It also refused to negotiate with the United States on exports of goods made by prison labor and on other bilateral issues. Nonetheless, the White House adopted unilateral compromise, and, in May 1991, it once again announced that it would support unconditional extension of MFN for China.

At the height of U.S. leverage in the post–Cold War era, the threat that costly economic sanctions might be imposed by a partisan and deeply committed U.S. Congress failed to coerce China to change its human rights policies. The reason the U.S. threat failed is that China's moderate leaders lacked the authority to impose controversial policies on domestic adversaries. In the aftermath of the Beijing massacre, Deng Xiaoping and his moderate colleagues yielded significant authority to conservative politicians. The threat of sanctions failed because no one in Chinese politics had the ability to compromise. As Secretary of State James Baker said in response to the question "Who's in charge?" the "situation is too clouded now . . . to answer," observing that "there is a power struggle going on in China."[4] Indeed, Chinese concessions might have made relations worse, insofar as they might have further undermined Deng's authority and contributed to more adversarial policies. Chinese policymakers released Fang Lizhi only after the White House agreed to extend MFN because they had to avoid charges of appeasement. Despite the combination of leverage and the threat of costly sanctions, Washington accommodated Chinese intransigence. The alternative was less attractive—impose sanctions and elicit PRC retaliation without gaining any change in China's domestic situation, because hard-liners would maintain repressive policies.

The second period of U.S. threats to retaliate against Chinese human rights abuses occurred from late 1991 to the end of the Bush administration. During this period, although China had reduced much of its post–June 4 international isolation and its economy had begun to grow at impressive rates, so that U.S. leverage had diminished, the threat of economic sanctions did lead to PRC conciliation. Once again domestic factors in both countries were decisive in determining credibility and leverage.

In 1991 President Bush experienced an unprecedented decline in popularity. At the start of the year he enjoyed greater popularity than any other post–World War II president. By the end of the year he was held responsible for the decline in the economy, and his reelection prospects had dimmed. This trend accelerated in 1992, so that his ability to enforce his China policy on a reluctant Congress had declined. In contrast, beginning in the second half of 1991, Deng Xiaoping gradually restored his political authority, reestablishing the moderate policy agenda and restoring his allies to policymaking roles. This trend culminated in Deng's January 1992 tour of China's southern provinces and his resurgence over his conservative adversaries. No longer was he incapable of making and enforcing compromises with the United States.

These shifting domestic fortunes yielded the United States leverage in U.S.-China relations. Because the White House could no longer guarantee MFN, the credibility of the U.S. threats had increased. Chinese leaders were compelled to compromise to mollify congressional critics and to reduce the risk of losing access to the U.S. market. U.S. partisan politics combined with policy divisions to compel Beijing to incur the cost of cooperation. Thus in late 1991 and early 1992, as the date for renewal of MFN approached, China adopted a relatively moderate posture. In January China released nine dissidents it had detained prior to trial. In April it released information regarding its most famous and longest imprisoned dissident, Wei Jingsheng. In addition, in February it pronounced relatively light sentences on 11 dissidents and did the same in August for political associates of former Premier Zhao Ziyang, who had been ousted for his conciliatory policies toward the demonstrators.[5] In June it reached agreement with the United States on exports of goods made by prison labor.

The Clinton Administration and Human Rights in China

The third and final period of U.S. efforts to use the threat of MFN suspension to obtain human rights concessions occurred during the first year and a half of Bill Clinton's presidency. This period is different from earlier periods in two ways. First, the president, rather than Congress, threatened sanctions. Second, during the Clinton administration, domestic politics in both China and the United States were not significant factors. In China Deng's leadership remained stable, and in the United States a new Democratic president enjoyed a Democratic-controlled Congress, minimizing the impact of partisan politics on policy. Thus the outcome of U.S. efforts reflected the ineffectiveness of threatening economic sanctions when Congress was not led by an opposition party with a politically inspired foreign policy agenda. The results indicate that without the leverage derived from domestic opposition, the threat of economic sanctions against Chinese human rights abuses does not work.

When the Clinton administration took office in January 1993, it struggled with the legacy of the June 4 crackdown and the presidential campaign on U.S. policy toward China. Rather than allow congressional politics to determine policy, in 1993 Bill Clinton issued an executive order linking continuation of China's MFN status with its human rights practices. But rather than free the White House from the politics of MFN, the order further politicized the issue, for the president had made a personal commitment to revoke China's MFN status should Beijing not conciliate U.S. demands. Yet even a presidential commitment and the political costs for the president of retreat could not make credible the threat to disrupt U.S.-China trade.

The administration made a strong effort to persuade China of its resolve. The president, Secretary of State Warren Christopher, and other senior officials pressured China to make reforms. In October 1993 Christopher warned Foreign Minister Qian Qichen that without quick progress on human rights, China would lose its MFN status. The president held a "frank" and "candid" discussion with Chinese President Jiang Zemin. After Beijing released a handful of dissidents, Christopher insisted that it had not done enough. In February 1994 Assistant Secretary of State for Human Rights John Shattuck held an unannounced meeting with Wei Jingsheng during a visit to Beijing. The next month Christopher visited China with the declared intention of withdrawing MFN unless China compromised. In May President Clinton told Chinese Vice Premier Zou Jihua that China had to make more concessions by June 3, the deadline for renewing China's MFN status, if it expected to maintain normal trade relations.[6]

Washington underscored its resolve with tough policies. The administration's annual human rights report underscored that China had yet to make significant political reforms. In 1993 Congress voted its disapproval of Beijing as the site for the Olympic Games in 2000 and voted funding for Radio Free Asia. The administration also coerced Chinese leaders into allowing a fruitless search of the shipping vessel *Yinhe*, which it suspected of carrying chemical weapons to Iran.[7] America seemed in no mood to tolerate Chinese intransigence.

President Clinton had done all he could to persuade Chinese leaders that the United States would revoke MFN if they did not meet U.S.

demands. The president had linked his personal credibility to this policy, suggesting that domestic political costs made compromise impossible. But Chinese leaders remained intransigent, adopting policies more hostile than those of 1992 and 1993. In meetings with administration officials, they expressed no willingness to meet U.S. conditions. Prior to Secretary Christopher's visit to Beijing, Chinese leaders rearrested or detained at least 13 dissidents, including Wei Jingsheng and Wang Dan. In their meetings with Christopher, they refused to discuss human rights. Premier Li Peng insisted that China would endure U.S. sanctions rather than succumb to pressure. In May, as the June 3 deadline approached, police arrested four Shanghai democracy activists.[8]

Washington's strenuous effort had failed to elicit concessions. Because the White House lacked leverage from domestic cleavages, Chinese leaders assessed American credibility solely by focusing on the costs and benefits of imposing sanctions for U.S. interests; they concluded that American interest in Chinese dissidents was far less than its interest in access to the Chinese market and stable U.S.-China political relations. They were correct. President Clinton, despite his commitment to retaliate against Chinese intransigence, flinched from the political costs and the national economic and security costs of disrupting U.S.-China trade. Thus Chinese leaders called the administration's bluff.

Denying MFN to China would have elicited PRC retaliation against American exports. Although American reliance on China's market is insignificant compared to Chinese reliance on the U.S. market, key sectors of U.S. industry and the labor force would have been affected. The economies of Washington and Kansas, for example, would have paid a substantial price were Beijing to cancel orders from Boeing and purchase European Airbuses instead. In 1994 China purchased 13 percent of Boeing's aircraft sales.[9] Many states would have been hurt were Beijing to decide to buy wheat from other countries. U.S. telecommunications, energy, and automobile corporations are in competition with their foreign counterparts for a share of China's infrastructure and transportation sectors. Chinese leaders understood the importance of the Chinese market to the U.S. economy and threatened to retaliate against U.S. sanctions.[10]

Economic and political interests pressured the Clinton administration to accommodate Chinese intransigence. Executives from AT&T, General Electric, and Dow Jones sharply criticized the administration's human rights policy during Secretary of State Christopher's March 1994 visit to Beijing. Executives of 450 California companies signed a petition urging the White House to delink trade relations. Nearly 800 companies wrote to the president to urge him to separate trade from human rights.

Secretary of the Treasury Lloyd Bentsen and director of the National Economic Council Robert Rubin distanced themselves from the State Department's position, also advocating delinkage. Under Secretary of Commerce Jeffrey Garten argued that the "economic stakes with China are enormous" and that the United States needed "to inject commercial considerations more into the policy." In Congress, Democratic Representative Lee Hamilton, chairman of the House Foreign Affairs Committee, called for a "broader understanding of the national interest." Leading Democratic and Republican senators, including Max Baucus (D-Mont.), Bill Bradley (D-N.J.), and John Danforth (R-Mo.), advised Secretary Christopher to eschew sanctions, no matter how intransigent China might be. In the House of Representatives, 106 members, including Speaker Tom Foley (D-Wash.), Minority Leader Robert Michel (R-Ill.), and Minority Whip Newt Gingrich (R-Ga.), advised President Clinton to approve unconditional renewal of China's MFN status.[11]

Security considerations were also influential. Representative Hamilton warned that "single-minded emphasis" on human rights had interfered with U.S. pursuit of security interests. Former Secretaries of State Henry Kissinger, Cyrus Vance, and Lawrence Eagleburger criticized the threat of sanctions as a failure and advised the administration to place greater emphasis on such issues as arms control and regional security. Even Assistant Secretary of State Winston Lord, who had played a major role in developing the Clinton administration's sanctions policy, acknowledged that U.S. preoccupation with human rights had undermined other American interests in U.S.-China relations and in regional affairs.[12]

In the weeks prior to the president's decision, administration officials met many times to consider their options. The president spoke with former presidents and senior foreign policy advisers and met with members of Congress. On May 18, eight days prior to his announcement of delinkage, Clinton met with his senior political and foreign policy advisors to elicit their advice. It was widely acknowledged that China had made only minimal concessions. Nonetheless, the president decided to retreat from the brink. On May 26 he announced delinkage of China's MFN status with its human rights policies.[13]

U.S. threats failed to change Chinese behavior because U.S. interest in Chinese dissidents was less important than U.S. economic and security interests in U.S.-China relations. Indeed, China closely observed the pressures on the White House from both the business sector and political leaders. It called the administration's bluff because it understood the American calculus; China's leaders correctly assessed the relative importance of human rights in U.S. policy and the repercussions of disrupted U.S.-China trade for the president's political situation. As one report characterized the administration's dilemma, the president was "working furiously" to get himself out of the "self-inflicted trap" of linking MFN to human rights.[14]

It is important to stress that the failure of the threat of economic sanctions was not due to the overwhelming importance of stability and power to Chinese leaders or to any Chinese unwillingness to compromise in order to protect access to the U.S. market. Chinese leaders had made concessions in the past, including releasing dissidents and other humanitarian actions, to improve U.S.-China relations. As noted earlier, they did so in 1992 when it appeared that U.S. domestic politics might lead Congress to apply economic sanctions. They also did so in early 1993, apparently trying to influence the new administration to forgo linkage and adopt a long-term cooperative China policy, releasing Wang Dan and two other dissidents.[15]

Especially significant, China made important human rights concessions for a brief period in early 1994, when it appeared that the Clinton administration would adopt a more conciliatory policy. In September 1993 the White House launched its policy of "engagement." For the next four months, in the aftermath of heightened tension surrounding the *Yinhe* incident and China's unsuccessful effort to secure the Olympic Games, Washington expanded high-level exchanges with China. In addition to agreeing to visits to China by Lloyd Bentsen, Secretary of Agriculture Michael Espy, and Chairman of the Federal Reserve Board Alan Greenspan and to a meeting between Presidents Clinton and Jiang Zemin at the November meeting in Vancouver of the forum on Asia-Pacific Economic Cooperation (APEC), it also conducted the first dialogue with the Chinese military since 1989. In January National Security Adviser Tony Lake met with Chinese Vice Foreign Minister Liu Huaqiu, the first step toward renewing the U.S.-China strategic dialogue. The two sides also reached an important textile agreement, removing a source of considerable tension from the relationship.[16]

It seemed that the White House might reconsider linking MFN with human rights.[17] China reciprocated with concessions. From January to early March 1994, Chinese leaders assured a congressional delegation that it would improve its human rights record, released two Tibetan political prisoners and a number of prominent democracy activists, including Wang Xizhe, released information on imprisoned activists, and granted Western reporters access to Chinese prisons. China also opened negotiations with the International Red Cross regarding prison visits and with U.S. officials regarding exports of goods made by prison labor.[18] But when the White House intensified its pressure with Shattuck's meeting with Wei Jingsheng and with threats to suspend MFN prior to Christopher's visit to Beijing, China reversed course. It renewed its harsh domestic policies, arresting numerous dissidents over the next three months. Only in the weeks before the deadline, in a transparent effort to make it easier for the president to accept failure, did China release some dissidents.[19]

Perhaps China would have been more responsive if Washington had the support of other advanced industrial countries. Multilateral sanctions would inflict greater costs on China, insofar as Beijing would not be able to find substitutes for U.S. high-technology products and would lose additional foreign markets. Yet the prospect of multilateral sanctions against China's human rights abuses is an illusion. Other advanced Western countries do not agree that linkage is appropriate policy. They also enjoy the advantages of U.S.-China conflict. Washington would have to coerce western European countries and Japan to follow its lead, imposing strains on bilateral relations with these countries and undermining cooperation in other areas. The cost of friction between the United States and its most important economic and strategic partners is not worth the benefit of improved Chinese human rights policies. Indeed, Washington has not tried to use its leverage to develop a multilateral approach. It has relied on cost-free ineffective moral arguments.

But this experience also reveals that Chinese leaders can be cooperative. In the aftermath of the 1997 Washington summit, Beijing allowed Wei Jingsheng, the most famous dissident, to leave China. That decision by Chinese leaders reflected their willingness to release dissidents when it would contribute to enhanced U.S.-China cooperation. In this case, the release reduced the cost to President Clinton of holding the Washington summit and facilitated U.S. cooperation toward holding the expected 1998 Beijing summit. On the other hand, had Chinese leaders released Wei prior to the summit, they might have encouraged ongoing U.S. coercive diplomacy.

The obstacle to Chinese cooperation is not the inherent cost to China of compromise. China has released dissidents when the quid pro quo was improved U.S.-China relations. Yet by measuring improved human rights by counting dissidents released from jail, U.S. policy has produced two perverse affects. First, it has reduced jailed dissidents to bargaining chips, demeaning the dissidents and the United States. Chinese dissidents deserve constant support, and American values should not be manipulated by Chinese leaders. Second, by transforming dissidents into bargaining chips, the United States can prolong their time in jail. When Beijing believes that release of dissidents can improve relations, it is prepared to do so. But if it appears that the United States will not reciprocate, dissidents remain in jail until their value increases. In spring 1994, when it became clear that the United States had not abandoned linkage, China returned to repressive policies. Prior to Vice President Al Gore's 1997 visit to China, Beijing seemed prepared to release Wang Dan. But when "donor-gate" locked the administration into a noncompromising posture, Wang remained in jail.

The Threat of Sanctions and Chinese Proliferation Activities

The United States has also threatened economic sanctions to try to influence China's proliferation policies. In this case, U.S. leverage has not been significantly influenced by domestic political circumstances. Thus U.S. policy toward China's proliferation practices has been more consistent than its policy toward PRC human rights violations. The antiproliferation policies of the Bush and Clinton administrations are nearly identical. They also have been more effective than policy toward Chinese human rights abuses. This effectiveness reflects the relative interests involved and the associated U.S. credibility to inflict costly sanctions on China.

American credibility to sanction Chinese missile proliferation has not derived from the severity of the sanctions it has imposed or threatened to impose. The United States has imposed only limited sanctions on missile proliferation, so that the impact on the Chinese economy has been negligible. Nonetheless, the sanctions remind Chinese leaders that Washington keeps a watchful eye on their behavior, that it takes proliferation seriously, and that it is prepared to adopt the most severe, albeit informal and implicit, sanction should Chinese proliferation harm vital U.S. interests—deterioration of the overall relationship and heightened adversarial relations.

U.S.-China friction over Chinese arms exports emerged in 1987 when Iran fired Chinese Silkworm missiles on U.S. warships in the Persian Gulf. The Reagan administration responded by freezing ongoing liberalization of regulations limiting technology exports to China. In March 1988, after China assured the United States that it would end Silkworm shipments to Iran and supplied Washington with the technical information necessary to defeat the missiles, the administration lifted the sanction.[20] But within weeks of lifting the sanction, the White House learned that China had sold Saudi Arabia CSS-2 intermediate-range ballistic missiles. Quickly, China assured the United States that the missiles would not carry nuclear warheads. Satisfied that China now understood the importance of controlling arms sales to the Middle East, in September 1988 Secretary of Defense Frank Carlucci visited Beijing and announced that the United States would license export of satellites to China for launching and that it would consider selling China helicopters, radar systems, and other military equipment. In February 1989 the Bush administration announced liberalization of restrictions on technology exports.[21]

These discussions of proliferation and U.S. retaliation against the Silkworm sale to Iran educated Beijing on the importance the United States attached to Middle East stability. Since 1988 China has not exported a single weapon to any Middle Eastern nation that violates any international agreement or that significantly enhances the capabilities of any country against the United States or its regional allies. Yet Chinese consideration of American interests in the Middle East has required persistent U.S. reminders of the consequences of ignoring U.S. warnings. Still, sanctions have failed to constrain China's security relationship with Pakistan.

In early 1991 Washington learned that China had shipped to Pakistan launch vehicles for the M-11 missile and that it was preparing to sell Syria M-9 missiles. Both missiles have sufficient range to destabilize regional balances. The Bush administration responded by denying export to China of satellite components and then imposing sanctions on exports of high-speed computers, U.S. participation in Chinese satellite launches, and sales of missile technologies to the Chinese corporation suspected of transferring the missile launchers. In June Secretary of State James Baker warned that there would be "profound consequences" if China sold the missiles to either Syria or Pakistan.[22] Nonetheless, after Under Secretary of State Reginald Bartholomew's visit to Beijing in August, China remained noncommittal.

The issue came to a head in November 1991 when Baker visited Beijing. China had made it clear that it wanted him to visit—it would be an important step toward regaining international legitimacy for China in the aftermath of its June 4, 1989, crackdown on the city's democracy movement. But it could be a costly visit for the Bush administration, for the president continued to face criticism for "coddling" Chinese leaders. It was clear that Baker wanted a quid pro quo and that his priority was missile proliferation. He wanted a PRC commitment to abide by the Missile Technology Control Regime (MTCR), which, according to U.S. interpretations, prohibited export of both the M-9 and the M-11 missile. After prolonged negotiations requiring Baker to spend an additional six hours in Beijing, Foreign Minister Qian agreed that China would abide by MTCR "guidelines and parameters" and that it would not sell M-11 missiles to Pakistan. But the next day the foreign ministry spokesman said that China would "consider" adhering to MTCR. On this contentious issue, debate still raged, and Beijing could not cancel its missile sales agreements.[23] U.S. sanctions remained in place.

Subsequent public Chinese statements appeared to reaffirm Beijing's original assurances to abide by MTCR, but Baker pressed for a written commitment. When Qian finally wrote to him on February 1, 1992, committing China to abide by MTCR guidelines and parameters, Washington lifted its sanctions. After learning that China had canceled its agreements with Pakistan and Syria, the administration expressed satisfaction with Chinese cooperation.[24] The threat of sanctions and the potential reward from compromise combined to affect PRC behavior. Aware that following through on the transfers would harm overall U.S.-China relations and enhance congressional opposition to China's MFN status, Beijing compromised.

China's cancellation of its agreements with Syria and Pakistan was a politically controversial decision. It required the reestablishment of moderate authority following Deng Xiaoping's tour of the southern provinces. Most important, for even moderate Chinese leaders, the agreement was made in the expectation that it would stabilize U.S. cooperation, thus meeting an important Chinese national interest. But when U.S. arms sales infringed on an important Chinese interest, the deal fell apart. On September 2, 1992, the Bush administration announced that it had agreed to sell 150 F-16s to Taiwan. Not only did this violate the August 17, 1982, U.S.-China joint communiqué regulating the quality and quantity of U.S. arms sales to Taiwan, it also substantially reduced the benefit to Beijing of reducing its own arms transfers, for the F-16 transfer would improve Taiwan's political and military capability to withstand PRC pressure to acknowledge PRC sovereignty over Taiwan.[25] China retaliated by transferring the M-11 missiles to Pakistan. It also withdrew from the talks among the five permanent members of the United Nations Security Council on arms exports to the Middle East.[26]

Thus, there began another round of U.S. sanctions and negotiations. In August 1993, after negotiations in which Chinese leaders insisted that there had been no violation, the Clinton administration announced that licenses would not be given to export to China advanced electronic equipment, technology and equipment for space systems, and technology for military aircraft.[27] Negotiations continued through October 1994. China never acknowledged that it had violated the U.S.-China agreement on missile exports, and the United States never acknowledged that it had violated the August 1982 communiqué. Finally, in October 1994, Beijing and Washington reached a new agreement clarifying the 1992 agreement on Chinese missile exports. Washington lifted the sanctions it imposed in August 1993 and Beijing agreed not to export missiles "featuring the primary parameters of the Missile Technology Control Regime—that is, inherently capable of reaching a range of at least 300 km with a payload of at least 500 kg."[28]

The October 1994 agreement added important specificity to China's February 1992 nonproliferation commitment. The "inherent capability" clause prevents China from arguing that because the M-11 missile has not been tested with payload weights and at ranges specified by MTCR, it is not governed by MTCR. On the other hand, China did not clarify its 1992 commitment to apply "inherent capability" on technology exports. Moreover, the communiqué only clarified China's 1992 commitment, which referred to the missile export restrictions contained in the original 1987 MTCR agreement. It did not commit China to abide by the expanded restrictions agreed upon by MTCR signatories in January 1993. These revised guidelines cover all delivery vehicles for all types of "weapons of mass destruction" including chemical and biological weapons as well as nuclear weapons.[29]

Since October 1994 the United States has tried to resolve the ambiguities in the U.S.-China agreements and to achieve full Chinese compliance with MTCR, but Beijing has refused to negotiate. Washington also has probed Chinese interest in formal membership in MTCR.[30] But the stumbling block has been U.S.-Taiwan relations. Each time Washington raises missile exports, China raises conventional arms exports, including U.S. exports of F-16s. By withholding full commitment to MTCR, China threatens to make additional transfers should the United States not limit arms sales to Taiwan. Indeed, the M-11 missiles it transferred to Pakistan in December 1992 have not been deployed—they remain in their shipping crates.[31]

Most important, formal Chinese participation in the MTCR would not change China's posture toward full adherence to the regime. Past threats of sanctions have not prevented China from assisting Pakistan's deterrent capabilities. China assigns high strategic value to Pakistan's security, and the cost of compromise would be great. China's reluctance to clarify its commitment to MTCR guidelines regarding technology exports apparently reflected its plans to transfer M-11 manufacturing capabilities to Pakistan.[32] To realize full Chinese compliance with MTCR, the United States would have to make significant concessions regarding its Taiwan policy, the only conceivable compensation to Beijing for the cost of reduced Pakistani security. But for the United

States, full Chinese compliance with MTCR is not worth the sacrifice of important elements of its Taiwan policy. Without this quid pro quo, Chinese leaders will continue to argue that MTCR serves only U.S. interests and that China should not contribute to U.S. interests without receiving corresponding U.S. concessions.[33]

Outside of South Asia, however, Beijing continues to exercise restraint. It has not exported MTCR-regulated missiles to the Middle East or elsewhere. It did not retaliate against the F-16 sale to Taiwan by renewing its agreement to provide Syria with M-9 missiles. That agreement has remained dead since March 1992. The only missile export to the Middle East since 1988 is transfers to Iran of C-802 and C-801K cruise missiles. These are early-generation cruise missiles with a range of slightly more than 20 miles. Then Secretary of Defense William Perry compared them to German World War II V-2 rockets and said that they have little military significance. Nonetheless, during the 1997 Washington summit and during Secretary of Defense William Cohen's January 1998 visit to Beijing, Chinese leaders expressed interest in curtailing the export of cruise missiles to Iran.[34]

Beijing understands that transfer of advanced weaponry to the Middle East would lead inevitably to U.S. sanctions and that these sanctions would be far graver than those imposed against Chinese transfers to Pakistan—political repercussions would affect the overall relationship. In addition, the cost of compromise is minimal, insofar as China has few strategic interests in the Middle East.[35]

The one major exception to this pattern is the sale by Chinese companies of chemical weapons precursors to Iran. Although the exports did not violate the Chemical Weapons Convention (CWC), as they were not on the list of proscribed chemicals, they nonetheless can contribute to Iran's chemical weapons program. In May 1997, after trying to persuade Beijing to end the exports, the Clinton administration imposed trade sanctions on the companies. It also has held discussions with Chinese leaders on chemical weapons proliferation, trying to encourage Beijing to develop more effective control over its chemical industries and their exports.[36] Although Beijing has not satisfied American demands regarding chemical exports to Iran, by late 1997 the administration was pleased with Beijing's progress in developing an export-control regime for chemical weapons precursors. Whether the combination of sanctions and negotiations will encourage PRC policy change remains to be seen.

The United States has imposed only limited sanctions against Chinese missile transfers to Pakistan. Apparently this is in recognition of limited U.S. ability to shape PRC policy in a region where China has vital security interests and where its Pakistani ally is involved in an incipient arms race with India. Also, U.S. post–Cold War interests are nominal there.[37] But repeated U.S. sanctions, no matter how ineffective, do remind China of America's constant vigil against destabilizing missile transfers to more sensitive regions, whether there exist pertinent international agreements or not. Given U.S. interests in the Middle East, China is confident that a destabilizing arms transfer there would seriously set back its effort to promote U.S.-China cooperation, would enhance congressional opposition to MFN for China, and would enhance U.S. political and strategic opposition to Chinese influence in Asia. Thus it has refrained from transferring to the Middle East not just MTCR-regulated missiles but all missiles that would significantly alter current force-on-force relationships.

The Threat of Sanctions and Chinese Nuclear Proliferation

The United States has tried to deter China from exporting nuclear technologies to selected states. As in the case of missile proliferation, the United States has been less concerned with Chinese compliance with international regimes than that its exports do not assist U.S. adversaries. The same is true for China. Chinese behavior has been shaped more by its assessment of the costs of U.S. retaliation and the costs of Chinese compromise for PRC interests than by whether U.S. demands conform to international principles.

Three countries have been the beneficiary of significant Chinese nuclear technology exports—Algeria, Iran, and Pakistan. The Chinese agreement with Algeria was concluded in 1988 or earlier, when the United States was not paying close attention to China's potential as an arms exporter. When the United States discovered the scale of the project in late 1990, it was too late to abort the agreement.[38] Although the nuclear reactor has been under constant supervision of the International Atomic Energy Agency (IAEA), the United States has been critical of Chinese practice.

The conflict over Algeria warned China of U.S. sensitivity to the transfer of nuclear technology to so-called rogue states. Nevertheless, Beijing concluded a nuclear energy deal with Iran. The timing of the announcement of the Iran agreement reveals that China used nuclear proliferation there as well as missile transfers to Pakistan to retaliate against U.S. arms sales to Taiwan. Beijing announced the agreement in early September 1992, on the heels of the Bush administration's decision to sell F-16s to Taiwan.[39] Similar to China's arrangement with Algeria, China and Iran agreed to place the Iranian reactor under IAEA supervision. Although the United States did not impose sanctions, the Sino-Iranian agreement was a constant source of friction. But, in November 1995, in the aftermath of Taiwan President Lee Teng-hui's May visit to Cornell University and subsequent U.S.-China efforts to improve relations, including China's release of Harry Wu and Hillary Clinton's August visit for the international women's conference, Foreign Minister Qian informed Secretary of State Christopher that Beijing had "suspended" its agreement to sell Iran two nuclear reactors. Then, in the weeks preceding the October 1997 Washington summit, China agreed to cancel the 1992 agreement and not to transfer any nuclear technologies to Iran.[40] Thus far there have been no new Chinese agreements to provide nuclear reactors to U.S. adversaries.

The final case of proliferation concerns Chinese transfer in late 1995 to Pakistan of $70,000 worth of ring magnets that can be used to produce enriched uranium, a key ingredient in nuclear weapons. Compounding the issue is the fact that the magnets apparently were destined for a Pakistani nuclear reactor that is not under IAEA supervision. In early 1996 Washington suspended consideration of U.S. Export-Import Bank loans for projects in China and threatened to impose restrictions of technology exports to Chinese military-owned enterprises suspected of cooperating with Pakistan.[41] Faced with the threat of sanctions, China compromised. Although Chinese leaders convinced the United States that they were unaware of the transfer, in a meeting with Secretary of State Christopher in April in The Hague, Foreign Minister Qian assured the United States that China would not assist nuclear facilities that were not under IAEA safeguards, precluding future Chinese assistance to the unsupervised Pakistani reactor. Beijing also agreed to cooperate with the United States in establishing more effective Chinese export controls. U.S. efforts culminated in 1997, when Beijing completed establishment of domestic regulations restricting the export of nuclear technologies and joined the Zangger Group, i.e., countries who have agreed not to export selected proliferation-relevant technologies.[42]

American experience in using sanctions to shape Chinese nuclear proliferation policy is similar to that concerning human rights and missile proliferation. When U.S. credibility is high, which is a function of the gravity of U.S. interests and its cost of imposing sanctions, and the cost to China of compromise is low, China has been willing to compromise. Regarding the transfer of ring magnets to Pakistan, China wanted to improve relations with Washington after the 1996 Taiwan Straits confrontation. Because U.S. domestic legislation (the "Glenn-

Symington amendment") required a sanction and the cost to the United States of imposing it would have been nominal, Beijing understood that without a concession, sanctions would have been imposed. Although the cost to Beijing of the sanctions might have been limited, the setback to U.S.-China cooperation would have been costly in an era when Beijing was trying to improve relations. Moreover, the cost of compromise was minimal. If China actually had not intended to transfer the magnets, it had little reason to object to refrain from exporting them.

This experience suggests that it would be a mistake to premise non-proliferation policy on the assumption that a "rogue" Chinese military controls PRC weapons exports. With minor exceptions, since the end of the Cold War Beijing has managed its missile exports policy in support of broader national objectives, including U.S.-China cooperation and its regional security interests. Remaining PRC intransigence is not due to U.S. failure to invite China to participate in the formation of the post–Cold War international order. There are many important reasons to encourage Chinese leadership in international institutions, including MTCR, but greater accommodation of U.S. interests is not one of them. Just as America's China policy has not been guided by whether China has complied with international norms but by its assessment of the impact of PRC policies on U.S. security, when international regimes call for behavior contrary to important national interests, China will not necessarily change its behavior. Rather, Chinese proliferation policies will reflect Beijing's assessment of the importance of the policy to Chinese interests, the costs of pursuing that policy, including the likelihood that the United States will impose sanctions on China, and the cost of compromise.

Conclusion: Crafting a Sanctions Policy for China

American experience in dealing with China's human rights and proliferation policies suggests a number of policy recommendations. First, limited sanctions are preferable to comprehensive sanctions, which impose excessive costs on U.S. interests and thus lack credibility and invite PRC intransigence. In addition, China's proliferation policies have been responsive to limited sanctions. The threat of limited sanctions is credible and the cost to China can be greater than the costs of compromise, especially when viewed in the context of the overall relationship. Moreover, even limited sanctions can serve to maintain U.S.

credibility by signaling its willingness to adopt more comprehensive sanctions against more destabilizing proliferation.

Second, the threat of sanctions has been most effective when the promise of the carrot is employed simultaneously. In the absence of politically significant policy differences in the United States, China has not compromised to avoid sanctions unless there also has been the expectation that the United States will cease using sanctions and that there will be an overall improvement in the relationship. One of the reasons why President Clinton's sanctions policy failed is that the administration did not make clear that it would end the policy should China compromise. On the contrary, Chinese leaders reasonably could presume that if the president's policy was successful, he would benefit from appearing as the strong president who made China's leaders cower and that he would have no incentive to change policy. Similarly, when it appeared that the repercussions from "donor-gate" would prevent U.S. reciprocity, Beijing did not release Wang Dan prior to Vice President Gore's visit to China.

On the other hand, when Chinese leaders believed that the United States was both wielding the stick of sanctions and proffering the carrot of improved relations, they compromised. This explains PRC cooperation in 1992 regarding missile exports to Syria and Pakistan, in the 1996 negotiations over Chinese assistance to nonsupervised nuclear reactors following the ring magnets transfer to Pakistan, and in the 1995–97 negotiations over Chinese nuclear energy cooperation with Iran. This was the case concerning human rights diplomacy at the start of the Clinton administration in early 1994 and in 1997 following the Washington summit.

Third, the threat of costly sanctions can be effective when the domestic policy debate suggests that the president's flexibility is undermined by the partisan agenda of a Congress controlled by the opposition party. This is the case even when the threatened sanctions would affect important U.S. interests, such as denial of MFN. The presidential campaign in the final year of the Bush administration was responsible for considerable PRC flexibility in a wide range of areas.

The implications of partisan politics also apply to Chinese policymaking and PRC negotiating flexibility. Washington will not be able to use sanctions to extract concessions when China is experiencing heightened domestic political infighting because Chinese leaders will have neither the authority nor the will to make and enforce compromises with the United States. In these circumstances, the result is heightened U.S.-China tension and, thus, reduced overall cooperation, without any compensating benefit to the United States, such as progress in human rights. In these circumstances, it is best to wait until PRC politics stabilize before threatening to impose sanctions to promote PRC cooperation.

Fourth, it is difficult for the president to manufacture domestic political costs in order to enhance the credibility of an otherwise costly sanctions threat. By attaching his personal prestige to the outcome of U.S.-China conflict and by manufacturing the personal political costs to backing down before PRC intransigence, President Clinton boosted the American resolve to deny China MFN. But because he also would have incurred the political costs from Chinese retaliation against U.S. economic and security interests, the threat lacked credibility and did not alter PRC behavior. Only when the threat of sanctions comes from the autonomous behavior of the political opposition can it affect the policy calculations of the target state.

China can resist the threat of sanctions because it can impose high costs on important U.S. interests. America's stake in stable U.S.-China relations involves not only economic growth but also the security of allies and the peace of Asia. The result is that the United States cannot challenge Chinese interests except for the most important reasons. Most countries do not have China's power and retaliatory capability. This makes the U.S.-China case unique. But great powers always have treated each other differently. U.S. policy toward China, whether from design or from Chinese threats of retaliation, reflects the "realpolitik" implications of great power relations.

Notes

1. For a similar argument concerning the efficacy of sanctions per se using formal quantitative methodologies, see T. Clifton Morgan and Valerie L. Schwebach, "Fools Suffer Gladly: The Use of Economic Sanctions in International Crises," *International Studies Quarterly* 41, no. 1 (March 1997).

2. These seven demands called for China to allow free emigration, to comply with the U.S.-China agreement on prison labor, and to make progress in adhering to the Universal Declaration of Human Rights, releasing political prisoners, ensuring "human treatment" of prisoners, protecting Tibet's "distinctive religious and cultural heritage," and ending jamming of international broadcasts into China.

3. Wayne M. Morrison and John P. Hardt, "Major Issues in U.S.-China Economic Relations," in *Joint Economic Committee,* Congress of the United States, ed. (Armonk, NY: M.E. Sharpe, 1997), pp. 473, 477–78.

4. *Congressional Quarterly Weekly,* June 10, 1989, pp. 1428–30; *Weekly Compilation of Presidential Documents,* June 8, 1989, p. 867; *State Department Bulletin,* August 1989, p. 58.

5. *New York Times,* January 28, 1992; *New York Times,* February 29, 1992; *New York Times,* April 8, 1992. Also see *New York Times,* May 6, 1992; *The Standard* (Hong Kong), May 29, 1992, in *Foreign Broadcast Information Service, Daily Report: China* (hereafter *FBIS*), May 29, 1992, p. 29; *Far Eastern Economic Review,* August 6, 1992, p. 10; *Far Eastern Economic Review,* September 10, 1992, p. 13.

6. *New York Times,* October 1, 1993; *New York Times,* October 21, 1993; *New York Times,* November 20, 1993; *Far Eastern Economic Review,* December 2, 1993; *New York Times,* January 24, 1994; *New York Times,* February 28, 1994; *New York Times,* March 12, 1994; *Far Eastern Economic Review,* March 24, 1994, pp. 18–20; *New York Times,* May 3, 1994.

7. *New York Times,* September 6, 1993.

8. *Far Eastern Economic Review,* March 17, 1994, p. 16; *New York Times,* March 5, 1994; *New York Times,* March 12, 1994; *Washington Post,* March 13, 1994; *Wall Street Journal,* May 10, 1994.

9. *Dow Jones Newswires,* June 25, 1996.

10. See, for example, *Zhonguo Tongxun She,* March 20, 1994, in *FBIS,* April 1, 1994, pp. 4–5; *Xinhua,* May 4, 1994, in *FBIS,* May 5, 1994, pp. 8–9; also see the coverage of Foreign Minister Qian Qichen's statement in the *New York Times,* March 21, 1994.

11. *New York Times,* March 14, 1994; *Far Eastern Economic Review,* May 12, 1994, p. 16; *New York Times,* March 19, 1994; *New York Times,* March 20, 1994; *New York Times,* March 27, 1994; *New York Times,* January 30, 1994; *New York Times,* May 11, 1994; *New York Times,* May 20, 1994; *New York Times,* May 25, 1994.

12. *New York Times,* March 18, 1994; *New York Times,* May 11, 1994; *New York Times,* March 18, 1994; *Washington Post,* March 28, 1994; *Washington Post,* May 5, 1994; *Asian Wall Street Journal,* May 11, 1994; *Far Eastern Economic Review,* May 19, 1994.

13. For a close analysis of the decision-making leading to delinkage, see David M. Lampton, "America's China Policy in the Age of the Finance Minister: Clinton End Linkage," *China Quarterly,* no. 139 (September 1994), pp. 597–621.

14. Chen Dawei, "Clinton Faced with Decision on Problem of China's Most-Favored-Nation Status," *Zhongguo Xinwen She,* May 16, 1994, in *FBIS,* May 17, 1994, p. 9. For other Chinese commentaries on the domestic politics of MFN, see, for example, *Xinhua,* March 26, 1994, in *FBIS,* March 28, 1994, pp. 3–4; *Xinhua,* May 4, 1994, in *FBIS,* May 5, 1994, pp. 8–9; *Xinhua,* May 5, 1994, in *FBIS,* May 5, 1994, p. 8; *Xinhua,* May 6, 1994, in *FBIS,* May 9, 1994, pp. 4–5; *Xinhua,* May 11, 1994, in *FBIS,* May 11, 1994, p. 7; *Xinhua,* May 18, 1994, in *FBIS,* May 19, 1994, p. 6.

15. *New York Times,* February 18, 1993.

16. *New York Times,* October 2, 1993; *Far Eastern Economic Review,* October 14, 1993, p. 13; *New York Times,* November 3, 1993; *Far Eastern Economic Review,* November 11, 1993; *New York Times,* November 17, 1993; *New York Times,* January 23, 1994; *Xinhua,* January 29, 1994, in *FBIS,* January 31, 1994, p. 8; *Zhonguo Tongxun She,* January 18, 1994, in *FBIS,* January 19, 1994, p. 5.

17. See, for example, Li Peng's comments in *Xinhua,* January 2, 1994, in *FBIS,* January 3, 1994, p. 4; Foreign Broadcast Information Service, *Trends,* October 27, 1993, pp. 1–2; *New York Times,* January 16, 1994.

18. *Far Eastern Economic Review,* January 27, 1994, p. 15; *Far Eastern Economic Review,* February 17, 1994; *New York Times;* February 2, 1994; *New York Times,* March 2, 1994; *New York Times,* March 6, 1994; *New York Times,* January 22, 1994; *New York Times,* January 21, 1994.

19. FBIS, *Trends,* May 25, 1994, pp. 1–5.

20. *Far Eastern Economic Review,* February 25, 1988, p. 13; *Far Eastern Economic Review,* March 24, 1988; *New York Times,* March 13, 1988; Ross interview with U.S. government official.

21. *Christian Science Monitor,* August 4, 1998; *Far Eastern Economic Review,* September 29, 1988, p. 29; *Los Angeles Times,* March 1, 1989. On the missile sale to Saudi Arabia, see Yitzhak Shichor, *East Wind over Arabia: Origins and Implications of the Sino-Saudi Missile Deal, China Research Monograph,* no. 35 (Berkeley, CA: Institute of East Asian Studies University of California, Berkeley, 1989).

22. *Washington Post,* April 6, 1991; *New York Times,* May 1, 1991; *New York Times,* May 28, 1991; *New York Times,* June 10, 1991; *New York Times,* June 13, 1991; *New York Times,* June 13, 1991; *Far Eastern Economic Review,* June 27, 1991, p. 12; *Xinhua,* August 2, 1991, in *FBIS,* August 2, 1991, p. 3.

23. On China's interest in the Baker visit, see *Washington Post,* October 26, 1991; *Xinhua,* November 7, 1991, in *FBIS,* November 7, 1991. On the course of Baker's meetings with Chinese officials, see *New York Times,* November 16, 1991; *New York Times,* November 17, 1991; *Xinhua,* November 17, 1991, in *FBIS,* supplement, November 20, 1991, p. 6. Regarding the initial agreement and China's subsequent retreat, see *Renmin Ribao* (People's Daily), November 18, 1991, in *FBIS,* supplement, November 20, 1991, p. 7; interview with a U.S. State Department official.

24. *Zhongguo Xinwen She,* November 21, 1991, in *FBIS,* November 21, 1991, p. 1; *Beijing Radio,* January 16, 1992, in *FBIS,* November 23, 1992, p. 2; *Xinhua,* February 1, 1992, in *FBIS,* February 3, 1992, p. 8; *U.S. Department of State Dispatch,* March 9, 1992, p. 189; interview with a U.S. State Department official. On the Chinese cancellations, see *Far Eastern Economic Review,* May 28, 1992; interview with U.S. State Department official. Although the sanction was lifted in February, it took another seven months before the administration issued licenses for the export of the technology.

25. *Far Eastern Economic Review,* September 17, 1992; *New York Times,* September 4, 1992; on the 1982 communiqué, see Robert S. Ross, *Negotiating Cooperation: U.S.-China Relations. 1919–1989* (Stanford, CA: Stanford University Press, 1995), chap. 7.

26. Ross interviews with U.S. government officials; Deborah A. Ozga, "A Chronology of the Missile Technology Control Regime," *The Nonproliferation Review* 1, no. 2 (Winter 1994); *New York Times,* May 6, 1993; *New York Times,* September 20, 1992.

27. *International Herald Tribune,* July 22, 1993; *New York Times,* August 25, 1993; *New York Times,* August 26, 1993; *Far Eastern Economic Review,* September 9, 1993.

28. *Joint United States–People's Republic of China Statement on Missile Proliferation,* October 4, 1994, in *U.S. Department of State Dispatch* 5, no. 42 (October 17, 1994), p. 702.

29. See the report by the U.S. General Accounting Office, *Export Controls: Some Controls over Missile-Related Technology Exports to China Are Weak,* April 17, 1995 (Washington, DC: USGAO Report #29 NSIAD-95-82, 1995).

30. Ross interviews with U.S. Department of State officials.

31. Ross interview with U.S. Government officials; *Washington Post,* February 7, 1996.

32. *New York Times,* August 27, 1996; *Washington Times,* November 26, 1996; *Jang* (Rawalpindi, Pakistan), January 20, 1997, in *FBIS, Daily Report: South Asia,* January 22, 1997. For a discussion of PRC motives for arms transfers, see Karl W. Eikenberry, *Explaining and Influencing Chinese Arms Transfers, McNair Paper,* no. 36 (Washington, DC: Institute for National Strategic Studies, National Defense University, 1995).

33. Ross interviews with Chinese government analysts. Also see, for example, the statements by the spokesmen of the Chinese Foreign Ministry on October 10, 1996; in *FBIS,* October 11, 1996, and on November 5, 1996, in Kyodo, November 5, 1996, in *FBIS/China,* November 21, 1996.

34. For a discussion of these developments, see the June 17, 1997, briefing by a "senior Department of Defense official." Perry's comments are reported in the *Far Eastern Economic Review,* September 11, 1997, p. 12. For Chinese comments during the summit, see the October 29, 1997, White House Fact Sheet "Accomplishments of U.S.-China Summit," and Secretary of Defense William Cohen's November 25, 1997, briefing on the release of the Department of Defense report "Proliferation: Threat and Response." On the Chinese remarks during Cohen's visit to Bejing, see *New York Times,* January 20, 1998.

35. Ross interview with White House official.

36. Statement by U.S. Department of State Spokesman Nicholas Burns, May 21, 1997; *New York Times,* May 23, 1997; Ross interview with U.S. Department of State official. On China's efforts on chemical exports, see the October 29, 1997, White House Fact Sheet "Accomplishments of U.S.-China Summit" and the transcript of Robert Einhorn's January 7, 1998, interview on China/nonproliferation published in January 1998 in the United States Information Agency's electronic journal *U.S. Foreign Policy Agenda.*

37. For a discussion of the strategic importance to China of Sino-Pakistan relations and China's extensive military relationship with Pakistan, see John W. Garver, "Sino-Indian Rapprochement and the Sino-Pakistan Entente," *Political Science Quarterly* 111, no. 2 (Summer 1996).

38. *New York Times,* November 15, 1991.

39. The agreement was first announced in September 1992. See *New York Times,* September 11, 1992.

40. *New York Times,* September 28, 1995; *New York Times,* November 10, 1995. On China's pre-summit nuclear agreement regarding Iran, see the October 29, 1997, White House background press briefing by senior administration officials on nuclear cooperation with China.

41. *Financial Times,* February 29, 1996; *New York Times,* February 21, 1996; *New York Times,* March 29, 1996.

42. See U.S. Department of State, Daily Press Briefing, "Special Briefing on U.S.-China Discussions on Non-Proliferation and Nuclear-Related Exports," May 10, 1996; interview with Warren Christopher on *News Hour with Jim Lehrer,* June 17, 1996. On Chinese export controls and membership in the Zangger Group, see the October 29, 1997, White House background briefing by senior administration officials on nuclear cooperation with China and the October 29, 1997, White House Fact Sheet "Accomplishments of U.S-China Summit."

2

Cuba

Susan Kaufman Purcell

THE U.S. ECONOMIC embargo against Cuba has been in place for 36 years. During that period, its rationale and goals have changed. For the most part, its principal purpose was either to modify the international behavior of Fidel Castro and his Communist government, which Washington regarded as a threat to U.S. strategic interests, or to eliminate the regime entirely. As long as those goals proved unattainable, Washington settled for a secondary goal of isolating and containing Cuba. Since the collapse of the Soviet Union and the end of Moscow's substantial economic aid to the island, Washington has tried to take advantage of Cuba's new economic vulnerability by tightening the embargo in order to prevent the Castro government from replacing Soviet aid with foreign investment and other capital. The goal of Washington's policy remains the disappearance of the Castro regime, by forcing either reform or revolt on the island.

Washington's post–Cold War policy toward Cuba has been caught up in a larger debate concerning the effectiveness of economic sanctions in general and of unilateral sanctions in particular as a way of producing change in the nature and behavior of hostile regimes. Critics of the administration's Cuba policy argue that U.S. sanctions against Cuba have not worked for decades and that it is "time for a change," particularly now that the Cold War is over and Havana is no longer a serious threat to U.S. interests. They believe that the Castro government would respond better to incentives rather than to punishment. Supporters of U.S. policy, in contrast, argue the opposite. They claim that the embargo could not work during the Cold War, when Havana received billions of dollars annually from Moscow. Now that this aid has disappeared,

Washington's ability to influence Castro's behavior, and perhaps even to topple him, has increased. Their conclusion: The U.S. embargo should not only be continued but tightened.

Who is right? To a large extent, it is impossible to resolve this argument, not only concerning Cuba but in regard to any other country that is the object of economic sanctions. If the Castro government were to collapse tomorrow, supporters of the recently tightened U.S. embargo would proclaim the success of their policy preference. Critics of U.S. policy toward Cuba, on the other hand, would argue that the regime's collapse had less to do with Washington's policy than with the end of Soviet aid, the imperatives of the new global economy, the information revolution, and/or the policy of engagement pursued by Europeans and others in Cuba.

Furthermore, critics of U.S. sanctions against Cuba have a debating advantage. All they need to charge is that the policy has not produced the overthrow or collapse of the Castro regime. They are under no obligation to prove that their preferred policy option—a policy of engagement—would cause the Castro government to collapse or become more democratic and less hostile to U.S. interests. Because their policy of engagement has not been tried over an extended period, therefore, the critics usually are given the benefit of the doubt.

Despite current differences in opinion regarding U.S. policy toward Cuba, for much of its history the policy did not generate strong opposition within the United States. Particularly during the Cold War, which shaped U.S. policy toward Cuba during the first 27 years of the embargo, it was not difficult to convince the U.S. public that the Castro regime posed a threat to U.S. interests. This was especially true in the aftermath of the Cuban missile crisis of 1962 and during the following decade, characterized by a growing Soviet influence over the island. Only since the Soviet collapse has any significant opposition to the embargo developed within the United States. It has been fueled not only by the demise of the Soviet bloc but also by the normalization of U.S. relations with other formerly hostile communist regimes, such as Vietnam and, to a lesser extent, North Korea.

Ultimately, the charge of inconsistency in U.S. policy will not prove effective in ending the embargo. Each country provides different opportunities and constraints for U.S. policy. As long as U.S. goals are consistent, Washington will be able to justify using different means to achieve a common end. What may prove more of an obstacle to sustaining the embargo against Cuba, however, are the growing costs of doing so. Specifically, we are alienating our friends and allies whose cooperation is needed on other issues of importance to U.S. and global security.

One final aspect of the Cuba sanctions debate concerns the strong and unwavering support for sanctions on the part of the Cuban American population, whose voting power is concentrated in two important states, Florida and New Jersey, and whose main lobby, the Cuban American National Foundation, is well organized and financed. Critics of Washington's Cuba policy often imply or state that the sanctions are illegitimate because they "only" or "mainly" reflect the views of a small but powerful minority. Or the critics assume that the U.S. public does not really care about Cuba and would be willing to go along with a U.S. policy of engagement with the Castro government.

U.S. foreign policy, of course, always has been shaped to varying degrees by domestic interest groups. As the United States is a representative democracy, its foreign policy must, to some extent, reflect domestic values and institutions. During the Cold War, however, when Washington and Moscow were engaged in what many U.S. citizens saw as a life-or-death global competition, the U.S. president could defeat even well-organized domestic groups in the name of larger strategic concerns. Since the Soviet collapse, doing so is much more difficult. The power of the Cuban American lobby on the Cuba sanctions issue reflects the more general phenomenon of the increased clout of domestic actors in shaping foreign policy in the post–Cold War era.

Origins of the Economic Embargo

The embargo, which dates from 1962, was the culmination of unilateral U.S. responses to a series of developments in Cuba during the height of the Cold War, developments that the Kennedy administration interpreted as having put Castro's Cuba squarely in the Soviet camp.[1] The Cuban leader called off promised elections in April 1959 and announced shortly thereafter that Cuba did not want U.S. economic assistance. In May Cuba adopted an agrarian reform law that led to the expropriation of U.S.-owned properties on the island. In February of the revolution's second year, Moscow and Havana signed a trade agreement under which the Soviet Union agreed to purchase sugar from Cuba and to supply Cuba with crude oil. In March 1960 President Dwight Eisenhower secretly ordered the Central Intelligence Agency to begin training Cuban exiles for an invasion of Cuba. In June the Castro government asked foreign-owned oil refineries to process Soviet crude oil. When they refused to do so, they were nationalized. In response, the U.S. Congress authorized President Eisenhower to cut off the yearly quota of sugar to be imported from Cuba under the Sugar Act of 1948. Two days later, on July 5, the Cuban government authorized the nationalization of all U.S. property in Cuba, valued at some $1.8 billion. The next day Eisenhower cut Cuba's remaining sugar quota for 1960 by 95 percent. Between August and October, the Cuban government nationalized U.S.-owned banks, industrial and agrarian enterprises, and wholesale and retail enterprises. In December Eisenhower fixed Cuba's 1961 sugar quota at zero.

On January 1, 1961, Cuba restricted personnel in the U.S. Embassy in Havana to a maximum of 11 and gave the remaining embassy staff two days to leave the country. The United States then broke off diplomatic relations with Cuba, and travel by U.S. citizens to Cuba was forbidden shortly thereafter. The Commerce Department had embargoed U.S. exports of goods and technical data to Cuba in October of the preceding year. On April 17, 1961, the day after Castro openly proclaimed his revolution to be "socialist," the Bay of Pigs invasion occurred. It failed to topple Castro.

On September 4 Congress passed the Foreign Assistance Act of 1961, prohibiting aid to Cuba and authorizing the president to establish and maintain "a total embargo upon all trade between the United States and Cuba." President John Kennedy already had similar authority under the Trading with the Enemy Act of 1917. On February 7, 1962, he declared an embargo on all trade with Cuba. On August 1 Congress amended the Foreign Assistance Act to prohibit U.S. aid "to any country which furnishes assistance to the present government of Cuba." Implementing authority lay mainly with the Treasury Department, first under the Cuban Import Regulations issued in 1962 and then under the Cuban Assets Control Regulations issued in 1963.

The unilateral U.S. embargo targeted only Cuba and did not prohibit third parties from trading with the island. It did have extraterritorial aspects, however, in that it prohibited the reexportation from third countries to Cuba of commodities or technical data of U.S. origin. In early 1963, moreover, National Security Action Memorandum 220 prohibited shipments of cargoes paid for by the U.S. government on foreign flag vessels that had called at a Cuban port on or after January 1, 1963. And in December 1963 Congress amended the Foreign Assistance Act to prohibit U.S. aid to countries that failed to take steps to prevent aircraft or ships under their registry from engaging in trade with Cuba.[2] Initially foreign subsidiaries of U.S. corporations were not prohibited from trading with Cuba, although the Treasury Department "vigorously pursued an informal policy of applying pressure to United States parent companies to ensure that their foreign affiliates 'voluntarily' refrained from engaging in any transactions with Cuba."[3]

Despite its unilateral nature, the embargo became multilateral in practice within most of the Western Hemisphere. The Organization of American States, meeting in Punta del Este in January 1962, first imposed limited sanctions on Cuba and excluded its "present government" from participating in the inter-American system. Two years after the Punta del Este vote, the Organization of American States (OAS) voted to require its members to break diplomatic relations with Havana, to impose a collective trade embargo on Cuba (excluding foodstuffs, medicine, and medical equipment for humanitarian purposes), and to suspend sea transportation with the island. The vote was partly the result of U.S. pressure. However, Latin American governments also were responding to the Castro government's efforts to spread Communist revolution to their countries.

The main rationale for the economic embargo was the threat to U.S. national security posed by a Communist Cuba that, by February 1962, had become allied economically and militarily with the Soviet Union. The embargo, however, was at best a second-choice policy that was implemented in the aftermath of the previous year's failed Bay of Pigs invasion. The embargo therefore represented Washington's effort to make the best of a bad situation. The Castro threat was real, yet the tools that Washington had at its disposal to overthrow, or even contain, Castro were at best limited and, at worst, inadequate for the task.

The fact that Cuba was an island provided some hope that an embargo might at least contain the Castro government. On the other hand, the recognition that Soviet trade with and aid to the island would not be affected by the embargo made it difficult to believe that it could "work." Of course, in 1962, when the United States unilaterally imposed its embargo against Cuba, it was still unclear how much economic aid the Soviet Union would provide to the island over the long term. It is important to stress, however, that the embargo was never considered the best possible policy that Washington could implement against the Castro regime. Instead, it was deemed better than doing nothing. At least it signaled Washington's disapproval of Havana's behavior.

The embargo also was never intended to be the only U.S. response to the threat presented by Castro's Cuba; rather it was to be one of several approaches. It followed by one year the creation of the Alliance for Progress, a $20 billion aid program aimed at helping Latin America achieve higher levels of economic development and thereby reduce the poverty and misery that were thought to make Communist revolutions possible or even probable. In addition, the Kennedy administration launched an ambitious counterinsurgency program in order to help

Latin American militaries prevail against Cuban-trained and armed Marxist guerrillas operating in the region.

Early Impact of the Embargo

Until the revolution, Cuba's economy had been closely linked with that of the United States. The United States had been Cuba's main trading partner and its principal foreign investor. In addition, it was the principal market for sugar, Cuba's chief export. Cuba also had earned substantial amounts of dollars from its tourist industry—and tourism from the United States far exceeded that from any other country.

By suddenly depriving Cuba of its main market and source of hard currency, the U.S. embargo caused great hardship for both the Cuban government and people. It also may have accelerated the process whereby Cuba became more dependent on the Soviet Union. On the other hand, there is ample evidence that Castro had no desire to maintain a capitalist economic system or Cuba's close economic ties with the United States. In order to eliminate both, however, he needed first to dismantle the Cuban military, so as to avoid a coup against him, and then get the Soviet Union to back his regime. While the U.S. embargo may have given Castro a rationale for forging closer ties with Moscow and may have given the USSR a good excuse for strengthening its alliance with "the enemy of its enemy," it also can be argued that the Cuban-Soviet alliance would have developed more or less as it did even without the embargo, since it served the interests of both Moscow and Havana.

The embargo also proved costly to the United States, specifically to those companies that had been heavily involved in trade with Cuba or that already had made substantial investments on the island. More costly than the embargo, however, were other aspects of U.S. policy that were adopted to offset or counter the threat that the Castro regime posed to U.S. interests in the hemisphere. Included here is the $20 billion Alliance for Progress, the costs of the counterinsurgency program, as well as other forms of U.S. military aid to the region.

On the positive side, there were no additional Marxist revolutions in the Western Hemisphere until 1979. Whether this was primarily the result of the embargo, or of the combination of policies that Washington implemented following the Cuban revolution, or of other developments having little or nothing to do with U.S. policy remains debatable. If the embargo did play a role in containing the spread of Cuban communism, it did so only in combination with the economic and military aid that the United States provided to the rest of Latin America as part of its overall policy of containment.

Détente and the Loosening of the Embargo

Two developments in the 1970s changed Washington's thinking on the embargo. Most important was détente with the Soviet Union, which reduced Washington's concerns regarding Soviet expansion in the Western Hemisphere. The fact that Latin America's Marxist guerrilla movements had been defeated by the end of the 1960s—the result of action by the region's U.S.-aided militaries—contributed to Washington's diminished preoccupation.

The other important factor was the U.S. defeat in Vietnam, which made the United States look less powerful to Latin American governments and encouraged them to chart a more independent course. In 1975, for example, the Organization of American States voted to lift its embargo of Cuba and instead to allow each member country to decide what kind of trade relations it wished to have with the island. The administration of President Gerald Ford then partially relaxed its prohibition against foreign subsidiary trade with Cuba, explaining the decision as an effort to improve U.S. relations with third countries and to conform to the OAS resolution regarding trade with Cuba. Washington also relaxed its prohibition against third-country exports to Cuba that contained U.S.-origin parts, allowing such countries to request licenses to export goods containing up to 20 percent of such parts. The denial of aid to third countries that permitted their ships to trade with Cuba also was revoked. These limited efforts of the Ford administration to improve relations with the Castro regime were halted abruptly when Cuba sent tens of thousands of troops to Angola to help the Popular Movement for the Liberation of Angola (MPLA) in its struggle against Jonas Savimbi.

President Jimmy Carter, who had criticized the United States' inordinate fear of communism, chose to downplay the extent to which Cuba's intervention in the Angolan civil war constituted a threat to U.S. interests. He therefore further liberalized the embargo and made clear his desire to work toward a normalization of relations with Cuba. In 1977 Washington allowed passport restrictions on travel to Cuba to lapse, thereby enabling U.S. citizens to go to the island as tourists. It also allowed U.S. travelers to spend dollars if such expenditures involved travel and living expenses within Cuba. The following year Treasury regulations were changed to permit U.S. residents to send money to relatives in Cuba. The Carter administration also agreed to the opening of U.S. and Cuban interest sections in Havana and Washington, respectively. These were expected to lead to the exchange of ambassadors at a future date.

Carter's plans for improved relations between Washington and Havana were undermined when Castro sent Cuban troops to fight on the side of Marxist rebels in Ethiopia in late 1977. Carter felt that the Cuban leader had betrayed him. The Cuban government asserted then—and continues to claim—that conflicts between Havana and Washington over international issues can be negotiated but are not relevant to discussions regarding the possible normalization of relations between the United States and Cuba.[4]

Although the changes in U.S. policy toward Cuba in the mid-1970s corresponded to new international realities, they also were based on a series of assumptions regarding the determinants of Castro's attitude and behavior toward the United States. Supporters of a more relaxed embargo had argued that Castro's behavior was a reaction to U.S. hostility toward him and his regime. They therefore assumed that better treatment by Washington would lead to less provocative and hostile behavior on the part of Castro. Instead, Castro's behavior seemed to validate those who had argued that he would interpret a more liberal policy toward Cuba as a sign of U.S. weakness, which he would turn to his advantage.

Perhaps more important in explaining Castro's behavior, however, was the willingness of the Soviet Union to continue bankrolling his exploits abroad, despite the existence of U.S.-Soviet détente. As a result, Washington's loosening—or tightening—of the embargo remained largely irrelevant to the Cuban regime as long as Castro could count on receiving billions of dollars of Soviet economic and military aid annually.

The End of Détente and the Tightening of the Embargo

Cuba's exploits in Africa were but a prelude to resumed revolutionary activity in the Western Hemisphere. In 1979 two Marxist groups triumphed in the Caribbean Basin—the New Jewel Movement in Grenada and the Sandinistas in Nicaragua. Castro played a particularly crucial role in training the Sandinistas. Within days of their triumph, he sent Cuban advisers to Nicaragua to advise and organize the new Marxist government. He also continued to aid the Marxist guerrillas in El Salvador.

In response to two successful Marxist revolutions in Washington's "backyard," the Carter administration began pursuing—reluctantly—a more hard-line policy in the Caribbean Basin. Carter cut off aid to the Sandinista government (after being forced by Congress to do so) and increased military aid to El Salvador during the final months of his administration.

Policy toward Cuba, however, remained essentially the same until the election of Ronald Reagan as president in 1980. After Secretary of State Alexander Haig vowed to "go to the source" of the Central American unrest—that is, Cuba—Washington once again severely restricted travel to the island, initially by limiting the ability of U.S. citizens to spend dollars there. In 1982 the restrictions were tightened further so that only a narrowly defined group of professionals were permitted to travel to Cuba for research purposes. In 1988 Congress asked the administration to submit recommendations for tightening the embargo against Cuban-origin imports. The Treasury Department also launched an initiative to block access to U.S. ports by Cuban shipping companies operating in third countries.

The embargo was tightened in order to increase the costs to Castro of fomenting revolution abroad—essentially the same rationale that Washington used for supporting counterrevolutionary movements in Nicaragua, Afghanistan, and Angola. Unlike the situation in the early 1960s, serious thought no longer was given to invading Cuba. The U.S.-Soviet agreement that had ended the missile crisis had included a U.S. promise not to use force to overthrow the Cuban government. In addition, the fact that the Cuban military had become one of the largest, best-trained, and most experienced militaries in the hemisphere had made the costs to the United States of any attempted military invasion prohibitive. On the other hand, although a tightened embargo would increase the costs to Castro of spreading revolutionary unrest, the fact that the Soviets were providing him with billions of dollars annually made it doubtful that his efforts would be seriously undermined. Instead, increased sanctions should be seen more as a symbolic move, indicating Washington's disapproval of Cuba's behavior.

This does not mean that the embargo had no economic impact during the Cold War. One European study claims that it cost Cuba approximately $40 billion over this 30-year period.[5] A preliminary study by the Institute for Economic Research of Juceplan, Cuba's central planning board, reached a similar conclusion.[6] The fact remains, however, that whatever the economic cost of the embargo to Cuba in dollar terms, it was largely irrelevant since the Soviet Union, not Cuba, was paying for Castro's revolutionary crusades. The embargo therefore should be measured in terms of its costs to the Soviet Union. To the extent that it helped draw Moscow into a closer and very costly relationship with the Castro government, it contributed somewhat to the USSR's growing economic problems in the 1980s. On the other hand, the Soviets got good value for their investment in terms of the problems that Castro caused for the United States and the effort, time, and cost involved in dealing with them.

The Soviet Collapse and the Cuba
Democracy Act of 1992

The collapse of the Soviet Union in 1989 led longtime critics of the U.S. embargo to hope for a liberalization of U.S. policy toward Cuba. They assumed that since the embargo was intimately linked to the Cold War and the Soviet threat to U.S. national security, the end of the Cold War would make the embargo obsolete. They also assumed that the fact that the embargo had never "worked," in the sense of overturning Castro or making him behave in a manner less hostile to U.S. interests, would strengthen the rationale for "trying something new."[7] Supporters of the embargo, however, came to exactly the opposite conclusion. They reasoned that the embargo had never "worked" because the Soviets had provided the Castro government with approximately $6 billion of aid each year. Without Soviet aid, they concluded, Castro would be more vulnerable to U.S. economic sanctions.[8]

The administration of George Bush, having worked out a diplomatic solution to end the Nicaraguan civil war, seemed to lean more toward the argument that it was time to adopt a less hard-line policy toward Cuba. On the other hand, the upcoming presidential election in which Bush was seeking to be reelected ultimately led him instead to support some tightening of the embargo in order partially to accommodate hard-line Republicans within his party, including many Cuban Americans. Early in 1992 Bush therefore barred from U.S. ports any ships that served routes to or from Cuba. He also tightened regulations regarding the sending of money and parcels by Cuban Americans to their relatives in Cuba. Bill Clinton, the Democratic presidential candidate, went even further, supporting passage of the Cuba Democracy Act, which sought to penalize U.S. companies whose foreign subsidiaries traded with the island nation. Bush followed suit. Neither he nor Clinton could afford to write off Florida's 25 electoral votes and New Jersey's 15.

The focus on foreign subsidiaries was the result of a growing realization that trade between foreign subsidiaries of U.S. multinational corporations and Cuba was undermining the impact the U.S. embargo could have in the absence of Soviet aid. Between 1980 and 1990 the total number of license applications to the U.S. Treasury for purposes of exporting to Cuba had increased from 164 to 321. More significantly, the value of subsidiary trade increased from $292 million in 1980 to $705 million in 1990. Of this amount, 76 percent were Cuban imports, and 71 percent of these imports were foodstuffs. The countries that accounted for most of this subsidiary trade were Switzerland, Argentina, France, Canada, and Great Britain.[9]

The Cuba Democracy Act—or, informally, the Torricelli bill, named after Democratic Congressman Robert Torricelli of New Jersey—further discouraged trade with Cuba by prohibiting ships entering Cuban ports for purposes of trade from loading or unloading freight in the United States for 180 days. It also sought to reduce Cuba's access to dollars by more tightly restricting the kinds of U.S. citizens who could spend money in Cuba without special permission from the U.S. Treasury, and required those seeking to send remittances to the island to get licenses from the Treasury's Office of Foreign Asset Controls. The act also authorized, but did not require, the president to declare any country providing assistance to Cuba ineligible for aid under the Foreign Assistance Act of 1961, ineligible for assistance or sales under the Arms Export Control Act, and ineligible under any program providing for the forgiveness or reduction of debt owed to the U.S. government.

These efforts to tighten the U.S. embargo against Cuba represented the "stick" side of the Cuba Democracy Act. There was also a "carrot" side that allowed the president to waive the prohibitions on foreign subsidiary trade or the restrictions on third-country vessels trading with Cuba if and when he determined that the Cuban government had held free, fair, and internationally supervised elections; had allowed opposition parties sufficient time to organize and campaign; and had given them full access to the media, showed respect for civil liberties and human rights, and was moving toward the establishment of a market economy. On the assumption that increased communication between the United States and Cuba would strengthen internal opposition to the Castro regime, the bill also authorized expanded telephone and mail service to the island.

The passage of that act also reflected the new post–Cold War era. With the collapse of the Soviet Union, the U.S. embargo could no longer be justified by reference to the Soviet threat. Nor could it be justified as punishment for Cuban support for revolution abroad, since the loss of Soviet aid had made it all but impossible for Cuba to "export revolution." (Cuba steadfastly had denied charges that it was supporting Marxist guerrillas during the Cold War; after the Soviet collapse, it claimed it had stopped doing so.) As a result of the disappearance of the Soviet threat, therefore, Washington began to explain its Cuba policy in terms of the need to bring democracy, respect for human rights, and a market economy to the island.[10]

The U.S. government also believed that the continued isolation of the Cuban government was a good thing. Most of Latin America's relatively new democracies were still fragile, and the region was in the process of opening and reforming its formerly statist economies. This involved the implementation of economic stabilization programs that, at least in the short run, reduced living standards and increased unemployment. In this context, it was deemed better to deprive the Castro government of the resources that would have enabled it to cause additional problems for Latin America's already beleaguered governments. Given that Castro's adventures in Latin America had depended greatly on his ability to fund them, this conclusion was reasonable.

At the same time, however, Washington favored establishing more contact with, and providing assistance to, the Cuban people. This contact and assistance would help offset their dependence on the Castro government for information and enable the regime's opponents to communicate and organize more effectively. This, then, became the rationale for the so-called Track II of the Cuba Democracy Act, which encouraged an increase in contact and communication with nongovernment groups and individuals on the island via telecommunications, visits by authorized U.S. travelers, and the like.

The hard-line provisions of the Cuba Democracy Act appear to have accomplished some of their goals. By July 1993 the Cuban government had admitted that the law had raised its shipping costs by 42 percent. A study published by the Institute of European-Latin-American Relations (IRELA), a European Union think tank, found that by December 1993 the act had cost Cuba about $1 billion, resulting from the higher prices that the country had to pay for imports and because of difficulties in exporting, problems with fleets, and so on.[11]

The Cuba Democracy Act took effect in 1992, the same year in which all Soviet aid remaining in the pipeline to Cuba dried up. The year 1993 marked the beginning of Cuba's efforts to attract foreign capital in order to offset the loss of Soviet aid. Between 1993 and 1996 (when the so-called Helms-Burton law further tightened the U.S. embargo), the Castro government allowed Cubans to hold and use dollars and other foreign currencies, permitted self-employment by individual Cubans in more than 100 job categories, and approved the creation of free farmers' markets and a number of retail markets for handicrafts and surplus products made by state enterprises. The government also began welcoming foreign investment, particularly in the tourism industry, while strictly controlling the hiring and payment of workers as well as the ability of ordinary Cubans to use the new recreation facilities.

Since one of the goals of the Cuba Democracy Act was to move Cuba toward a market economy, the implementation of these and related reforms can be regarded as a positive impact of the legislation. On the other hand, the need for hard currency in the absence of Soviet aid was undoubtedly a more direct cause of Cuba's limited economic opening. Nevertheless, the act exacerbated Cuba's hard-currency shortage by raising the costs of production and trade. As a result, Cuba was forced to make more extensive economic reforms than it had intended originally.

The conclusion that the U.S. embargo did significant damage to Cuba after the implementation of the Cuba Democracy Act is also evident from the Castro regime's energetic campaign, following its passage, to have the embargo lifted. During the Cold War, Castro and his colleagues repeatedly had minimized the embargo's impact, claiming that they did not care whether Washington lifted it or not. After the Soviet collapse and the tightening of the embargo, Cuban officials announced that the removal of the embargo was their top international priority.[12]

It is important to note, because of what came later, that the Europeans, Canadians, and Mexicans in particular had strongly opposed the Cuba Democracy Act and had threatened to fight it. They objected particularly to the legislation's extraterritorial reach, in that it stopped U.S. subsidiaries in foreign countries from trading with a third country.[13] The actions of the three governments, however, never matched their early rhetoric. Instead, they seemed to resign themselves to the third-party sanctions contained in the new legislation—possibly because they soon realized that their own companies would benefit economically from the act. Although the legislation barred U.S. subsidiaries from trading with Cuba, it did not forbid foreign-owned enterprises from engaging in such trade. The Torricelli bill therefore ended up benefiting foreign economic enterprises at the expense of U.S. companies.

A second reason why Europeans and others did not fight strongly against the act was their belief that U.S. policy toward Cuba would change during the Clinton administration. Despite the fact that Clinton had supported the act during the campaign, a number of his key Latin American policymakers had favored normalization of relations with the Castro government when they had served in the Carter administration. As a result, the Europeans and others may have decided that it was not worth making an issue of the Cuba Democracy Act, since it would be rescinded soon. Still another possibility is that they believed that Clinton would emphasize the so-called Track II part of the legislation, which called for increased contact and communication with the Cuban people, rather than the harder-line Track I, or third-party sanctions part of the law. Whatever the explanation, the fact that the Europeans and others did not follow their verbal opposition to the act with concrete action undoubtedly left the Clinton administration unprepared for their very different behavior with regard to the Helms-Burton law.

The Further Tightening of the Embargo and the Cuba Libertad Act

The limited economic reforms implemented by the Castro government after the Soviet collapse achieved their goal of increasing Cuba's access to at least a portion of the hard currency needed to keep its economy functioning, albeit at a relatively low level. The reforms made it attractive for foreign companies to invest in sectors such as tourism, mining, and telecommunications without having to worry about U.S. competitors. Furthermore, Cuba's desperate economic straits and its inability to enter the U.S. market allowed these foreign companies to drive a hard bargain with the Castro regime. As a result, foreign investment in Cuba increased dramatically between 1993 and 1996.

What was particularly disturbing to the representatives of the Cuban American community in Congress was the fact that many of these investments involved former U.S. properties that had been confiscated by the Castro government shortly after it took power. The combination of the influx of foreign capital (which helped offset the Castro government's loss of Soviet aid) and its use of expropriated U.S. property led in February 1996 to the passage of the Cuba Liberty and Democratic Solidarity (Libertad) Act, or the so-called Helms-Burton Act. President Clinton originally had opposed several of its most punitive provisions but felt obliged to sign the legislation following the shoot-down by Cuban MiGs in international waters of two small private planes piloted by Cuban Americans.

The bill, which passed both houses of Congress with overwhelming support, was signed by Clinton on March 12, 1996. The two most controversial provisions of the new law are Title III and Title IV. Title III enables U.S. nationals to bring lawsuits in federal court against foreign governments, companies, and individuals who "traffic" in expropriated U.S. property. However, it gives the president the power to delay implementation indefinitely (six months at a time) if he determines that the delay would be in the national interest of the United States and would facilitate a democratic transition in Cuba. Title IV denies entry into the United States of foreigners who traffic in expropriated property claimed by U.S. citizens. Corporate executives, owners, controlling shareholders and their immediate families, and agents would be prohibited from entering the United States except for medical reasons or to contest legal action taken against them because of their trafficking. Another important provision of the law codifies all existing economic sanctions against Cuba, including the embargo. It will now take an act of Congress to change the embargo. Helms-Burton also authorizes cuts in U.S assistance to countries providing aid to Cuba, such as Russia, in an amount equal to the aid supplied by these countries.

The most evident impact of the new legislation has been not on Cuba but on the Europeans, Canadians, and Mexicans, all of whom have objected strongly to the provisions that allow the United States to impose sanctions on countries that traffic in confiscated U.S. property. In contrast to their limited response to similar types of provisions in the earlier Cuba Democracy Act, the Europeans, Canadians, and Mexicans in particular have implemented so-called antidote legislation to counter whatever sanctions are applied against them under Helms-Burton.

In addition, the Europeans have brought the case before the World Trade Organization (WTO), despite the fact that Washington claims that Helms-Burton is not a trade issue but an issue of U.S. national security. Under the organization's rules, this would place the case outside of the WTO's jurisdiction, at least as far as Washington is concerned. The United States also has repeatedly pointed out that Helms-Burton does not prohibit or penalize third-country trade with, or investment in Cuba, as many critics of the legislation claim or imply. Instead, it targets trade or investment involving former U.S. properties that have been confiscated illegally by the Castro government. In addition, the law does not provide for U.S. sanctions resulting from such trafficking to be applied *in* foreign countries (i.e., extraterritorially) but rather only *within* the United States. Thus, foreign companies "trafficking" in confiscated U.S. property in Cuba cannot be sued under Helms-Burton in the country in which their headquarters are located. Instead, legal claims can be made only against foreign subsidiaries of such companies within the United States. These arguments have done little to assuage the Europeans. For their part, the Canadians and Mexicans have announced that they are planning to contest the compatibility of Helms-Burton with the North American Free Trade Agreement (NAFTA).

The more immediate and strident reaction from Europeans to Helms-Burton may have more to do with Middle Eastern oil than with Cuba. At the time that Helms-Burton became law, other legislation involving sanctions against third countries that trade with Libya and Iran was making its way through the U.S. Congress. It was easier to object to the third-party sanctions embodied in the Cuba law, which had been passed already, than to a law that did not yet exist. More important, the U.S. national security rationale for third-party sanctions could be challenged more easily in the case of Cuba than in the cases of states currently engaged in terrorist activities, such as Iran and Libya.

Washington apparently was caught off guard by the strong negative European reaction to Helms-Burton and has tried to work out a subsequent compromise. The Europeans have agreed temporarily to suspend their litigation over Helms-Burton in the WTO and to work with Washington to develop "binding disciplines" that would "inhibit and deter" new investment in illegally confiscated property in Cuba and other countries. If no agreement was reached by October 15, 1997, the Europeans said they would revive their case before the World Trade Organization. (In fact, the deadline passed without an agreement or a renewed WTO challenge.) As of this writing, the Europeans have been willing to apply such new rules only to private property confiscated in the future rather than to already confiscated property. This continues to be unacceptable to the United States.

If an agreement satisfactory to the United States is reached, the Clinton administration has promised to ask Congress to suspend the visa restriction provisions of Title IV. Washington also would like the Europeans to press Castro more strongly to respect human rights and hold free and fair elections. So far they have agreed to do so in principle, although how the principle will be implemented remains to be seen. If the Europeans and others really do help develop new international rules regarding confiscated property, this would have to be regarded as an important positive impact of Helms-Burton.

The same point can be made regarding a more active stance by the Europeans in support of human rights and free and fair elections in Cuba. Until now the Castro government has been able to play the Europeans and the Americans against each other. In the process, Cuba has avoided becoming the object of a concerted effort on the part of Western democracies to force Castro to end his dictatorial rule. It is unlikely that European rhetoric, unsupported by actions, would have any major impact on his behavior. It could, however, further weaken Castro's already diminished legitimacy and perhaps encourage more action on the part of his opponents within Cuba.

In the meantime, it is difficult to come to a definitive conclusion regarding the impact of Helms-Burton on the Cuban economy. The law has been in existence for over two years. It is generally conceded, even by critics, that economic sanctions act much more slowly than military force, for example, the alternative whose unacceptability or unfeasibility has often led to the adoption of economic sanctions as a second best option. To date, there is no consensus regarding what constitutes a reasonable waiting period before evaluating whether sanctions have worked. It seems doubtful, however, that any conclusion could be reached reasonably before five years or more have elapsed. Second, it is difficult to come by accurate data that would allow a realistic assessment of the legislation's impact, since the Cuban government has stopped publishing information regarding foreign investment on the island. Havana has justified its decision as motivated by a desire to protect foreign investors from being sanctioned under Helms-Burton. This may well be true. On the other hand, it is equally plausible that the

Castro government is refusing to publish such data because they show a significant decline in new foreign investment.

Based on media accounts as well as reports from foreign diplomats based in Cuba, few of the biggest foreign investors have withdrawn from the island as a result of Helms-Burton. What some companies, such as Sherritt or Melia Hotels, have done is sell or spin off their U.S.-based subsidiaries so as to avoid incurring sanctions under Helms-Burton. The Mexican telecommunications company, Domos, has backed out of its deal with the Cuban government, in part because of Helms-Burton and in part because of its own economic difficulties. Anecdotal evidence shows that a number of European banks have reneged on promised loans out of fear of incurring sanctions under Helms-Burton. Those that continue to lend to Cuba are charging interest rates ranging between 16 and 20 percent, and the loans are for less than a year.

What is more difficult to measure is how the size and pace of new foreign investments in Cuba since Helms-Burton compare with what occurred prior to the implementation of the law. One is hard put to cite new, big foreign investments in Cuba since mid-1996, apart from one or two exceptions in the mining and tourism sectors. At the same time, there is growing evidence that Cuba's economic difficulties are increasing, despite the limited number of economic reforms implemented after the Soviet collapse. After announcing that the 1997 harvest would exceed the 1996 one by 20 percent, the harvest proved smaller than that of the preceding year. The Cuban government also has claimed that the 7.5 percent economic growth achieved in 1996 was proof that Helms-Burton was not working. Carlos Lage, Cuba's economic "czar," admitted in December 1997, however, that the gross domestic product increase for 1997 equaled only 2.5 percent, or less than half the growth rate of the preceding year.[14] In addition, it is doubtful that the Cuban government will be able to repay the $330 million loan that it incurred at 16 percent interest to finance the necessary inputs for the 1997 harvest. And the $1.7 billion trade deficit that Cuba accrued in 1996 is expected to be even larger in 1997. This represents the fifth consecutive year in which Cuba's trade balance has deteriorated.[15]

Tourism has been cited as the bright spot in the Cuban economy, with the government predicting that gross income from tourism in 1997 would generate $1.6 billion. The impression that the Castro government wants to leave is that increases in revenues from tourism will more than offset any damage done to Cuba by Helms-Burton. It is important to note, however, that although gross income from tourism has been increasing, so have the costs of imports and other inputs necessary to sustain the tourism industry. Specifically, such costs have increased from 38 percent of gross revenue in 1990 to 67 percent in 1996. Adjusting for this, net revenue from tourism in 1996 was only about $429 million, an amount that does not even begin to compensate for the income that Cuba will lose as a result of the decline in the 1997 sugar harvest.[16]

The extent to which Cuba's recent economic problems are specifically the result of Helms-Burton or, for that matter, any of the earlier legislation, including the embargo and the Cuba Democracy Act, will remain debatable. This reinforces a point made earlier. If Cuba's economic performance had shown a sustained improvement, or at least had avoided a decline over a number of years, critics of U.S. economic sanctions likely would have proclaimed them a failure. Now that Cuba's economic performance shows a noted decline over the first year of the existence of Helms-Burton, however, sanction critics will be tempted to attribute the weaker economic performance to the Cuban government's own misguided economic policies, poor weather in Cuba, low world sugar prices, high world oil prices, the continuing fallout from the end of Soviet aid, and the globalization of the world economy, among others.

The fact remains, however, that the first year of Helms-Burton coincides with a dramatic fall in Cuba's economic growth rate over the preceding year from 7.8 percent in 1996 to 2.5 percent in 1997. This fact will leave the Castro government with no alternative but to undertake a new round of economic reforms. Fidel Castro loathes capitalism but wants and needs capital. He therefore will try to have his cake and eat it too, mainly by implementing economic reforms that encourage the entry of new capital or increase his government's hard-currency earnings without seriously undermining his control over the Cuban economy or people. In a sense, Castro is seeking his own version of the Chinese reform process, but without going as far in allowing private ownership as the Chinese have gone. He is restricting the reform process because he knows that it is easier for an opposition movement with access to resources to overthrow the government of an island of 11 million people than to overthrow the government of a huge country like China with a billion inhabitants.

Conclusion

During the past 36 years, the strongest supporters of economic sanctions against Cuba have hoped, if not believed, that the sanctions would lead to the overthrow or collapse of the Castro regime. Measured against these goals, the sanctions clearly have failed.

Measured against the less ambitious goal of transforming the behavior of the Castro government, however, the sanctions have produced mixed results. They were least effective during the Cold War, when Cuba received billions of dollars in Soviet aid annually. Since the collapse of the Soviet Union and the termination of Moscow's aid, the sanctions have had more of an impact. They have not been definitive in explaining recent changes in Cuban economic policy. They have, however, helped exacerbate Cuba's hard-currency crisis, thereby adding to the pressures on the Cuban leader to liberalize parts of the economy. The embargo also has imposed economic costs on both sides; one study, for example, concludes that trade between Cuba and the United States could reach $6.5 billion a year after the first few years following the lifting of the embargo.[17]

The maintenance of the U.S. embargo against Cuba has, however, become increasingly controversial since the Soviet collapse, particularly among U.S. allies. Their criticism has grown in direct proportion to the degree to which Washington's Cuba sanctions directly have affected their interests. Had the United States not tightened the embargo several years after the Cold War ended, it is likely that the Europeans, Canadians, and others would have tacitly accepted its remaining in place. The Cuban American community, however, with the support of significant numbers of Democratic and Republican legislators, viewed the end of Soviet aid to Cuba as an opportunity to force change on the island. Therefore the embargo was tightened, first in 1992 by the Torricelli bill and then in 1996 by the Helms-Burton bill.

The time covered by these bills coincides almost perfectly with the period during which the Castro government has experimented with limited reform. The year 1992, however, also coincides with the end to Soviet aid. It is, therefore, difficult to sort out the degree to which the Torricelli bill contributed to Cuba's hard-currency problems. What became clear rather quickly, however, was that the bill was keeping U.S. subsidiaries from trading with and investing in Cuba while allowing foreign ones to do so. This fact explains the essentially rhetorical opposition to the bill on the part of the Europeans, Canadians, and Mexicans who then took no significant actions to follow through on their threats. The fact that the Torricelli bill did not affect foreign subsidiaries enabled Cuba partially to offset the loss of Soviet aid with capital from non-Communist countries. In reaction to this situation, some U.S. businesses began to mobilize against the embargo.

Efforts to close this loophole began to be made even before the shootdown of the U.S. private planes by the Cuban MiGs in February 1996, although it is not clear that the most controversial parts of the Helms-

Burton bill would have survived intact were it not for the groundswell of support generated by this incident. Precisely because Helms-Burton raised the costs to foreign companies of dealing with Cuba, however, it generated significant opposition on the part of the Europeans, Canadians, and Mexicans. On the other hand, the greater effectiveness of Helms-Burton in tightening the embargo could force the Cuban government to implement even more liberal economic reforms in the coming years. One unanswerable question is, therefore, whether the benefits of Helms-Burton ultimately will justify its costs.

Assuming for the moment that Helms-Burton succeeds in forcing Cuba to open its economy further in order to attract more foreign capital, an additional question is whether such reforms ultimately will lead to a change of government in Cuba. Such a question may never be answerable. Indeed, even if the Castro regime were to collapse suddenly, supporters of the tightened embargo would claim victory while opponents would argue its essential irrelevance and attribute Castro's fall to other factors.

One other important question concerning the effectiveness of the embargo has, to date, received little attention. This is the issue of Cuba after Fidel and whether a transition to democracy and a market economy in a post-Castro Cuba would be easier or harder to achieve if the embargo remains in place.

Most embargo opponents argue that its removal would make for a more peaceful and successful transition to democracy in Cuba. Usually they have refrained from asking that the embargo be lifted unconditionally. Instead, they have advocated a quid pro quo approach, that is, a partial lifting of the embargo in response to some change for the better in the Castro regime in the area of human rights, democracy, and the like.[18] This approach—essentially one of conditional or constructive engagement—has failed in the past and likely will fail in the future, since Castro will never willingly allow himself to be seen as succumbing to Washington's directives. He may play with the idea of normalization, but at the moment he perceives his control threatened, he will act in a way so as to trigger U.S. backtracking. Therefore, those who really believe that the lifting of the embargo will further U.S. interests should be willing to press for its unconditional lifting.

It also should be pointed out that there is no guarantee that Castro's behavior would change for the better in the absence of the embargo. At least during the Cold War, whenever Castro had surplus or even barely adequate resources, he chose to embark on new adventures that invariably caused problems for the United States. There is no reason to believe that this option would no longer be available to him, given Latin America's many social problems.

Embargo supporters argue that by keeping it in place, it will be harder for any future leader or for the Cuban military to maintain "Fidelism" after the latter's departure from the scene. Stated differently, keeping the embargo in place should help ensure that something else is tried after Fidel. Opponents, in turn, claim that by maintaining the embargo, the most likely result of Fidel's departure would be civil war and either chaos or a military takeover.

In the end, the debate over the embargo and related sanctions may be less about what works but rather about the political clout of those in the United States who care strongly about the issue. This is particularly true in the aftermath of the Cold War, when a U.S. president has a much harder time going against domestic political interests in the name of a larger U.S. security interest. As a result, as long as Cuban Americans remain politically powerful and united in their support of the embargo, it will remain in place. And when change finally comes to Cuba, they will argue that their tenacity finally paid off. The embargo's opponents will reach exactly the opposite conclusion.

Notes

1. For a more detailed chronology of the events leading to the U.S. embargo against Cuba, see Michael Krinsky and David Gorove (eds.), *U.S. Economic Measures Against Cuba* (Northampton, MA: Aletheia Press, 1993), pp. 107–13; and Jorge I. Domínguez, *Cuba: Order and Revolution* (Cambridge, MA: Belknap Press of Harvard University Press, 1978), pp. 146–48.

2. Krinsky and Gorove, *U.S. Economic Measures,* pp. 112–13.

3. Ibid, p. 114.

4. Philip Brenner, *From Confrontation to Negotiation: U.S. Relations with Cuba* (Boulder, CO and London: Westview Press, 1988), p. 50.

5. Gerardo Trueba González, "Los Efectos del Bloqueo de Estados Unidos en Cuba: Características y Perspectivas," in *Cuba: Apertura Económica y Relaciones con Europa* (Madrid, Spain: Instituto de Relaciones Europeo-Latinoamericas (IRELA), 1994), p. 84.

6. Krinsky and Gorove, *U.S. Economic Measures,* p. 139.

7. For examples of these kinds of arguments see Andrew Zimbalist, "Dateline Cuba: Hanging on in Havana," *Foreign Policy,* no. 92 (Fall 1993), pp. 151–167, and Donald E. Schulz, *The United States and Cuba: From a Strategy of Conflict to Constructive Engagement* (Carlisle Barracks, PA: Strategic Studies Institute–U.S. Army War College, May 12, 1993).

8.   See Mark Falcoff, *Cuba and the U.S.: Thinking About the Future* (Carlisle Barracks, PA: Special Report of the Strategic Studies Institute–U.S. Army War College, December 9, 1992), pp. 3–9, and Susan Kaufman Purcell, "Collapsing Cuba," *Foreign Affairs* 71, no. 1 (America and the World, 1991/92), pp. 130-145.

9.   Purcell, "Collapsing Cuba," p. 132.

10. See the speech by Michael E. Ranneberger, the U.S. Department of State's Coordinator for Cuban Affairs, delivered at Friedrich Hayek University in Coral Gables, Florida, November 17, 1997, available on the Internet at http://www.state.gov/www/regions/ara/97117_ranneberger.html. For a statement of the consistency between U.S. support for democracy, human rights, and a market economy in Cuba and U.S. policy toward the rest of the Western Hemisphere, see the speech by Jeffrey Davidow, assistant secretary of state for inter-American affairs, delivered to the American Enterprise Institute and Friedrich Hayek University (Cuba Vision Series) in Washington, DC, July 28, 1997, available on the Internet at http://www.state.gov/www/regions/ara/970728_davidow.html.

11. Gerardo Trueba Gonzalez, "Los efectos del bloqueo de Estados Unidos en Cuba: Caracteristicas y perspectivas," p. 83.

12. Edward Gonzalez, *Cuba: Clearing Perilous Waters?* (Santa Monica, CA: RAND, 1996) p. x.

13. Andrew Zimbalist, "Magnitud y costos del Embargo de Estados Unidos en Cuba y Terceros Países," in *Cuba: Apertura Economica y Relaciones con Europa* (Madrid, Spain: IRELA, 1994), p. 96.

14. *Latin American Advisor* (New York, NY: International Advisory Group, Inc, December 15, 1997), p. 2.

15. "Cuba: The Last Communists," *The Economist*, January 17, 1998, pp. 19–21.

16. Carmelo Mesa-Lago, "Short on Sweet," *Hemisfile: Perspectives on Political and Economic Trends in the Americas* 8, no. 4 (July/August 1997), p. 5.

17. Krinsky and Gorove, *U.S. Economic Measures*, pp. 130–31.

18. See, for example, Gillian Gunn, *Cuba in Transition: Options for U.S. Policy* (New York: The Twentieth Century Fund Press, 1993); Wayne S. Smith, "Cuba's Long Reform," *Foreign Affairs* 75, no. 2 (March/April 1996), pp. 99–112; Jorge I. Dominguez, "The Secrets of Castro's Staying Power," *Foreign Affairs* 72, no. 2 (March/April 1993); and Inter-American Dialogue, *Cuba in the Americas: Breaking the Policy Deadlock* (Washington, DC: Second Report of the Inter-American Dialogue Task Force on Cuba, September 1995), p. ii.

3

Haiti

GIDEON ROSE

FOLLOWING THE 1986 departure of dictator François "Baby Doc" Duvalier, Haiti was governed by a succession of short-lived authoritarian regimes. In internationally monitored elections held in December 1990, however, leftist priest Jean-Bertrand Aristide won the presidency by a decisive majority and assumed office two months later, after the army suppressed a coup attempt. As the champion of Haiti's masses, Aristide sought major changes in the way the island was governed and its meager resources distributed. Haitian elites grew increasingly worried about his encroachment onto their prerogatives and his countenance of extraparliamentary intimidation, and so seven months into his term the charismatic cleric was deposed by his armed forces, led by Lieutenant General Raoul Cédras.

The coup against Aristide raised two key questions for U.S. policymakers. The first was *whether* outsiders should intervene in Haitian affairs in order to shift the balance of power among local political factions—or, more specifically, to prevent the disruption of Haiti's transition to democracy. The second question was *how* they should intervene, what goals the intervention should have, and what means it should adopt. To Bush administration officials and many others at the time of the coup, the answers seemed relatively obvious: There should indeed be an intervention, its goal should be the restoration of Aristide, and its means should include regional diplomatic and economic sanctions against Haiti in order to pressure the post-Aristide regime into stepping aside.

This initial consensus proved short-lived, however, because it was based on a serious overestimation of the power and efficacy of the sanctions chosen and a serious underestimation of Haitian social and political divisions. Soon these miscalculations became clear, and the humanitarian costs of the initial policy began to mount—leading to the emergence of still another problem, a rising tide of Haitian refugees trying to escape to Florida. When Aristide, the coup leaders, and their Haitian supporters all proved recalcitrant, American policymakers found themselves caught in a dilemma, unhappy with staying the course and yet unwilling to move either forward or backward. The Bush administration coped by forcibly repatriating the refugees and shifting Haitian policy to a back burner; the Clinton administration, ruling out that course because of pressure from key domestic constituencies, eventually decided to restore Aristide by force.

Despite Haiti's poverty and lack of strategic importance, this case raises questions that have significance for various debates. Some center on democratization—why it begins and why it falters, whether fair elections or fair governance produces political legitimacy, how to manage transitions in countries with vast social and economic cleavages. Others center on foreign intervention—what the proper roles are of regional versus global institutions, what the proper criteria are for committing American troops abroad. After providing a comprehensive treatment of U.S. decision-making during the Haiti crisis, however, this chapter will focus primarily on what the Haitian experience reveals about economic sanctions as a policy tool.

Unfortunately, the lessons are mostly cautionary ones, for it is hard to conceive of a worse outcome: The sanctions did not achieve their main objective; they hurt the people they were intended to help; and they created an intolerable situation that led, eventually, to policy choices no one would have selected initially on their own merits. The U.S. officials who crafted and implemented the sanctions faced a complex problem and acted with the best of intentions, but ultimately—as F. Scott Fitzgerald said about Tom and Daisy Buchanan—they were careless people, and the effect of their carelessness and confusion was that things and creatures were smashed up and left worse off than before.

Bush I: The Response to the Coup

Jean-Bertrand Aristide differed from his predecessors in many ways, but the manner of his removal from office was not one of them: Haitian leaders historically have been unceremoniously deposed, like the several figurehead rulers serving in the late 1980s.[1] The most important question to ask about the sanctions against Haiti, therefore, is what made this coup different from all the others, and the occasion for a dramatic international intervention?

The answer lies less in Haiti itself than in the broader historical and regional context. The 1970s and 1980s witnessed what has been termed the "third wave" of democratization in modern history, as authoritarian regimes across the globe liberalized and gave way to democratic successors.[2] The political face of Latin America was transformed during these years, and by 1991 all nondemocratic regimes in the region other than Cuba had been eliminated. Several of the new democracies had shaky foundations, however, and many observers feared that the wave could be reversed quickly should any of the regimes stumble. In June 1991, therefore, the Organization of American States (OAS) passed Resolution 1080 (the Santiago Commitment), a pledge of collective defense of the region's democratic institutions. In the event of any "sudden or irregular interruption of the democratic institutional process," the organization declared, OAS foreign ministers would convene an emergency meeting and somehow address the situation.[3]

Aristide's ouster on September 30, 1991, was the first test of this new regime, and the OAS rushed to follow through on its commitment. Within days OAS foreign ministers demanded Aristide's immediate reinstatement and recommended that the coup leaders face diplomatic, economic, and financial isolation. A high-level OAS mission was dispatched quickly to Haiti to help resolve the crisis, but it found the situation more intractable than it had expected. After the mission's efforts at mediation proved fruitless and the coup leaders declared the start of a new Haitian government, the OAS declared Aristide's ouster illegal and any replacement government unacceptable.[4]

The Bush administration had invested substantial effort and diplomatic capital over the years in facilitating Haiti's democratization and in spearheading the drive for the Santiago Commitment, so it also reacted negatively to the coup. As Secretary of State James Baker said during the initial OAS deliberations, "it is imperative that we agree—for the sake of Haitian democracy and the cause of democracy throughout the hemisphere—to act collectively to defend the legitimate government of President Aristide. Words alone are not going to suffice. This is a time for collective action."[5]

Officials saw the coup as significant not because they felt Haiti was important for U.S. strategic interests but because they feared an ideological "domino" effect. As Assistant Secretary of State for Inter-American Affairs Bernard Aronson put it on October 1, "Every time democracy is threatened by the military in this hemisphere it sends off potential shockwaves and we want to make clear that this kind of behavior has a terrible price."[6] President Bush would telegraph the point at a later press conference: "Our interest is this: There was a democratic process. A man was elected. He was overthrown. The hemisphere's moving toward democracy and Haiti started moving back toward totalitarian dictatorship. We have a keen interest in that."[7]

Although the Bush administration soon would hesitate, during the first days after the coup it rushed to take what seemed a forceful stand. The president met with Aristide in the Oval Office to show support for his beleaguered counterpart. The administration canceled $91 million in economic and military aid to Haiti scheduled for the next fiscal year, sent home Haitian officers enrolled in International Military Education and Training (IMET), and blocked arms exports. It froze Haitian government assets in the United States and went on to establish bilateral trade sanctions. (On humanitarian grounds, food staples and medicines were exempted from the embargo, and U.S. foreign assistance continued for humanitarian purposes through nongovernmental and international organizations.)[8] The administration also helped get the U.N. General Assembly to condemn the coup, demand Aristide's return, and ask members to support the OAS resolutions. As Aronson told Congress, "We face many difficult choices in our policy toward Haiti, none attractive; all fraught with difficulty and risk. But the one choice that the democratic community of the Organization of American States never contemplated was to stand by and do nothing when Haiti's first democratically elected government was violently overthrown."[9]

Nevertheless, because the level of U.S. interests involved seemed low and because of regional sensitivities regarding past U.S. behavior, the administration had no desire to become engaged militarily.[10] Few considered the use of force seriously, moreover, because most casual observers thought that given Haiti's poverty and dependence, economic sanctions soon would work. "U.S. officials believe," reported the *Washington Post,* "that Haiti . . . cannot withstand tough sanctions for any sustained time and the junta soon will be forced to look for a face-saving way to surrender power."[11] Congress generally agreed, thinking that—as one Republican member put it—"the economic sanctions that have been ordered by the Bush administration, in cooperation with our allies, should convey to the military government in Haiti and its supporters that there will be severe economic and social costs if democracy is not restored. As the poorest nation in the hemisphere, Haiti cannot long stand the type of economic pressure it faces with the OAS-mandated sanctions and U.S. economic embargo."[12]

At this point the United States supplied 62 percent of Haiti's imports and received 85 percent of its exports. Haiti, as Aronson testified on October 31, "is largely an agricultural and subsistence economy. So, in one sense, [foreign trade] is not important. But to run the macro economy—fuel, basic food staples, and the like—to employ people, it is virtually totally dependent." When the embargo started to work, he argued, "the formal economy will begin to suffer severe constrictions. They will not be able to generate power at the same levels. They will run out of and have to ration gasoline. The part of the economy which depends on exports, the assembly sector which employs about 35,000 Haitians, will be subject to the embargo. All kinds of consumer goods will be unavailable. So, I think there will be a severe impact." On the basis of such reasoning, he predicted that there was a six in ten chance that Aristide would be back in power within two months.[13] Asked when the administration would lift or revise the embargo and other sanctions, Aronson replied that there were no "halfway measures": "We want to see the OAS resolutions complied with and that means President Aristide restored to authority."[14] In the event, it would take three years and a military invasion before these goals were achieved.

Bush II: From Activism to Frustration

The sanctions against Haiti were adopted in the belief that when they began to bite, the coup plotters would relent and allow Aristide to return. This logic had three central flaws, however. It ignored the depth of Haiti's sociopolitical divisions, it misjudged the ability of Haitian elites to withstand modest external pressure, and it underestimated the difficulty of managing a democratic transition against the will of most local parties. The result was that the sanctions did not resolve the crisis, although they did prevent the new regime from consolidating itself or gaining foreign recognition.

From the start, American policymakers failed to conceptualize clearly the challenge they were facing. Samuel Huntington has argued that democratic transitions can be grouped into three broad categories: those in which elites take the lead in liberalizing the existing regime, or so-called "transformations"; those in which the opposition takes the lead and the authoritarian regime collapses or is overthrown, or so-called "replacements"; and hybrid situations in which the authoritarian elites and their opposition jointly negotiate the transfer of power, or so-called "transplacements."[15] During the course of the crisis, U.S. officials sometimes seemed to envision Aristide's restoration as a "*re*placement," in which the authoritarian coup leaders would be ousted and succeeded by the democratically elected president. At other times, however, U.S. officials seemed to envision a *"trans*placement," in which the various Haitian factions all would sign on to a plan for a gradual transition, with the coup leaders and their backers agreeing to cede some of their prerogatives in return for amnesty, a say in future governance, and so forth. The failure to distinguish between these two scenarios intellectually—and to pick one and stick with it in practice—led to confusion and resentment on all sides, and minimized what little leverage the sanctions might have provided.

Part of this confusion stemmed from the suddenness and unexpectedness of the coup and the haphazard way in which American policy evolved during the first days afterward. Aristide had not been American officials' favored candidate in the 1990 Haitian elections, but once he won the Bush administration quickly offered recognition and assistance in order to demonstrate its support for the democratic process. During 1991 officials in Washington occasionally chided the new regime for human rights abuses committed by its supporters, but they did not pay a great deal of attention to what was, after all, a small, poor, and strategically insignificant country. The coup took Washington by surprise, and the administration's initial response was driven by a perceived need to uphold the Santiago Commitment and support an assertive OAS stance.[16] During the first days after the coup, as noted, senior U.S. officials viewed the anti-Aristide forces as both evil and weak: A touch of the whip, it was felt, would be enough to make them back down.

Only when the OAS mediation mission got to Haiti in early October did senior U.S. policymakers begin to realize the depth of opposition to Aristide and his government throughout the Haitian upper and middle classes, and the difficulty they would have in negotiating any kind of compromise between these forces and the recalcitrant priest. For the coup leaders, the armed forces, and their chief backers—the MREs, or "Morally Repugnant Elites," as some U.S. diplomats termed them— what was at stake was nothing less than control over a predatory state apparatus. They believed that Aristide's return to real power would threaten their political and economic dominance and, given his previous advocacy of mob violence by supporters, might threaten their lives as well. As a result, "Everyone who is anyone opposes Aristide," said one Haitian businessman, "except for the people."[17] The initial postcoup sanctions, in contrast, were viewed by the MREs as an inconvenience, and probably a temporary one at that: The Haitian upper classes found it hard to believe that U.S. officials really cared about putting Aristide back in power simply because a bunch of peasants had voted for him.[18]

What transpired in the months after sanctions were imposed, therefore, was precisely the opposite of what had been intended. European countries did not participate in the embargo (partly because they could not be bothered to and partly because they claimed an obligation to continue trading with Haiti under the Lomé convention dealing with former European colonies), and sanctions were not enforced militarily against OAS members (because doing so was not considered necessary and would have smacked of gunboat diplomacy). Enough supplies of goods and fuel reached Haiti for the richest sectors of society to survive relatively unscathed. At the same time, the sanctions pushed the large mass of Haitian poor even closer to or below the subsistence level.[19] Fuel shortages led to an ecological catastrophe (as peasants chopped down trees to make charcoal, thus hastening the country's deforestation), and soon a surge of refugees set sail in hopes of finding haven in the United States.[20] The nascent Haitian middle class, finally—which U.S. policymakers had nurtured for a decade and saw as the key to the country's long-term economic development—was practically wiped out. After four months of sanctions an estimated 100,000 Haitians had lost their jobs, with many of these losses coming from the evisceration of the assembly sector, previously the darling of American efforts to create an internationally competitive Haitian economy.[21]

This last development, because it hurt certain Americans as well as Haitians, produced the first significant shift in post-coup U.S. policy. Responding to intensive lobbying from business interests, at the beginning of February 1992 the Bush administration loosened the sanctions slightly by permitting some American companies connected with Haiti's assembly sector to ship components there and bring finished products back to the United States.[22] In practice, this move probably had little effect either way on the broader course of events—because most of the assembly sector jobs were gone for good—but many perceived it to signal the Bush administration's weakening of resolve. "When Washington announced that it would begin selectively removing sanctions against industrial concerns to help revive a choking economy," reported the *New York Times*, "the mood of optimism among many who supported the coup turned to bravado and frankly expressed glee."[23]

Three months later, the growing number of Haitian boat people produced the second significant shift in U.S. policy. The Bush administration initially had sought to screen the intercepted refugees according to standard U.S. practice, determining whether they were "politically" motivated (and thus allowed to remain) or "economically" motivated (and thus sent home). Within six months of the coup, however, more than 30,000 Haitians had been picked up at sea, over-whelming a temporary refugee camp set up at Guantanamo. As the human tide flowed into Florida, pressure on the administration to do something about the situation grew intense. Unwilling either to lift the sanctions or to solve the problem at its roots, President Bush ordered that the boat people be returned to Haiti without screening.[24] This move got Haiti out of the headlines and allowed the administration to put the whole problem onto a back burner, where it stayed until after the election. As Deputy Secretary of State Lawrence Eagleburger said about the administration's policy during this period, "If you're look-ing for a clear, precise roadmap of how this is going to change the sit-uation, I can't give it to you. Sooner or later it will be settled in the way we want it to be settled."[25]

Clinton I: To Governors Island and Beyond

During the 1992 presidential campaign Bill Clinton attacked George Bush's Haiti policy as heartless, particularly his stance on refugees. After the election, nonetheless, Clinton decided that he had no practical alternative and so kept the repatriation effort in place.[26] More than their predecessors, however, the Clinton team was uncomfortable with the situation.

The Bush administration, once its senior officials realized that Aris-tide was not a poster child for democratic rule and faced deep opposi-tion at home, had settled into a policy of halfhearted efforts to mediate a negotiated settlement among all parties concerned.[27] The Clinton administration's first Haiti policy was essentially to pursue a similar goal with greater intensity. The administration's special advisor on Haiti, Lawrence Pezzullo, worked closely with representatives from the OAS and United Nations to find some compromise solution. The scheme they devised, centered around the provision of a few interna-tional police officers and some foreign aid, was at once so detailed and yet so vague, so precise and yet so full of holes at crucial points, that it is worth quoting at length:

> The police volunteers . . . are intended to reassure Haitian officers and rank-and-file soldiers that they would be protected from mob attacks. Some of these volunteers are expected to begin training substantial num-bers of Haitian soldiers to serve as the nucleus of a new, professional police force. That would be the first step in what U.S. and U.N. officials describe as an ambitious, many-sided international aid program aimed at helping the poverty-stricken republic improve its economic situation and

build the institutions necessary for democracy. With the help of other outside advisers, plans would be drawn to reform the justice system, create a free labor movement, and persuade scaled-down armed forces to turn their energies to road building and other improvements in Haiti's primitive infrastructure. "All this would take place against a background of a transition in power," said the senior U.S. official. "We can't say yet precisely at what stage it would happen. But if the negotiations succeed, somewhere in there—between the deployment of the police force and the move to other reforms—the present, military-controlled government would give way to civilian rule; laws would be passed to establish democratic reforms, and the new regime would gain recognition by the world community. Also, as part of that mix, Aristide would return home and reclaim the presidency."[28]

Taken at face value, this plan seems to rely on an assumption that the deeply divided Haitian factions, traditional players in a brutal, zero-sum political culture, would voluntarily and miraculously change their spots simply because it was the most sensible route to national progress. A more charitable if cynical interpretation of the plan holds that the foreign police contingent would have acted like the soldiers inside the Trojan horse, covering key points and by their presence giving the United States great leverage over future developments—thus helping American officials impose a solution on the Haitian parties whether they changed their spots or not. If the first interpretation of the plan is correct, U.S. officials were guilty of naïveté; if the second, they were guilty of overconfidence in their ability to manipulate events.

When neither the coup leaders nor Aristide embraced the scheme, the Clinton administration decided to coax and pressure them into going along with it anyway. Cédras and his cohorts would be prodded by further sanctions, the strategy went, while Aristide would be made to see that half a loaf was better than none, and the maximum he could expect to get. In June 1993, accordingly, the administration ratcheted up pressure on Haitian elites supporting the coup by introducing more targeted sanctions denying them and their families access to the United States (and in some cases freezing their personal assets in the country).[29] Following the lead of the United States, moreover, the U.N. Security Council passed Resolution 841, which mandated the imposition of a universal oil and arms embargo against Haiti unless immediate steps were taken to return Aristide to power.[30]

Since by this point, despite American entreaties, 90 percent of Haiti's fuel was being supplied by Europeans (particularly from the Netherlands), the threat of U.N.-imposed sanctions did indeed bring the coup leaders to the negotiating table, albeit grudgingly. Aristide was bullied into coming along too, although the Haitian principals refused to deal directly with each other. The result of this inauspicious process was that on July 3 a sullen Cédras and a no less sullen Aristide both signed the Governors Island Agreement, a variant of the plan just quoted under which a new prime minister and government of reconciliation would be named, Cédras would step down and receive amnesty, and Aristide would return on October 30. Both Haitian parties wanted a significantly better deal and signed under duress; almost immediately they began sparring over just what had been agreed to. Nevertheless, when the first steps of the plan proceeded according to schedule, the U.N. oil embargo was suspended in late August, along with some of the targeted U.S. sanctions, and in late September a United Nations Mission in Haiti (UNMIH) was established to oversee implementation and soothe tensions after Aristide's return.[31]

Under the agreement's terms the Haitian military would be retrained to serve as a combination police force and corps of engineers, and eventually a boatload of U.S. and Canadian military experts was dispatched to preside over this process. When the *USS Harlan County* approached Port-au-Prince on October 11, however, armed gangs loyal to the coup leaders created disturbances on the docks. The ship promptly sailed away instead of continuing forward, because the foreign troops' mission was predicated on a benign, consensual environment and because a disastrous confrontation in Somalia the previous week had made U.S. military officials adamantly opposed to (and administration officials extremely wary of) participation in any potentially dangerous Haiti mission.

As prospects for the fulfillment of the Governors Island Agreement evaporated, the deadline for Aristide's return passed unheeded, and so the U.N. oil embargo was reimposed. In a new development, however— following U.N. Security Council Resolution 875, which authorized member states to ensure implementation of the U.N. sanctions— President Clinton ordered six destroyers to patrol the waters surrounding Haiti and enforce the embargo more strongly than before.[32] The president also issued yet another executive order designed to target coup supporters, this one blocking the property of anyone found to have obstructed the Governors Island Agreement, contributed to violence in Haiti, or supported these activities.[33]

Clinton II: Bush Redux

At this point, nine months into its term, the Clinton administration was back where it had begun on Haiti, except with a much stiffer package of sanctions in place (thanks to the U.N. oil embargo, the military enforcement of that and the general OAS embargo, and the unilateral U.S. measures designed to punish rich coup supporters). With no appetite to press forward or to track back, the administration saw little choice but to sit tight and adopt the Bush strategy of hoping that somehow the situation would solve itself. "We're just going to let the military stew in their own juices, that's the policy," said one official. "I hate to say it," said another, "but the military has us boxed into a corner, and no one has any idea of what to do except let the situation ride for a while and hope something breaks our way."[34]

Attempts to forge a diplomatic solution to the crisis continued to founder as both Aristide and the Cédras regime held to their maximalist positions. Another compromise plan was scuttled in December when Aristide withdrew his support at the last minute, and afterward the Clinton administration issued an ultimatum declaring that the sanctions would be tightened yet again unless the Cédras regime lived up to its obligations under the Governors Island Agreement by January 15, 1994. The deadline passed without any progress, but the administration could not bring itself to make good on its threat—and so it shifted gears once more, to a new tack of distancing itself from Aristide.[35] In February this new course produced still another compromise plan,[36] which again was rejected by Aristide, but the administration decided not to bring on domestic political trouble for itself by trying to force it down his throat.

By then, even though Pezzullo wanted to continue pursuing the transplacement route ("There was always another initiative," said a colleague, "the second cousin of the head of the Parliament who believed he could get to Cédras"), it had become clear to the White House that "we were just chasing butterflies."[37] At this point, moreover, three new factors began pushing the administration to seek a *re*placement. The first was a deterioration in the humanitarian situation in Haiti; the second was an increase in Haitian immigration; and the third was a brewing political storm within some of Clinton's critical constituencies.

The Cédras regime, in keeping with Haitian tradition, always had been brutal and unsavory, but during the spring of 1994 the country's domestic situation began to worsen significantly. This was due in part to a stepped-up campaign of terror against Aristide's supporters.[38] It was also due, however, to the cumulative impact of the sanctions, which had by this point devastated the country, hastened the ravaging of its environment, and helped to unravel its general social and economic fabric.

The most powerful members of the traditional elite had been able to protect themselves from most of the sanctions' effects, using their wealth to procure enough contraband so as not to be unduly put out. Even the harshest sanctions often worked perversely to the MRE's advantage, such as when the embargo of everything but basic food products allowed Haiti's traditionally wealthy families to extract still greater rents through their monopolies over such staples as flour, sugar, rice, and cooking oil.[39] A new class of sanctions profiteers had sprung up, moreover, representing the drug dealers, the black marketeers, and the most ruthless of the military. "The army," as one reporter noted, "once largely dependent on the economic elite for money, has developed an independent financial network based on contraband and extortion that makes its leaders less reliant on the business community."[40] By controlling the spot market in smuggled oil, the military reaped windfall profits from practically all buyers, including U.S. embassy staff.[41]

For ordinary Haitians, however, the sanctions materially worsened what was already the most abject poverty in the hemisphere.[42] Inflation rose each year during the crisis, while the country's gross domestic product fell by 13.5 percent from 1991 to 1993 and by another 10.6 percent the year after.[43] The only good thing the sanctions produced was the construction of Haiti's one decent highway—in order to facilitate the endless passage of trucks carrying contraband oil from the Dominican Republic to Port-au-Prince.[44] (During mid-1994 Clinton administration officials announced a high-profile attempt to restrict that flow of oil; the measures had little practical impact but allowed U.S. policymakers to say that all options other than force were being actively pursued.)

The deteriorating conditions in Haiti, combined with the political stalemate, helped generate a new wave of Haitian boat people, who nevertheless were met on the seas by U.S. ships and forcibly repatriated. This was when Haitian affairs intersected with U.S. domestic politics, producing the true catalyst for the administration's policy shift. On one side, the administration came under increasingly harsh attack from the Congressional Black Caucus, which demanded that the Haitian refugee policy be loosened; on the other side, it was pressed by the electorally critical state of Florida, which refused to tolerate any more Haitian immigrants. Seizing the moment, activist Randall Robinson began a hunger strike to publicize the refugees' concerns and put Haiti at the top of the administration's agenda.[45] The administration now finally decided to abandon the search for a compromise settlement; Pezzullo was replaced with former Congressman William Gray as the administration's Haiti point man, and somewhere in Washington a clock started counting down to the use of force.[46]

Clinton III: The Shift
to Military Intervention

The first step in the new policy was the adoption of a looser approach to refugee repatriation. This temporarily satisfied the president's critics on the left, but it also soon produced more immigrants than the political market could bear. The administration responded, accordingly, by tinkering with the refugee handling process and by ratcheting up the sanctions yet again, this time considering it as a step onto the lower rungs of one final ladder of escalation that would end the crisis once and for all. On May 6 the U.N. Security Council, led by the United States, adopted Resolution 917 imposing a total trade embargo on Haiti, to be enforced by an international naval blockade, as well as a cut-off of air travel to and from Haiti. In the United States these measures were enacted—along with further sanctions, including a complete cut-off of all financial transactions between the United States and Haiti, a complete freeze of U.S. properties and assets held by all Haitian nationals, and a revocation of all nonimmigrant visas given to Haitians prior to May 1994—in a series of executive orders announced in May and June.[47] These measures constituted, in the words of one administration official, "as close to a smart bomb financially as we could get."[48] They were targeted at identified coup supporters and at Haitian nationals still resident in the country who had U.S. holdings; the assumption behind the latter provision was that any Haitian prosperous enough to have holdings in the United States was a de facto member of the elite, and that any such person still resident in Haiti in mid-1994 was either supporting or at least cooperating with the coup regime. (The tightened sanctions were combined, it is worth noting, with efforts to step up humanitarian aid to the Haitian poor.)

As the impasse continued, the Clinton administration moved closer toward a military option, and on July 31 it secured passage of U.N. Security Council Resolution 940, which authorized member states to form a multinational force (MNF) and "use all necessary means" to reverse the coup and implement the Governors Island Agreement. The plan was that after an intervention "the multinational force will terminate its mission and UNMIH will assume the full range of its functions . . . when a secure and stable environment has been established and UNMIH has adequate force capability."[49]

Soon afterward the final plans for an invasion of Haiti began to take shape. President Clinton approved the timetable for intervention on August 19 and gave formal approval to the invasion plans on

August 26.[50] During this period the administration was trying simultaneously to threaten leaders in Haiti (in hopes that they would step down without an invasion) and to deflect congressional criticism at home; neither strategy worked particularly well, although congressional moves to prevent the administration from invading were defeated.

The plans called for a brief operation in which an amphibious attack would secure the Port-au-Prince pier while airborne troops took the airports; forces would then pacify key targets around the city and soon spread out to secure the remaining objectives around the country. About 20,000 U.S. troops would be involved, along with a few thousand other participants; having conquered the country, they would switch to humanitarian assistance, training, and multilateral peacekeeping for some months, at which point they would hand off to the UNMIH.

On September 15 President Clinton told the nation that diplomatic efforts had been exhausted and that unless the coup leaders left voluntarily, they would soon be deposed and Aristide restored to power by a U.S.-led invasion: "Leave now," he told them, "or we will force you from power." In a hastily arranged move, however, Clinton agreed to permit a final mission by former President Jimmy Carter, former Joint Chiefs of Staff chairman General Colin Powell, and Senator Sam Nunn (D-Ga.) to resolve the crisis. Negotiating under the threat of invasion, with the go-ahead order actually sent during their final discussions, the trio managed to craft a deal in which Aristide would return and the coup leaders step down in return for amnesty and an unfreezing of their personal assets. En route to Haiti the troops' task changed from invasion to occupation, and on September 19 they landed without opposition, quickly securing their initial objectives.

At the end of the month the Security Council declared that the sanctions against Haiti would be lifted the day after Aristide's return, which proved to be October 15. Cédras resigned a week earlier, and he and his cronies soon departed for Panama or the Dominican Republic.[51] Aristide designated a new prime minister, and with the support of the legislature the new government took office in early November.

By the third week of the operation MNF troop levels were being drawn down. During the fall and winter the U.S. and coalition presence expanded throughout Haiti, and helped coordinate international humanitarian assistance. Troops restored essential public services, helped in the (re)building of Haitian government institutions, helped repatriate over 13,000 Haitians who had fled, and reduced the number of illegal weapons in Haiti.[52] They did not undertake large-scale disarmament of the population, however, because of fears that such "mission creep" would produce Somalia-style resistance.[53] The key issues involved in determining when to transition from the MNF to the UNMIH were policing, devising a timetable for forthcoming legislative elections, and establishing a secure and stable environment. Whereas the MNF had been largely American, moreover, only about one-third of the UNMIH force was.

The transfer of responsibility from the MNF to the UNMIH occurred smoothly as planned at the end of March 1995, and over the summer the Security Council extended UNMIH's mandate for another half year. Its tasks throughout this period were, first, to help the Haitian government maintain a secure and stable environment so free elections could be held, followed by an orderly transition to a new government, and, second, to professionalize the Haitian Armed Forces and create a separate police force capable of maintaining order on its own.

Prohibited by the Haitian constitution and external pressure from running for a second term, Aristide sponsored the candidacy of Rene Préval in the presidential election of December 1995. Préval won in a landslide (he garnered 88 percent of the vote, with 28 percent popular participation) and took office in February 1996. He soon requested that the mandate for the UNMIH, which was set to expire, be extended. The Security Council agreed, although authorizing a decreased level of troops and police.[54] After subsequent extensions the UNMIH presence in Haiti finally ended in late 1997, although a small contingent of police trainers remained behind, along with a several-hundred-strong deployment of U.S. troops ostensibly devoted to civil engineering and other nonsecurity-related functions.

The total cost of U.S. military participation in Haiti-related operations up to early 1996 (including MNF, UNMIH, sanctions enforcement, and the rest) amounted to just over $1 billion; the annual cost of maintaining the preinvasion policy in its mid-1994 form would have been $200 million.[55]

Conclusion

To judge the wisdom of employing sanctions in any particular case, one must answer two separate questions: How effective particular sanctions are likely to be in the circumstances at hand, and how they compare in terms of cost and effectiveness to other potential policy options. The sanctions against Haiti fare poorly on both counts.

Diplomatic spin aside, U.S. policymakers might have responded to the coup against Aristide in three basic ways: by grudgingly accepting it, by moving decisively to reverse it, or by punishing Haiti until the situation somehow improved. The first course would have been easy to implement and probably would not have carried a significant material price, although it would have involved accepting an ideological and humanitarian defeat. The second course would have been more difficult to implement but still feasible, although it would have carried real if uncertain costs. Bush administration officials were reluctant to accept *either* ideological *or* material costs in the short term, however, and so after the initial OAS mediation attempts failed they selected the third course, gambling that sanctions could reverse the coup on the cheap. To the administration's chagrin, given the intractability of Haitian politics and leaders, the sanctions proved politically ineffective, morally costly, and ultimately domestically unsustainable. In the Haitian case, therefore, sanctions were not a wise middle course but rather the worst of the three alternatives available.

The coup presented U.S. policymakers with a much more difficult choice than they appreciated at the time.[56] The transition from authoritarianism to democracy is rocky and complex in the best of situations; Haiti's divided society, backward economy, and dearth of healthy political and civic institutions created something approaching a worst-case scenario. Democratization, furthermore, is notoriously difficult to manipulate from the outside, except on the margins. And Aristide's own characteristics, finally—his stubborn resistance to compromise, his inability to embrace and internalize liberal principles—helped scuttle whatever slim chances existed for a real transplacement. For all these reasons, it was unwise to commit U.S. prestige so vociferously at the start of the crisis to reversing the coup and restoring Aristide to power. However unpleasant it may have been, U.S. officials should have limited themselves to expressing their sorrow and disapproval, combined perhaps with a distant stance toward the coup regime and an offer to help mediate some compromise settlement to Haiti's problems. Such a course probably seemed heartless and weak, however—and would have involved acknowledging that "the end of History" had not come to Latin America—and so it was rejected.

Two legitimate arguments can be offered, nevertheless, for opposing the coup firmly: that it was symbolically and practically important for the United States to put teeth into the Santiago Commitment and be seen defending democracy in the Americas, and that a postcoup Haitian refugee crisis might have arisen *even without the impact of the sanctions.* Even those who accept such arguments and believe that it was appropriate to commit U.S. prestige to reversing the coup, however, would be hard-pressed to defend the actual policy course adopted.

The proper activist response would have been to sit down and devise some realistic strategy to accomplish the central goal within a manageable time frame. Swift, powerful, targeted sanctions against the coup leaders, combined with credible threats to escalate beyond sanctions to the use of force if necessary, might conceivably have persuaded them to relent; more likely, an actual invasion would have been required to dislodge them and solidify Aristide's control. The period from fall 1991 to spring 1992, in this scenario, should have witnessed what actually occurred from spring to fall 1994. The result probably would have been roughly the same, but without all the suffering of the intervening years. Few if any voices, however, were prepared to embrace such an activist approach at the beginning of the crisis, because there seemed no commensurable American interests at stake.

In the end, the Bush administration chose to articulate ambitious goals but to devote only modest means to achieve them. The means in question, moreover—broad-based economic sanctions—were not merely ill-suited to pressuring entrenched authoritarian elites within a short time period; they were also *guaranteed to work against all other U.S. goals in Haiti apart from democratization.* The greatest challenges Haiti faces are rampant population growth, economic underdevelopment, and environmental degradation. As might have been predicted, the sanctions gutted family planning programs, destroyed the Haitian assembly industry, and hastened the country's deforestation. They practically wiped out what small Haitian middle class existed, thus rendering future political and economic development that much more problematic. As if injuring others were not enough, however, the sanctions—again, as might have been predicted—generated the unintended consequence of an immigration tidal wave washing on to U.S. shores. The original policy was thus not sustainable for domestic reasons, quite apart from its impact on Haiti.

A variety of generalizable conclusions can be drawn from this case about sanctions as a tool of statecraft for the United States and in some cases others. The first is that determined authoritarian rulers can manage to shield themselves from a great deal of harm when broad-based measures are taken against their country. Small loopholes in sanctions can be enough to provide sustenance for regime leaders, since they can monopolize whatever resources the society possesses, and eliminating all such loopholes is practically impossible—especially if the sanctions are not global in scope and not militarily enforced. Even after both those conditions were met in the Haitian case by late 1993, however, a steady trickle of oil made its way (by the truckload, or the skiffload, or even the individual bucketful) across or around the border between Haiti and the Dominican Republic. The total amount of oil involved was tiny, but given Haiti's nonindustrialized conditions, it was still enough to blunt the sanctions' impact and fuel a coup regime bent on staying in power at all costs.

Like Vietnam a generation earlier, therefore, the Haitian case should serve as a reminder not to underestimate one's foes: Just because a country is weak, poor, and strategically insignificant does not mean that its leaders will cave in quickly to moderate outside pressure. With regard to sanctions as to force, policymakers should be wary of overconfidence and should take the time to develop a clear, realistic strategy setting out how their actions will produce results. They need to pay careful attention to the balance of power *and* the balance of interests at stake.[57]

A second lesson is that a policy of sanctions designed to achieve a specific political objective can leave the sanctioner in an uncomfortable position if the objective is not achieved quickly. In the first weeks after the coup, for example, various congressmen pressed Assistant Secretary Aronson to say what the administration would do if the sanctions did not produce results: "One of the things that, of course, is in the minds of all of us that are interested in this is what is going to happen if the sanctions put in place do not work," said one. "My concern is whether the time has not come for us to think of military intervention."[58] "If indeed in the coming days or weeks," said another, " . . . there is wide-scale suffering, contamination of water or food, or other disease that might result in massive suffering . . . I trust . . . that there are contingency plans to deal with that."[59] Aronson was able to deflect such questions at the hearing, but neither the Bush nor the Clinton administration could deflect them forever. The Haiti sanctions may have appeared to policymakers at first as a low-cost, low-risk option, but they started a clock ticking that would force officials down the road either to walk away from a commitment or to escalate.[60]

A third lesson is that sanctions generate undesirable consequences and side effects that need to be anticipated and planned for. In Haiti, for example, the combination of political repression and economic crisis after the coup led inexorably to increased emigration. This was hardly unforeseeable—in fact, it was predicted by many in October and November 1991—and yet neither the Bush nor the Clinton administration ever came up with a solution to the problem that addressed American interests and American values simultaneously.

A fourth lesson is that for both practical and humanitarian reasons, sanctions always should be targeted as precisely as possible and frontloaded rather than adopted incrementally. As for targeting, it is barely possible, as mentioned earlier, that hitting the Haitian coup leaders and their backers with the toughest measures conceivable right at the start of the crisis might have convinced them to step aside, and at less cost to the general Haitian population—not least because such measures would have sent clearer signals to the de facto government that waiting out the Americans was not a realistic possibility.[61] One of the few positive precedents of the Haitian experience, moreover, might be the creation, in 1993–94, of appropriate legal procedures and mechanisms for implementing "designer sanctions" against foreign elites: denying entry to the United States, freezing individuals' holdings and accounts, and so on. They were not very effective at producing significant behavioral change in this particular case—in fact, the chief purpose of instituting them was a desire to demonstrate that all options short of intervention had been tried—but it is possible that under certain circumstances they might be more effective in the future and might also represent a useful way of making unrepentant targets into true international pariahs. Unless one is confronting a true democracy where leaders must be responsive to broad-based constituencies, sanctions should be designed as creatively as possible to strike at key decisionmakers where it hurts.

A fifth lesson, finally, is that regional sanctions are unlikely to be very effective but can serve a minor constructive role in stigmatizing the target, in preventing the consolidation and widespread recognition of a pariah regime, and in helping to keep an international coalition together. Sanctioners should be cynical and recognize from the start that any opportunities available to circumvent the restrictions probably will be seized, by one's friends if not by one's enemies.

The sum total of these conclusions is that policymakers considering the use of economic sanctions should not necessarily reject them but should think far more carefully before proceeding than is generally the case. Precisely because it *was* treated as a more serious affair by all concerned, the 1994 Haitian military intervention—in contrast to the tortuous history of the Haitian sanctions—went smoothly. By breaking the exit into several gradual phases and avoiding abrupt departures or transitions, moreover, the planners enabled practically all of the outside troops to withdraw while leaving behind a situation in Haiti that has proved stable for at least the short term and is certainly more democratic than ever before. This demonstrates that a well thought out, carefully planned military operation—combined with some luck and, if necessary, the inducement of an appropriate "golden parachute" for departing strongmen—can be more humane and effective than supposedly benign economic sanctions.[62]

Nevertheless, Haiti remains a potential failed state, and its political future is unclear. Per capita income is only $250; the task at hand is not economic recovery but initial development—something made even more difficult by the sanctions' destruction of Haiti's nascent middle class. What the country truly requires is sustained nation-building, precisely that which few are willing to sponsor. The political, social, and economic tensions that gave rise to the 1991 crisis persist, and the intervention's success might be only temporary. Aristide and his chosen successor Préval have parted ways, the MREs remain, the new democratic institutions have practically ceased to function, and violence and disorder have begun to proliferate.[63] As one author has argued, therefore, the chief lesson of the Haiti intervention may be that those desiring success in the tricky situations of the post–Cold War environment should "define [their] goals so minimally that it will be easy to meet them, declare victory, and go home."[64]

Notes

1. A survey of the fates of Haitian rulers since independence reads like a sick joke: "fled," "shot," "overthrown," "taken hostage," "blown up," "poisoned," "dismembered," and so on. See "The Nightmare Next Door," *Economist,* September 24, 1994, p. 19.

2. Samuel P. Huntington, *The Third Wave: Democratization in the Late Twentieth Century* (Norman, OK: University of Oklahoma Press, 1991).

3. See Richard J. Bloomfield, "Making the Western Hemisphere Safe for Democracy? The OAS Defense-of-Democracy Regime," *Washington Quarterly* 17, no. 2 (Spring 1994), and Tom Farer (ed.), *Beyond Sovereignty: Collectively Defending Democracy in the Americas* (Baltimore, MD: Johns Hopkins University Press, 1996). For the Haitian case as a possible precedent, see John C. Pierce, "The Haitian Crisis and the Future of Collective Enforcement of Democratic Governance," *Law and Policy in International Business* 27, no. 2 (June 22, 1996), and Anthony P. Maingot, "Haiti: Sovereign Consent versus State-Centric Sovereignty," in Farer.

4. Domingo E. Acevedo, "The Haitian Crisis and the OAS Response," in Lori Fisler Damrosch (ed.), *Enforcing Restraint: Collective Intervention in Internal Conflicts* (New York: Council on Foreign Relations, 1993), pp. 119–155. For background on the coup and the events surrounding it, see Pamela Constable, "Haiti's Shattered Hopes," *Journal of Democracy* 3, no. 1 (January 1992), pp. 41–51.

5. Thomas L. Friedman, "The O.A.S. Agrees to Isolate Chiefs of Haitian Junta," *New York Times,* October 3, 1991, p. A1.

6. Thomas L. Friedman, "U.S. Suspends Assistance to Haiti and Refuses to Recognize Junta," *New York Times,* October 2, 1991, p. A1. This feeling was widely shared in Washington; in the words of Representative Robert Tor-

ricelli at a congressional hearing later that month, "There was and now remains the danger that the entire democratic trend could unravel as quickly and as decisively as it was assembled. . . . The test has arrived, and it is in Haiti. It tests the entire proposition of whether there is an inevitability to democracy in our hemisphere and whether this point of common democracy throughout the hemisphere shall indeed remain permanent." Remarks by Representative Torricelli, "Update on the Situation in Haiti," Hearing before the Subcommittee on Western Hemisphere Affairs of the House Committee on Foreign Affairs, October 31, 1991, 102nd Congress, 1st Session (Washington, DC: U.S. Government Printing Office, 1992), p. 1.

7. December 19, 1991, *Weekly Compilation of Presidential Documents* 27, no. 51 (Washington, DC: U.S. Government Printing Office, 1991), p. 1870.

8. Executive Order 12775, of October 4, declared a national emergency because of the Haitian coup and blocked the property and funds of the Haitian government in the United States. Executive Order 12779, of October 28, added trade sanctions against Haiti while permitting the importation into the United States until December 5 of goods within the Haitian assembly industry's pipeline. The measures were enacted under presidential authority deriving from the International Emergency Economic Powers Act, the National Emergencies Act, and section 301 of title 3 of the U.S. code. See *Weekly Compilation of Presidential Documents* 27, no. 40 (Washington, DC: U.S. Government Printing Office, 1991), pp. 1406–7, and 27, no. 44, pp. 1532–33. The humanitarian exemptions permitted relief operations to continue, and throughout the crisis organizations such as CARE fed hundreds of thousands of Haitians each day.

9. Remarks by Aronson, "Update on Haiti."

10. As the president said, "I've learned . . . that you've got to be very, very careful of using United States forces in this hemisphere." October 4, 1991, *Weekly Compilation of Presidential Documents* 27, no. 40 (Washington, DC: U.S. Government Printing Office, 1991), p. 1399.

11. John M. Goshko, "Aristide, Bush Agree to Push Diplomacy in Haiti," *Washington Post,* October 5, 1991, p. A14. One official in the Bush White House would later recall that "little thought went into the decision to impose economic sanctions on Haiti. It seemed to be the easiest thing to do, and many . . . thought that the regime would succumb to sanctions within a matter of months. This was seen by some as a slam dunk." Interview with author, May 1997.

12. Representative Robert Lagomarsino, "Update on the Situation in Haiti," p. 3. "Few countries are as vulnerable to a trade embargo as Haiti," reported the *Washington Post.* "Analysts say it might not hold out more than a few weeks if the embargo is anywhere near as sweeping as that which the United States has maintained against Cuba for 30 years." Lee Hockstader, "Stiff Embargo Seen Crippling Haiti Quickly," *Washington*

Post, October 14, 1991, p. A27. Even after the fact some felt such arguments were not unreasonable: "'If ever economic sanctions were going to work, Haiti, in a way, was an ideal situation,' [sanctions expert Gary C.] Hufbauer said, 'because it was so poor, so dependent on the United States and the impact was so great.'" Dick Kirschten, "Economic Sanctions," *National Journal,* January 4, 1997, p. 14.

13. "Update on Haiti," pp. 30, 32.

14. Ibid, p. 35.

15. Huntington, *Third Wave,* p. 114.

16. Many Haitians believed (and some still do) that U.S. officials were complicit in the coup; this erroneous view was not based on any evidence but rather on a common assumption in Haiti that nothing of importance in the country's politics can happen against U.S. wishes. For an occasionally perceptive but fundamentally wrong-headed radical argument that the coup fit squarely within "the very logic of the U.S.-transnational project" for Haiti, see William I. Robinson, *Promoting Polyarchy: Globalization, U.S. Intervention, and Hegemony* (Cambridge: Cambridge University Press, 1996), pp. 256–316; the quotation is on p. 294.

17. Lee Hockstader, "Inside Misery's Kingdom," *Washington Post,* November 10, 1991, p. C1.

18. This view was bolstered by the fact that historically, U.S. authorities had far better relations with the Haitian elites than with the Haitian masses. "Countries always look for local allies in their foreign policy and protect them no matter what," one diplomat pointed out. "Unfortunately, in the case of Haiti, the United States' old friends are precisely the people responsible for this crisis." Howard W. French, "Despite Embargo, Haiti's Rich Seem to Get Richer," *New York Times,* May 25, 1994, p. A3.

19. "Between November 1991 and March 1992, according to the U.S. General Accounting Office, ships from Latin America, Europe, and Africa supplied Haiti with goods ranging from Argentine steel to French perfume. Most significantly, tankers from half a dozen countries delivered almost a million barrels of oil." Pamela Constable, "Dateline Haiti: Caribbean Stalemate," *Foreign Policy* no. 89, (Winter 1992/3), pp. 175–90. For the effects of sanctions, see Lee Hockstader, "Haiti Embargo Raises Specter of Famine; Rich Still Dine," *Washington Post,* February 11, 1992, p. A18; Maureen Taft-Morales, "Haiti's Troubled Path Towards Democracy and U.S. Policy Concerns," in *The Caribbean Basin—Economic and Security Issues: Study Papers Submitted to the Joint Economic Committee of the Congress of the United States,* edited by Mark B. Sullivan (Washington: U.S. Government Printing Office, 1993), pp. 104–21; and Anthony P. Maingot, "Testimony," in Hearing Before the Select Committee on Hunger, House of Representatives, June 11, 1992 (Washington, DC: U.S. Government Printing Office, 1992). For a discussion of the problems with the OAS embargo, see Acevedo,

"The Haitian Crisis," pp. 119–55; see also Claudette Antoine Werleigh, "The Use of Sanctions in Haiti," in David Cortright and George A. Lopez (eds.), *Economic Sanctions* (Boulder, CO: Westview, 1995), pp. 161–72.

20. By late November the Coast Guard had intercepted more than 3,000 refugees at sea, and by the end of January, almost 14,000. For an excellent analysis of how Haitian demographic and environmental trends create pressures for migration, see Ernest H. Preeg, *The Haitian Dilemma* (Washington; DC: Center for Strategic and International Studies, 1996).

21. Lee Hockstader, "For Haiti's Rulers, A Key Signal," *Washington Post*, February 5, 1992, p. A26. For how the assembly sector fit into U.S. long-term plans for Haiti, see Preeg, *The Haitian Dilemma*. For radical critiques of such efforts and the neoliberal project they embodied, see Robinson, *Promoting Polyarchy*; and Deirdre McFadyen, et al. (eds.), *Haiti: Dangerous Crossroads* (Boston, MA: South End Press, 1995).

22. "We acted to prevent what we concluded would have been disastrous and lasting damage to the Haitian economy through the bankruptcy of these companies or their transfer to third countries," an administration official explained to Congress. Deputy Assistant Secretary of State Donna Hrinak, "The Situation in Haiti and U.S. Policy," Hearing before the Subcommittees on Human Rights and International Organizations and Western Hemisphere Affairs of the House Committee on Foreign Affairs, February 19, 1992, 102nd Congress, 2nd Session (Washington, DC: U.S. Government Printing Office, 1992), p. 23. For details on the lobbying effort to ease the sanctions, see Al Kamen, "U.S. Eased Haiti Embargo Under Business Pressure," *Washington Post*, February 7, 1992, p. A1, and Carol Matlack, "Lobbying, PR War over Policy on Haiti," *National Journal*, April 25, 1992, p. 1002. For details on the pro Aristide lobbying effort in Washington, see John M. Goshko, "Aristide Finances Government-in-Exile with Frozen Haitian Assets," *Washington Post*, January 15, 1994, p. A18, and—with caution—Christopher Caldwell, "Aristide Development," *The American Spectator* (July 1994). For interest group involvement in Haiti policy in general, see John W. Dietrich, "Interest Groups and the Making of American Foreign Policy: U.S.-Haiti Policy," Paper prepared for the annual meeting of the Northeastern Political Science Association, November 9–11, 1995.

23. Howard W. French, "Democracy Push in Haiti Blunted," *New York Times*, February 7, 1992, p. A5. By the spring of 1992, "The military, the Parliament, and much of Haiti's elite had become convinced that the administration's growing disillusionment with Aristide would eventually lead to their acceptance of his ouster, providing an acceptable substitute could be found." Richard L. Millett, "Panama and Haiti," in Jeremy R. Azrael and Emil A. Payin (eds.), *U.S. and Russian Policymaking with Respect to the Use of Force* (Santa Monica, CA: RAND Corporation, 1996, CF-129-CRES) (Also available on their webpage:www.rand.org.).

24. The administration simultaneously expanded somewhat the facilities for screening at the U.S. Embassy in Port-au-Prince. The decision to return the refugees automatically was accompanied by an attempt, taken in support of a new OAS resolution, to tighten the sanctions somewhat by denying the use of American ports to ships violating the Haitian embargo. See Lee Hockstader, "Sanctions on Haiti Tightened," *Washington Post*, May 18, 1992, p. A1, and "Statement on Denying Use of United States Ports to Vessels Trading with Haiti," May 28, 1992, *Weekly Compilation of Presidential Documents* 28, no. 22 (Washington, DC: U.S. Government Printing Office), p. 941.

25. Lee Hockstader, "OAS Move Seen Unlikely to Trigger Shift in Haiti," *Washington Post*, May 20, 1992, p. A27.

26. See Iain Guest, "Refugee Policy Leading Up to Governors Island," in Georges Fauriol (ed.), *Haitian Frustrations* (Washington, DC: Center for Strategic and International Studies CSIS, 1995), pp. 75–82.

27. This did not achieve much, partly because the gulf between the administration's rhetoric and its actions contributed to "a belief among Haiti's current rulers that there are distinct limits to how far the United States is willing to carry its campaign against them . . . there is widespread feeling there that if the dictatorship sits tight, Washington will eventually tire of the struggle." The blatant hostility to Aristide in certain quarters of the government, such as the CIA, only fueled this impression. John M. Goshko, "U.S. Bid to Oust Regime Underlies Haiti Problem," *Washington Post*, May 27, 1992, p. A24.

28. John M. Goshko, "Administration Aides Defend Haiti Policy," *Washington Post*, May 21, 1993, p. A30.

29. The secretary of state and secretary of the treasury, respectively, were to decide who would be affected by the immigration and financial measures; OFAC disseminated a list of 35 entities and 83 individuals covered under the latter. These actions were taken under presidential authority derived from section 212(f) of the Immigration and Nationality Act of 1952, as amended, and section 301 of title 3, U.S. Code. "Proclamation 6569—Suspension of Entry as Immigrants and Nonimmigrants of Persons Who Formulate or Implement Policies That Are Impeding the Negotiations Seeking the Return to Consitutional Rule in Haiti," June 3, 1993, and "Statement on Sanctions Against Haiti," June 4, 1993, *Weekly Compilation of Presidential Documents* 29, no. 22 (Washington, DC: U.S. Government Printing Office, 1993), pp. 1025–6, 1029–30. There had been an earlier attempt during the Bush administration to introduce targeted sanctions involving the denial of visas, but it had to be scaled back because of legal problems. Why these problems were considered insurmountable by the Bush administration but were nevertheless overcome by the Clinton administration remains unclear. See John M. Goshko, "20 Haitian Coup Backers Have U.S. Visas Revoked," *Washington Post*, April 11, 1992, p. A19,

and Douglas Farah, "U.S. Tightens Sanctions on Regime in Haiti," *Washington Post*, June 5, 1993, p. A18.

30. The oil and arms embargo was enacted in the United States by Executive Order 12853, which also broadened U.S. authority to block the property of and prohibit transactions involving Haitian nationals who were found to be supporting the coup regime; see *Weekly Compilation of Presidential Documents* 29, no. 26 (Washington, DC: U.S. Government Printing Office, 1993), pp. 1206–7.

31. For discussion of events and policy during this period, see Georges A. Fauriol and Andrew S. Faiola, "Prelude to Intervention," in Fauriol, *Haitian Factions*, and Ian Martin, "Mangled Multilateralism," *Foreign Policy*, no. 95 (June 1994).

32. "President's News Conference," October 15, 1993, *Weekly Compilation of Presidential Documents* 29, no. 41 (Washington, DC: U.S. Government Printing Office, 1993), p. 2082, and "Letter to Congressional Leaders on Haiti," October 20, 1993, pp. 2125–26. Argentina, Canada, France, the Netherlands, and the United Kingdom helped to enforce the embargo.

33. "Executive Order 12872—Blocking Property of Persons Obstructing Democratization in Haiti," October 18, 1993, *Weekly Compilation of Presidential Documents* 29, no. 42 (Washington, DC: U.S. Government Printing Office, 1993), pp. 2103–4. On November 1, OFAC published a list of 41 individuals covered; in January 1994, OFAC listed the 523 known officers of the Haitian Armed Forces as covered, and in April it added 27 more officers and one civilian. During this period the administration also tried to get other countries to adopt similar targeted sanctions.

34. Thomas W. Lippman, "U.S. Relaxes Its Drive for Haitian Democracy," *Washington Post*, November 17, 1993, p. A36, and Douglas Farah, "Haitian Military Plans Years in Power," *Washington Post*, November 28, 1993, p. A1.

35. "I would not say that Aristide's return has been discarded," one U.S. diplomat declared, "but I would say there is a growing separation between the concept of returning Haiti to democracy and the return of Aristide. They are no longer necessarily synonymous." Douglas Farah, "Fuel Aid Sharpens Debate over Haiti," *Washington Post*, January 15, 1994, p. A13.

36. This one had Aristide appoint another prime minister, who would name a centrist government of national reconciliation, which would pass an amnesty for the military, which might lead to their stepping down, at which point negotiations might begin to discuss Aristide's return.

37. John Barry, "How Did We Get Here?" *Newsweek*, September 26, 1994, p. 26.

38. This was epitomized by a brazen massacre of 28 slum dwellers in late April. See Cathy Booth, "Hostage to Violence," *Time*, May 9, 1994, p. 39.

39. Howard W. French, "Prostrate Haiti Looking to Foreign Aid for a Lift," *New York Times*, July 11, 1993, p. A3. "The elite relies on rigged markets to

preserve longstanding monopolies, and the lack of tax collection and an institutionalized corruption that allows big importers to bring their goods into the country without paying dues or even standard port fees. 'Haiti has what you could call a franchise economy, where members of the elite have carved out their own niches and in effect employ the Government and the army to protect their holdings,' said one expert. . . ."

40. Douglas Farah, "Embargo Has Haiti's Economy Near Collapse, But Rulers Stand Firm," *Washington Post,* August 26, 1994, p. A20.

41. Douglas Farah, "U.S. Fills Up in Haiti with Smuggled Gas," *Washington Post,* April 19, 1994, p. A1.

42. For details see Carole Cleaver, "Notes from the Hell That Is Haiti," *The New Leader 77,* no. 1 (January 17, 1994); Douglas Farah, "Rural Haitians Reeling," *Washington Post,* November 27, 1993, p. A1; and Preeg, *The Haitian Dilemma,* p. 21.

43. Prices rose about 15 percent in 1992, 25 to 30 percent in 1993, and 40 to 50 percent in 1994. "Haiti: Quarterly Economic Indicators," *EIU ViewsWire,* May 19, 1995, and "Haiti: Latest Economic Indicators," *EIU ViewsWire,* November 22, 1996. The GDP numbers are drawn from Canute James, "Haitians Try to Bring Tattered Economy Back From the Dead," *Financial Times,* January 7, 1995, p. 4, and "Haiti Economy," *EIU ViewsWire,* June 23, 1995.

44. Howard W. French, "New Haiti Road Could Be Anti-Embargo Lifeline," *New York Times,* October 28, 1993, p. A1. On the oil trade with the Dominican Republic, see Howard W. French, "Embargo Creates 'Oil Boom' Near Haitian Border," *New York Times,* March 13, 1994, p. A3, and Douglas Farah, "Haiti: Fueled by Despair," *Washington Post,* May 6, 1994, p. A1.

45. To unravel the strands of U.S. refugee policy during this period, see Andrew S. Faiola, "Refugee Policy: The 1994 Crisis," in Fauriol, *Haitian Factions;* for the legal aspects of the refugee issue, see Julie Ann Waterman, "Note: The United States' Involvement in Haiti's Tragedy and the Resolve to Restore Democracy," *New York Law School Journal of International and Comparative Law* 15, No. 1 (1994).

46. On the way out, the bitter diplomat offered his objections to the policy change for all to read; see Lawrence A. Pezzullo, "Our Haiti Fiasco," *Washington Post,* May 5, 1994, p. A23.

47. Executive Order 12914 of May 7 established the air ban and blocked the U.S. funds and financial resources of coup leaders, coup supporters, and military officers. Proclamation 6685 of May 7 barred entry into the United States by coup leaders, coup supporters, military officers, and their families. Executive Order 12917 of May 21 established an absolute trade embargo (except for informational materials and certain food and medical supplies). Executive Order 12920 of June 10 completed the air ban and cut off financial transactions. And Executive Order 12922 of June 21 froze all

U.S. property and assets of Haitian nationals. See the following volumes of the *Weekly Compilation of Presidential Documents* (Washington, DC: U.S. Government Printing Office, 1994): 30, no. 19, pp. 1014–17; 30, no. 21, pp. 1147–50; 30, no. 23, pp. 1261–64; and 30, no. 25, pp. 1321–23.

48. "Background Briefing by Senior Administration Officials," White House Press Release, June 22, 1994.

49. U.N. Security Council Resolution 940 (1994).

50. Elaine Sciolino, "Mission to Haiti: Diplomacy," *New York Times*, September 20, 1994, p. A1. For a look at the administration's internal debates during this period, see Ann Devroy and R. Jeffrey Smith, "Debate over Risks Split Administration," *Washington Post*, September 25, 1994, p. A1, and David Bentley and Robert Oakley, "Peace Operations: A Comparison of Somalia and Haiti," *INSS Strategic Forum*, no. 30 (Washington, DC: National Defense University, May 1995).

51. For the fate of the coup leaders, see Douglas Farah, "U.S. Assists Dictators' Luxury Exile," *Washington Post*, p. A1. Cédras and company did not, in the end, receive all the benefits of the deal they had negotiated with Carter.

52. Statement by DOD Haiti Task Force Director John Christiansen to the Subcommitee on Western Hemisphere of the House International Relations Committee, February 28, 1996. For the administration's view of the mission, see the Statement by Deputy Secretary of State Strobe Talbott before the House International Relations Committee, February 24, 1995.

53. Donald Schulz, *Whither Haiti* (Carlisle Barracks, PA: US Army War College, 1996).

54. Renewal was almost blocked by China, which wanted to retaliate against Haiti for its relations with Taiwan. For details about the shifting positions of Security Council members, see David Malone, "Haiti and the International Community: A Case Study," *Survival* 39, no. 2 (Summer 1997), pp. 126–46.

55. Total mission cost from Christiansen statement; annual preinvasion figure from testimony of Deputy Secretary of Defense John Deutch before the Senate Foreign Relations Committee, Western Hemisphere and Peace Corps Affairs Subcommittee, March 9, 1995.

56. For an analysis that comes to similar conclusions, see Thomas Carothers, "Lessons for Policymakers," in Fauriol, *Haitian Factions*, pp. 117–23.

57. See Richard K. Betts, *Nuclear Blackmail and Nuclear Balance* (Washington, DC: Brookings Institution 1987).

58. Representative Jaime Fuster, in "Update" Hearing, October 31, 1991, p. 21.

59. Representative Torricelli, ibid., p. 18.

60. One implication of this point, interestingly, is that if you favor intervention but your own political climate is not yet ripe for discussion of it, dis-

guising your policy preference by pushing sanctions would be a clever move.

61.   This is the conclusion of Robert Maguire et al., *Haiti Held Hostage: International Responses to the Quest for Nationhood, 1986–1996* (Providence, RI: Watson Institute for International Studies, Brown University, 1996): "A serious and timely embargo, firmly imposed, tightly enforced, and backed up by credible military force, as it finally was, would have been the most humanitarian approach. Although ordinary Haitians might still have suffered, the end result would in all probability have entailed less suffering" (p. 56).

62.   Others have drawn a similar lesson: "The blunt weapon of sanctions might have been avoided by the earlier and surgical use of military force, more familiar in the lexicon of the military regime. In such a scenario . . . the international community would have retained credit for its major achievement—replacing the de facto regime with the constitutional authorities— while foreshortening suffering and reducing the reconstruction challenge. As many Haitians believe, swift and effective military action might have been the most humanitarian approach." Maguire et al., *Haiti Held Hostage*, p. 99.

63.   For discussion of postintervention developments in Haiti, see "Policy Toward Haiti," Hearing of the House International Relations Committee, December 9, 1997. See also Donald E. Schulz, *Haiti Update* (Carlisle Barracks, PA: U.S. Army War College, 1997) and Sidney W. Mintz, "Can Haiti Change?" *Foreign Affairs* 74, no. 1 (January/February 1995), pp. 73–86.

64.   Johanna McGeary, "Did the American Mission Matter?" *Time*, February 19, 1996, p. 36

4

Iran

PATRICK CLAWSON

T HE UNITED STATES has had economic sanctions of one sort or another in place against Iran since the Islamic Revolution of 1979. Nearly all those sanctions have been unilateral U.S. actions without multilateral support, which if nothing else makes Iran an interesting case study of the use of sanctions when the United States disagrees with its allies about how to proceed.

In reaction to the November 1979 seizure of the U.S. embassy in Tehran, President Jimmy Carter made it illegal for Americans to purchase goods directly from Iran and froze $12 billion in Iranian assets in the United States. In orders issued on April 7 and 17, 1980, he extended sanctions to include a ban on all commerce and travel between Iran and the United States, except for food, medicines, and newspeople.[1] Part of the January 20, 1981, Algiers Accord for release of the American embassy hostages was Washington's agreement to restore full normal economic relations with Iran. There were no special U.S. barriers to bilateral economic ties from then until January 1984, when Secretary of State George Shultz designated Iran as a supporter of international terrorism, which triggered a variety of restrictions.[2] Since 1984 the restrictions on economic ties with Iran have increased steadily.

On October 6, 1987, Congress, in response to U.S. Department of Energy purchases of Iranian oil for the U.S. Strategic Petroleum Reserve, passed resolutions unanimously in the Senate and 407–5 in the House calling for the banning of Iranian imports. On October 29 President Ronald Reagan, not wanting to be seen as less tough on terrorism than the Democrats who had just taken control of both chambers of Congress, signed an executive order prohibiting nearly all imports from Iran.

Iran had not been a matter of particular concern in the years from 1987 to 1992. In his inaugural address, President George Bush had extended Iran an offer, noting "Good will begets good will." Despite the November 1991 return to Iran of $285 million frozen since 1979 (for prepayment of arms purchases),[3] nothing came of American offers, repeated by the White House publicly and privately, to meet with Iranian officials quietly.[4]

The Iran-Iraq Arms Nonproliferation Act of 1992 significantly tightened restrictions on U.S. exports to Iran. The definitions of items subject to export controls are so broad that, to quote one respected business journal, they "could encompass everything developed in the computer age."[5] The act also included mandatory sanctions against any foreign government aiding Iran's acquisition of "chemical, biological, nuclear, or destabilizing numbers and types of advanced conventional weapons," including a ban on sale to Iran of items on the U.S. Munitions List, suspension of dual-use technical exchange agreements, and an end to any economic aid.[6] It also provided for measures against firms and individuals aiding the targeted Iranian programs.

From its early days, the Clinton administration took a somewhat harder line against Iran. The May 1993 proclamation of the policy of dual containment of Iraq and Iran put those two regimes on a rhetorically equal plane, no matter how much the administration was at pains to explain that the containment of Iran was of a qualitatively different character than that of Iraq: There were no overflights, no "no-fly zones," no U.N. inspections, no U.N. embargo, and no de facto insistence on a change of regime.[7] The Clinton team emphasized the national security threat posed by Iran, including its weapons of mass destruction programs, its organization of terrorism, its sponsorship of those bent on disrupting the Arab-Israeli peace process, and its subversion of moderate Middle Eastern regimes. European governments generally missed the signals of the change in policy, often dismissing Secretary of State Warren Christopher's comments on the issue as reflecting his personal pique dating from his 1980–81 role as chief negotiator of the Algiers Accord.

The initial policy of the Clinton administration was to confine its economic pressure against Iran to opposing politically motivated loans and aid. In practice, this meant vigorous opposition to the generous 1993–94 loan reschedulings—thinly disguised as new loans in order to avoid breaking the informal rules of the Paris Club of creditor nations, which require that reschedulings be given only to countries with economic reform programs approved by the International Monetary Fund (IMF)—initiated by Germany and copied by other industrial countries.

The Clinton administration was opposed to the soft treatment of Iran, noting that the United States had paid a heavy political price by insisting to Latin American nations that they had to follow IMF prescriptions, while now Germany was letting Iran off the hook.

The early Clinton policy toward Iran in the economic sphere was quite similar to that applied during the Cold War toward the Soviet Union; namely, it attempted to reduce foreign exchange available for the military, including encouraging import of consumer goods as a way to undermine the system and to drain off foreign exchange.[8] The distinction between encouraging selected economic relations with Iran while discouraging politically motivated ones did not work diplomatically. European leaders complained about what they saw as hypocrisy when the United States urged limiting some economic transactions with Iran while it continued with others. American commentators agreed; one called this U.S. policy "feel good containment—a policy that makes us feel good but doesn't make Iran feel bad enough to change its behavior."[9]

After their victory in the election of 1994, Republicans in Congress were eager to show that they were taking a firmer stance than the Democrats against sponsors of terrorism. Faced with congressional Republican pressure and adverse publicity about perceived U.S. hypocrisy, President Clinton decided to act. In March 1995 he banned any U.S. firm from investing in the development of Iranian petroleum resources, an action specifically aimed at a multimillion dollar deal already concluded by Conoco to develop the Sirri field in Iranian waters a few miles from its platform in waters of the United Arab Emirates. On May 6, 1995, he further banned U.S. economic transactions with Iran, with the exceptions required by Congress in its most recent renewal of the International Economic Powers Act—transactions for the purposes of travel, academic exchange, journalism, humanitarian purposes, religious reasons, and family matters.

In the summer of 1995, Senator Alfonse D'Amato (R–N.Y.), who had long been an advocate of economic sanctions on Iran, reworked his sanctions bill, with expert advice from the American Israel Public Affairs Committee (AIPAC), often referred to as the voice of the Israel lobby. AIPAC was concerned about the issue because of the Iranian government's vigorous role in working to undermine the Arab-Israeli peace process as well as the danger that Israeli leaders felt their country faced from the prospect that Iran might develop nuclear weapons. The influence of the Israel lobby on Iran sanctions often has been exaggerated.[10] In fact, the key factor in the success of the D'Amato bill was the 1994 Republican victory. Indeed, it could be argued that the most influential lobby on the matter was that of the families of the victims of Pan

Am Flight 103, who succeeded in adding Libya to an originally anti-Iran bill and then made the provisions on Libya tougher than on Iran, thanks to the insistence of Senator Edward Kennedy (D–Mass.).

While no member of Congress opposed the D'Amato bill, many members were uncomfortable with it and, indeed, with the unilateral U.S. embargo declared by President Clinton, because they placed high priority on open trade and because they were skeptical about the likely impact of the bill. These congressional opponents of the sanctions, while unsuccessful in killing the bill, succeeded in watering down many of the original provisions, notably by introducing a great deal of flexibility in what measures needed to be taken against those choosing to do business with Iran. Driven in good part by the same domestic political considerations that affected Congress, President Clinton agreed to support the D'Amato bill in May 1996 if it were revised to cover only investment, thereby reducing the potential for conflict with U.S. obligations under international trade agreements. On August 5 President Clinton signed the Iran and Libya Sanctions Act of 1996 (ILSA), the formal name of the D'Amato Act, which passed by unanimous vote in both chambers of Congress.

ILSA targets only investment, and then only substantial investments (above $20 million) in oil and gas development.[11] Such investment is described as against the national security interest of the United States. To quote the act: "The Congress declares that it is the policy of the United States to deny Iran the ability to support acts of international terrorism and to fund the development and acquisition of weapons of mass destruction and the means to deliver them by limiting the development of Iran's ability to explore for, extract, refine, or transport by pipeline petroleum resources of Iran."[12] Measures are authorized only against specific firms, not against all firms from a country. Great flexibility is authorized in how to target a firm. Not only does the president have the authority to waive any retaliation against a firm, but if he decides to take action, the list of measures he must impose is designed to allow him the option of applying purely theoretical punishments, such as a ban on being a primary dealer in U.S. government bonds, or take serious measures, such as denying access to the U.S. market.

In 1997 there were suggestions that U.S.-Iran relations might improve. One reason was that the firm U.S. stance against Iran's unacceptable behavior was closely associated with Secretary of State Warren Christopher; his replacement by Madeleine Albright led to expectations of a change in policy. A second reason that led some to expect an improvement in U.S.-Iran relations was the widespread criticism by former senior U.S. government officials of policy toward Iran.[13] The third and principal factor stimulating talk of a change in U.S.-Iran relations, however, was the May 22, 1997, election of Mohammed Khatemi as president of Iran. Khatemi campaigned for moderation in domestic policies, especially liberalizing cultural and lifestyle restrictions and reinforcing the rule of law by curtailing revolutionary excesses. Many believed that these trends would carry over into Iran's foreign policy.

In July 1997 the U.S. government announced it would not sanction Turkish firms for their role in building a gas pipeline that hooks up to a pipeline under construction in Iran.[14] This was widely interpreted as a signal to Tehran.[15] Yet it would have taken an aggressive interpretation of ILSA to say that the United States could sanction the firms involved in the pipelines. ILSA is aimed only at investment in Iran, not at trade with it—a feature essential to making the act consistent with treaties governing world trade. Therefore, the only issue is whether foreign firms were investing in the development of the Iranian oil and gas industry. In fact, the portion of the connector pipelines inside Iran are being paid for entirely by that country, without any foreign financing. The only way to claim the project fell under ILSA restrictions would be to maintain that investment outside Iran that helped the country also was subject to ILSA, and that would be a stretch. Moreover, and as a counterindication of a changing U.S. policy toward Iran, on August 19, 1997, President Clinton issued a new executive order explicitly banning U.S. exports to third countries when the goods are destined for reexport to Iran.[16] The order uses sweeping language to ban just about anything a U.S. national could do to trade with Iran indirectly.

Multilateral versus Unilateral Support

The United States has received only limited multilateral support for its policy of constraining trade and investment with Iran. The failure to secure broader support for these sanctions often has been interpreted in Washington as a product of European interest in selling to Iran irrespective of that government's misdeeds. In Europe, the usual explanations for the differences across the Atlantic on Iran policy are, first, that Washington's exaggerated hostility is based on domestic politics rather than strategic interests, and, second, that engaging Iran and encouraging moderates there will be the more effective route to changing unacceptable Iranian behavior.

The United States has not tried to secure U.N. approval for any sanctions against Iran. Any such effort would undoubtedly fail, because China and Russia disagree with the U.S. evaluation of Iran's behavior.[17] All the same, the United States has made limited progress in persuading each to limit trade with Iran, primarily by offering quid pro quos on other issues that are more important to Beijing and Moscow. In particular, China has agreed not to sell nuclear reactors to Iran in return for ready access to U.S. nuclear power reactor technology. Russia has agreed not to make *new* arms sales to Iran, but mostly because so much remains undelivered from the $6 billion 1989 agreement that no new sales would be needed for years. Indeed, substantial deliveries of conventional arms are proceeding, and Russia has not agreed to cancel the sale of a nuclear power plant to Iran despite strong U.S. pressure.

As for Western Europe and Japan, they have joined with the United States in implementing strict export controls on sales to Iran of arms and of militarily useful technologies, including a complete ban on nuclear-related technologies.[18] Allied cooperation on these export controls has been, in general, better than the cooperation on exports of sensitive technology to the Soviet Union during the Cold War. The problem is no longer securing cooperation from governments inclined to look the other way; indeed, West European governments and Japan are, on the whole, quite aware of the dangers of shipping arms and dual-use goods to Iran. As Bernd Schmidbauer, the German Chancellery minister in charge of intelligence coordination, put it, "There was no way the Germans were ever willing to provide German [arms] technology to help the Iranians. This has been our position and it is adhered to strictly."[19]

Enforcing restrictions is no easy matter. Germany is making a substantial effort to prevent such smuggling. For instance, in late 1994 the German Economics Ministry sent a notice to German firms warning, "You may encounter innocent-looking addresses in Iran, such as scientific institutes or industrial federations acting as purchases so that the arms connection is not apparent."[20] In February 1995 Chancellor Helmut Kohl said, "I have talked to German industry and we have agreed that we will do everything possible to make diversion [of goods into military programs by Iran] impossible."[21]

Nevertheless, Western Europe and Japan have taken strong exception to ILSA, which they criticize as impinging on the sovereignty of other states.[22] Some of the criticism reflects misreporting about ILSA and its effects. ILSA makes no claim to impose U.S. authority on U.S.-owned firms incorporated abroad or to apply U.S. law to firms operating outside the United States, which is what usually is meant by extraterritoriality. Nor does it refer to trade. Indeed, many supporters of the law would be delighted if European firms sold Iran as many consumer goods as they could, for that would reduce the foreign exchange Iran could spend on arms and on support for terrorists.

But the heart of the European and Japanese objections to ILSA relate to its politicization of trade. ILSA can best be described as a secondary boycott, that is, a boycott of firms that do not comply with the U.S. boycott of Iran (a primary boycott). In that way, the act is rather similar to the Arab League boycott of Israel. The irony is that for years the United States campaigned against secondary boycotts, going so far as to argue that they were contrary to the procedures of the General Agreement on Tariffs and Trade (GATT), while Europe took a more relaxed attitude, viewing such boycotts as unfortunate but understandable. (Indeed, Egypt was allowed to join GATT without making any provision to end over time its secondary boycott of Israel.)[23] With ILSA, the United States and Europe appear to have switched sides in this long-running debate.

Upset by both ILSA and the Helms-Burton Act, which introduces sanctions against individuals and firms doing certain types of business with Cuba, the European Commission filed formal complaints against the United States with the World Trade Organization (WTO). After discussions with the United States, a Memorandum of Understanding about the two acts was agreed to on April 11, 1997. The European Union (EU) interpreted the understanding as suspending the application of ILSA as well as Helms-Burton, a position with which the United States disagreed. The European Commission then warned, "If action is taken against companies or waivers as described in the Understanding are not granted or are withdrawn, the Commission will request the WTO to restart or reestablish the panel" examining its complaint.[24]

It is not clear how the WTO would react to the European Commission complaint. Senator D'Amato modeled his bill on U.S. legislation imposing retaliation on firms that export dangerous technologies, such as those useful for nuclear weapons, which has never been challenged under GATT or WTO procedures. In the past the United States has retaliated under these laws with few complaints from Europe—for example, when the United States limited access to its market by Toshiba in retaliation for exports by one of its affiliates of technology for submarine propellers to the USSR. However, that action was in the context of what both the United States and Europe agreed was a real threat, one against which they had adopted common Coordinating Committee on Export Controls (COCOM) rules. The situation is quite different with regard to Iran. European officials are skeptical that ILSA is a national security issue, as the U.S. government claims, and therefore outside the scope of WTO analysis. If the European Union proceeds with its complaint against ILSA, the WTO could be in the delicate position of having to rule on what is and is not a threat to U.S.

national security. Congress is unlikely to appreciate any suggestion that the WTO is better placed than the U.S. government to determine what constitutes such a threat.

The Clinton administration saw ILSA as means to deter firms from entering into high-profile deals with Iran. From this perspective, the law is most effective if no sanctions are ever applied, because that would mean that no large investments are made in Iranian oil and gas development and that a dispute with Europe is averted.

This strategy succeeded until September 1997. Then the French firm Total announced a $2 billion deal with Iran to develop, in partnership with Gazprom of Russia and Petronas of Malaysia, the South Pars gas field.[25] The project was well designed to challenge ILSA: The Russian participation raised the political stakes, the investment was strongly supported by the French government, and Total was not particularly vulnerable to sanctions, as three days earlier it had finalized the sale of nearly all its assets in the United States and made no secret that its business strategy involved withdrawing from the U.S. market. In addition, the deal was announced close to the October 15 deadline set six months earlier by the European Union for reaching agreement with the United States over ILSA and Helms-Burton, with the threat that failing an agreement, the European Union would proceed with its WTO complaint against Helms-Burton despite the continuing U.S. waiver of most of that law's provisions. Faced with the threat of a serious conflict with the European Union over trade, the Clinton administration let it be.

The Impact on Iran of U.S. Sanctions

U.S. sanctions on Iran have had both an economic and a political impact on that country.

The economic effect of sanctions came soon after Iran had run into serious economic difficulties because of its own policies. Excessive foreign borrowing in the early 1990s had driven debt up from less than $5 billion in 1988, at the end of the war with Iraq, to about $30 billion in 1993. (The data are imprecise because the issue became highly political.) Iran experienced a foreign exchange crisis by 1993, which caused it to seek debt reschedulings and which pushed the economy into recession in 1993–94. Furthermore, the government was refusing to implement the reforms necessary to relaunch economic growth, such as reducing subsidies on energy worth at least $10 billion a year, freeing exports from a welter of restrictions, and reducing controls on private enterprise. Under these circumstances, Iran's growth prospects would have been limited irrespective of U.S. action. But the economic difficulties of 1994 to 1996 often were ascribed to U.S. hostility by both the Iranian government and people.

The May 1995 ban on oil dealings by U.S. firms had an immediate economic impact on Iran, on the order of several hundred million dollars in the first year. That came primarily from problems adjusting to the cutoff in sales to U.S.-owned oil firms. In the first three months (May through July) after sanctions were imposed, Iran was not able to sell about 400,000 barrels a day, and it had to accept a discount of 30 to 80 cents on the oil it could sell, for a combined loss of $100 million to $200 million.[26] The sanctions also appear to have caused Iran some problems doing business in U.S. dollars; that is, non-U.S. firms worry that sanctions may affect their ability to be paid in dollars. Some Iranian firms have been going through middlemen, who charge a fee for their service. The extra cost may be as much as $100 million a year.

An additional immediate impact of the imposition of the trade ban was a collapse in the value of the Iranian currency, which lost a third of its value in the week after the ban was imposed. Tehran responded by introducing rigid controls on foreign exchange trading, which caused the foreign exchange market to dry up. At the artificial level of 3,000 rials to the dollar instead of the market rate (which was 6,000 before the controls and has been 4,000 to 5,000 since), it is unattractive to export, and so non-oil exports in 1995–96 and 1996–97 were $3 billion a year, or one-fourth less than their presanctions level. That only makes the foreign exchange shortage worse and compels Tehran to impose more and more controls in a downward spiral into a distorted and inefficient economy.

More important, Iran's access to foreign capital has been reduced. Foreign lenders, such as commercial bankers and government export credit agencies, are more cautious about lending to Iran because of the sanctions. The country has not been able to secure anything like the $2 billion in annual capital inflows forecast by the IMF presanctions.[27] Meanwhile, Tehran has decided that it cannot be sure of continued access to foreign capital markets, so it has put top priority on repaying its foreign debt as quickly as it can. Iran has gone from being a net borrower of about $5 billion a year during 1989–90 to 1992–93 to being a net repayer of about $2 billion a year in 1995–96 and $4 billion in 1996–97. The $7 billion to $9 billion turnaround from a borrower to a repayer has forced Iran to cut its imports in half, from $24 billion in 1992–93 to $12 billion per year in 1995–96 and 1996–97. Much of this change is due to inappropriate Iranian policy, which wasted so much of the borrowed money that the country would not have been able to make regular debt payments even in the absence of U.S. pressure.

While U.S. sanctions somewhat weakened Tehran's foreign exchange position in the short run, that effect was small relative to the impact of changes in Iran's fortunes caused by the world economy. More specifically, the higher oil prices in 1996 brought Iran about $3 billion more in oil revenues than in 1995. The U.S. government lacked the instruments to affect the Iranian economy relative to what world economic developments could do.

If oil prices recover, Iran is positioned to resume strong economic growth, thanks to the higher oil income in 1996 and to the belt-tightening between 1994 and 1996 that allowed repayment of much foreign debt. As Iran's economy picks up and as foreigners resume lending, the country can be expected to proclaim the failure of U.S. sanctions.

The largest economic impact of the U.S. actions over the longer term is likely to be discouragement of investment in the oil and gas industry. The National Iranian Oil Company (NIOC) makes extensive use of U.S.-built equipment, which it regards as better than any alternatives. NIOC, which does not have enough capital to maintain (much less expand) its output, has placed high priority on attracting foreign firms to invest in its fields. However, in the first two years after the ban on U.S. trade, only one firm oil deal was announced: the replacement of Conoco by the French firm Total shortly after President Clinton banned Conoco from proceeding with the development of the offshore Sirri oil field.

Turning to their political impact, it is clear that the sanctions have not persuaded Iran to change the behavior to which Washington objects. Secretary of State Christopher argued that Iran must be made to choose between its economic aspirations and its unacceptable political behavior. This target was not attained for two reasons. First, Iran harbors hopes that Europe and Japan will step in to replace any losses due to U.S. sanctions. So far those hopes have been realized only partially. The allies have traded with Iran while making few loans and essentially no investment. But the prospect of European and Japanese business ties has reduced Tehran's incentive to change its behavior. Second, the leaders of the Islamic Republic place great store on their radical foreign policy. It is one of the few remnants of revolutionary ideology that has not been abandoned. And the radical foreign policy does much to puff up Iranian nationalist pride, making more plausible Iran's claim to be a major force on the world scene, a player in Arab-Israeli matters and, to its mind, a leader of the world Muslim community.

On the other hand, one of the accomplishments of U.S. sanctions on Iran has been to reduce the income available to acquire weapons. Iran had to curtail its 1989 five-year plan for $10 billion in weapons purchases because of budget problems—problems due in significant part to

U.S. pressure against loans to Iran. In the period from 1989 to 1996, Iran announced agreements with various suppliers to purchase many more weapons that it actually acquired; for example, 1,000 to 1,500 tanks agreed to but only 184 acquired; 100 to 200 aircraft agreed to but only 57 acquired; and 200 to 300 artillery pieces agreed to but only 106 acquired.[28] The reason for the shortfall was generally lack of money. Tehran reported to the IMF that its total military expenditures, including operating costs as well as weapons purchases, were only $1.3 billion a year on average between 1991–92 and 1994–95, compared to the planned $2 billion a year just for weapons purchases.[29]

The shortfall in weapons acquisition has had a significant impact on the balance of power in the Gulf. With an extra $1 billion to $2 billion a year, Iran would have been able to add more weapons with which to threaten stability in the Strait of Hormuz. Cash constraints explain why Iran was not able to take delivery of its third submarine until 1997 even though construction was complete in 1994 as well as the delays in acquiring more missile launching boats and modern mines.[30]

In some countries, governments have used sanctions as an excuse for their own economic failings. There is little evidence that the Iranian government has used this argument. Iranian politicians and media frequently criticize the country's economic performance but rarely do either mention sanctions. Instead, they focus their attacks on the policies of their political opponents; for example, President Mohammed Khatemi stressed corruption in his 1997 campaign. Nor have Iranian politicians used sanctions as a means to rally nationalist sentiment to their side. The politicians who wish to present Iran as under assault from the West are much more likely to refer to cultural aggression from Western mass culture, a subject that deeply concerns them.[31] The firm U.S. policy against Iran may have caused some nationalist backlash, but the principal factor was something much more substantial than sanctions, namely, the perception that the United States might attack Iran— not an irrational concern in light of U.S. press speculation about retaliation for terrorism as well as House Speaker Newt Gingrich's call for "replacement of the current regime in Iran" and his support for covert operations to that end.[32]

Costs of the Sanctions

The direct costs to the U.S. economy of the sanctions on Iran were a loss of profits on trade and investment. The largest direct loss was on about $3 billion in oil trade involving Iranian crude destined for third-country markets and the proposed Conoco development of the offshore Sirri oil field. Less important was a reduction in U.S. exports. Such exports had not been large; in 1993 U.S. exports to Iran were $616 million.[33] And it appears that sales continue through reexports from Dubai in the United Arab Emirates, which reexports to Iran $1 billion of goods a year, perhaps half of which come originally from the United States.[34] Indeed, European diplomats complain privately that for many consumer products, U.S. goods continued in 1997 to dominate the Iranian market. Still, the total forgone profits on all types of trade and investment would seem to be on the order of several hundred million dollars a year.

Indirect costs are larger. One consideration is the increasing concentration of world oil production in the Gulf Cooperation Council (GCC) states that would result if the sanctions on Iran, Iraq, and Libya are sustained for the medium term. The U.S. interest is in a diversity of oil sources, so as to reduce the risk of overall market disruption were there to be a problem with access to oil from any one country. A policy that restricts development of oil in three major producers at the same time goes against the overall U.S. interest in diversifying oil sources.

Another side effect has been to complicate the search by Central Asian and Caucasian states for alternative trade routes so as to lessen their dependence on Russia. Iran is well positioned to provide routes for oil and gas pipelines to permit full development of the Caspian Basin oil and gas resources now largely sitting idle because of lack of access to markets. At least until the mid-1997 U.S. decision to tolerate a pipeline crossing Iran, U.S. pressure has impeded the investments necessary for Central Asia to use routes through Iran.

Also to be included as an indirect cost of sanctions is the effect U.S. actions against Iran have had on Russian suspicions about U.S. intentions. U.S. pressure not to sell a nuclear reactor to Iran was seen by some as an attempt to stop Russia from competing in one of the few high-technology industries in which it has a decent competitive position, namely, the nuclear power industry. U.S. actions were largely incompatible with its obligations under the Nonproliferation Treaty (NPT), which declares that the nuclear weapons states will make peaceful nuclear technology readily available to nonnuclear signatories that cooperate with the International Atomic Energy Agency.[35] What is more, Iran has a well-established record of excellent cooperation with that agency.[36]

A rather different issue is the cost to the U.S. oil industry if it comes to be seen as an unreliable partner. While perhaps not dominant as it once was, the United States is obviously a significant player in every aspect of the oil business, from exploration and production technology to investment and trading. The U.S. competitive edge could be dulled by the perception that dealings with the United States are subject to abrupt cutoffs for political reasons. The specific targeting of the petroleum industry—first in President Clinton's March 1995 executive order and then in ILSA—are a precedent that troubles the industry.

A related problem is the cost that comes from the politicization of trade. U.S. action against Iran, especially the secondary boycott mandated by ILSA, is an important example of making trade subject to political rather than market considerations. For reasons of efficiency, economists prefer to see trade separated from politics. Besides that general consideration, there is a more specific problem for the United States if traders worldwide come to consider it an unreliable and unstable trading partner.

Last and most important are alliance friction costs. European governments have been angered at what they see as American bullying. ILSA, combined with the Helms-Burton Act and noneconomic issues such as the vetoing of a second term for U.N. Secretary-General Boutros Boutros-Ghali, has been seen as evidence that the United States insists on dictating to Europe on those issues where the two disagree. The perception of unfair U.S. pressure has hurt the overall relationship and impeded agreement on specific issues, whether about the re-incorporation of France into the NATO military structure or the response to rogue regimes like Iraq and Iran.

Developments early in 1996–97 appeared to offer some prospect of reducing this cost of the Iran sanctions. In particular, European governments found that their policy of critical dialogue with Iran brought them little, and there is some willingness to consider a tougher policy. One important factor was the Iranian refusal to participate in a compromise over the Salman Rushdie affair, to which the European Union devoted considerable attention. Iran refused to sign a proposed letter committing it not to kill Rushdie on EU soil, even though that letter made no mention of actions elsewhere, nor by actions of Iranian citizens (the Iranian government insists that the bounty on Rushdie's head is from a private group unconnected to the government), nor to the murder of publishers and translators of *The Satanic Verses* (such as the attack on the Italian translator and the Norwegian publisher). The letter was controversial in Europe; after Iran refused to sign, the London *Times* noted, "Now that this squalid surrender document has been torn up, almost nobody will admit to having supported such a formula."[37] After a November 1996 flap over an appearance by Salman Rushdie, the Danish Folketing (parliament) mandated more distant relations with Iran and dialogue with the democratic opposition. Norwegian State Secretary Jan Egeland announced in March 1997 that "the Government of

Norway calls for international economic sanctions against Iran" over the Rushdie affair.[38]

Germany has been Iran's traditional European friend, and in 1993 the German government arranged the precedent-setting debt refinancing that rescued Iran from a foreign exchange crisis, undercutting U.S. efforts to pressure Iran economically. Starting in 1995, the German government came under domestic political pressure to abandon its policy of critical dialogue because of Iran's position on terrorism, specifically, Iran's "welcome" for the November 1995 assassination of Israeli Prime Minister Yitzhak Rabin[39] and the February–March 1996 terrorist bombings in Israel. ("The divine retribution on those who spread corruption and injustice on the earth will be severe.")[40] This was reinforced by the verdict in the Mykonos case, pertaining to the murder in a Berlin restaurant of that name on September 17, 1992, of Sadegh Sharifkandi, the leader of the Kurdish Democratic Party of Iran (KDPI), who was attending a meeting of the Socialist International at the invitation of the German Social Democratic Party. The suspects, quickly arrested, were thought to be operating on behalf of Iran. In March 1996 the German federal prosecutor issued an arrest warrant for Iran's information minister, Ali Fallahian, as a co-conspirator in the case.[41] In August, testimony in that trial of former Iranian President Abdolhassan Bani Sadr led Prosecutor Bruno Jost to say he was considering indictment of Iranian religious guide (the supreme leader of the government, under the constitution) Ayatollah Seyed Ali Khamenei. In November, Jost said in his closing statement that "it is not possible to avoid mentioning the state terrorist background of the murder" and "there cannot be the slightest doubt that the attack was planned and prepared by the Islamic Republic of Iran and its leading men."[42] On April 10, 1997, Presiding Judge Frithjof Kubsch read the verdict of the Berlin court: "Iran's political leadership made the decision . . . to liquidate the KDPI. The final decision on such operations lies with the 'Committee for Secret Operations' which lies outside the constitution and whose members include the state president, . . . the top official responsible for foreign policy [and] the 'religious leader' [who] is a political leader [rather] than the spiritual head of the Muslims."[43]

Following the Mykonos verdict, EU states withdrew their ambassadors from Iran and suspended the critical dialogue until July 1998 at the earliest.[44] Iran protested vigorously. When the EU Council of Foreign Ministers decided on April 29 that the ambassadors would return to Tehran, the Iranian reaction was swift. The next day religious guide Khamenei ordered the Foreign Ministry "not to allow the German Ambassador to return to Iran for a while,"[45] an order that also extended to the Danish ambassador. Foreign Minister Ali Velayati went a step further, saying, "The later they [the ambassadors] come, the better it will be for us. And even if they do not come at any time, we will not be worried." President Ali Akbar Hashemi Rafsanjani announced, "The critical dialogue they [the Europeans] are mentioning today was stopped some time ago."

Many in Europe were profoundly embarrassed by the Union's weak reaction and the Iranian slap in the face. The *Frankfurter Allgemeine* editorialized, "Europe does not seem to be able to react . . . other than by 'just do not show any toughness,'" while the London *Times* editorial was entitled "License to Murder."[46] In Berlin's *Tageszeitung*, Dieter Rulff, in a column headlined "Looking Like a Damned Fool," bemoaned, "European foreign policy has gone to the dogs . . . dogs that are striving toward the feeding bowl by jumping over any stick."[47] As European Commission Vice President Sir Leon Brittain said, "Critical dialogue is dead in the water . . . it is difficult to see the circumstances which could lead to its revival short of a fundamental change of policy and approach on the part of the Iranian regime."[48]

European (or at least French) embarrassment (and anger against Iran) quickly abated, however. As already noted, in September 1997, Total signed a new deal to develop Iran's natural gas fields. The French government applauded the move. What remained unclear was whether other French and European firms would follow suit—and how the American Congress would react.

Alternatives to Sanctions

ILSA states in general terms what Iran would have to do to end sanctions—cease its programs on weapons of mass destruction and stop supporting terrorism, which presumably would include stopping support for the disruption of the Arab-Israeli peace process and for the destabilization of moderate Middle Eastern regimes.[49] The United States has not explained in detail what it expects Iran to do, much less what might be a transitional path involving phased measures by each side toward the final goal. One supplement to the existing sanctions policy would be to provide such a road map. Given the lack of dialogue between the United States and Iran—and the continuing refusal of Iran's leadership to permit its officials to meet with U.S. officials—it will be difficult to design such a map because neither side has a good understanding of what kind of transitional steps the other may be prepared to accept.[50]

Engaging Iran becomes more appropriate as that nation's strategic importance increases. However, it would appear that Iran's geostrategic position is less important now than in the 1970s. Iran is no longer an oil superpower. Its oil fields are old, and its reserves are expensive to develop; indeed, Iran produces today less oil than it did in 1970, while production has soared in other parts of the world. And Iran's economic weight has declined; its imports in 1996–97 were less than in 1977–78. Nor does Iran have the influence that Tehran claims with the world's Muslims: Besides being the only Shia state in a Muslim world dominated by Sunnis, the Islamic Republic of Iran is a failure whose experience does not inspire many others. On the other hand, Iran has gained an additional geostrategic importance with the breakup of the Soviet Union, since it offers a transport route to the Central Asian and Caucasian states, by which those countries could reduce their reliance on Russia and could develop more quickly their substantial oil and gas reserves.

The final factor affecting the evaluation of whether to engage or contain Iran are the prospects that engagement would encourage moderation. Washington is skeptical, based on its reading of the presidency of Rafsanjani from 1989 to 1997. When first in power, Rafsanjani and his team of technocrats liberalized Iran's economy, introducing market-based reforms and welcoming more foreign involvement. Europe engaged Iran to the tune of $30 billion in lending between 1989 and 1993.[51] During that same period, Iran sent assassination teams to Germany, France, Switzerland, Austria, Italy, the United Kingdom, Norway, and Japan.[52] For those who think that economic and cultural engagement will promote a more acceptable foreign policy, this is not an encouraging record.

Another alternative to sanctions would be offering carrots to Iran in return for strategic concessions by Tehran. U.S. sanctions supporters argue that this was U.S. policy in the mid-1980s. What they are referring to is "Iran-Contra." A mere five years after the humiliating embassy hostage affair of 1980–81, the United States sold Iran arms for use in its war with Iraq as a means of gaining the release of U.S. hostages in Lebanon. This policy was not a success, to put it mildly. Iran did not carry through on its end of the bargain. Indeed, instead of releasing Americans held hostage in Lebanon, Iran arranged for more Americans to be seized. The failure of the 1984–85 arms sales to Iran seriously weakened a popular president, Ronald Reagan. The Iran-Contra experience is a major factor in shaping the attitudes of sanctions supporters. By contrast, those opposed to U.S. sanctions on Iran regard the Iran-Contra affair as largely irrelevant in deciding whether to offer Iran carrots.

Sanctions supporters contrast the failure of conciliation in the Iran-Contra affair with the success of a tough policy for securing the release of the U.S. hostages in Lebanon. Only when Iran realized that the hostage holding was hurting its own interests did the hostages go free. The lesson that many in Washington learned was that with Iran, conciliation makes problems worse. According to this view, and unlike Cuba and North Korea, which have been prepared to cut deals with the United States that they then respected, Iran reads conciliation as weakness. The principal barrier to offering Iran inducements is that that nation's domestic politics makes deals with the United States unattractive.

Another alternative to sanctions is the use of military force. U.S. policy toward Iran could become like that of the Reagan administration toward Libya, where the United States used bombing raids against President Muammar Qaddafi. If, for instance, Iran is determined to have supported directly or indirectly the June 1996 bombing of the Khobar Towers in Dhahran, Saudi Arabia, in which 19 U.S. servicemen were killed, the United States could respond with military force to discourage further terrorism and to penalize Iran. But the use of military force against Iran would be unlikely to lead to a change in Iranian policy, unless the force were truly overwhelming or sustained—either of which would be out of proportion to the problem Iran poses, would be politically unsustainable in the region, and would lead to retaliation. Furthermore, the use of military force almost certainly would rally Iranian public opinion behind the now-unpopular Islamic Republic.

Lessons from Iran Sanctions

Economic sanctions are not likely to change a target country's behavior if it thinks the price is acceptably low. Iran has thought the price low because Tehran expects that, despite U.S. opposition, it can acquire from others needed finance and technology, including military technology. Also, Iran is not convinced that the United States has the will to persevere with a policy of denial until the Islamic Republic changes its behavior. And Iran has been willing to live with lower capital inflows and lower export earnings. The sanctions may well have reduced Iran's ability to carry out parts of its plans, such as conventional rearmament, but they have not changed its intentions or its capabilities significantly.

Combining carrots and sticks may not be politically possible at this juncture. Antipathy toward Iran, fed by suspicions that it may have been involved in terrorist attacks on Americans, makes politically unattractive any initiative for a more flexible U.S. policy toward that country. As a further complication, both Iranian and American sides are convinced that the other has been dishonest in past dealings, particularly by not living up to tacit agreements during the maneuverings for the release of U.S. hostages in Lebanon. Those in the United States leery of dealing with Iran are concerned that a new initiative could become a repeat of the Iran-Contra fiasco. Meanwhile, Iran may not be prepared to do much to improve relations with the United States. Domestic politics make it dangerous for any Iranian politician to propose talks with the U.S government, much less a strategic compromise. In the continuing maneuvering between conservatives and technocrats, any initiative for talks with the United States would be seized upon by the other side as a sign of abandonment of the Khomeini legacy.

The United States and Europe are far apart on how to deal with rogue regimes. Europe is wedded to the approach of encouraging Iranian moderates, while the United States is committed to containing Iran. In theory, the two approaches could be reconciled, with Europe offering the carrots and the United States proffering the stick. In practice, that would be a recipe for name-calling on each side, with the Europeans regarding the United States as a bully and U.S. politicians complaining about lack of support from Europeans who were selling out Western interests for commercial contract. Regular consultations at the highest levels between the United States and Europe have done little to resolve the differences. Designing and carrying out a policy of constructive engagement is more easily advocated than implemented.

Unilateral sanctions can cause friction with allies. To be sure, one could argue that the sanctions caused friction only because metal was already rubbing on metal: The United States and Europe were far apart on how to respond to Iran even before the United States applied sanctions against Iran. But the U.S. sanctions complicated discussions with European governments on how to approach Iran, and U.S. pressure to join in those sanctions made the discussions extremely difficult. In the aftermath of the Mykonos verdict, European governments became more aware of the problems Iran represents, but that did little to advance an agreement with the United States on how to approach Iran.

Notes

1. Wayne Mapp, *The Iran-United States Claims Tribunal: The First Ten Years* (Manchester: Manchester University Press, 1993), p. 6.

2. For the measures adopted through 1993, see Geoffrey Kemp, *Forever Enemies? American Policy and the Islamic Republic of Iran* (Washington, DC: Carnegie Endowment, 1994), pp. 103–10.

3. Elaine Sciolino, "U.S. and Iran Sign a Compensation Pact," *New York Times,* November 28, 1991, p. A3.

4. As described by Brent Scowcroft, Petro-Hunt Corporation "Iran in Transition" conference, May 2, 1996. Dallas, TX.

5. Vahe Petrossian, "Iran Back in the Firing Line," *Middle East Economic Digest,* December 4, 1992, p. 3.

6. Milton Buffington, "Iran-U.S. Trade Regulations," *Iran Business Monitor,* September 1993, p. 10. Interestingly in light of the later European objections about secondary boycotts, there appear to have been no objections to this act. Perhaps that was in part because the law was interpreted by the Bush and Clinton administrations in ways that restricted its reach—it was not applied to any goods with less than 20 percent U.S. content.

7. Martin Indyk, "Clinton Administration Policy Toward the Middle East," special report of The Washington Institute for Near East Policy, May 21, 1993, and Anthony Lake, "Confronting Backlash States," *Foreign Affairs* 73, no. 2 (March/April 1994), pp. 45–55.

8. Stephen Grummon, "Strengthening U.S. Containment Policy Toward Iran," *Policy Watch* (The Washington Institute for Near East Policy), March 16, 1995. Later that year Mr. Grummon joined the National Security Council staff as the official responsible for the Gulf.

9. Thomas Friedman, "Wednesday News Quiz," *New York Times,* March 29, 1995, p. A23.

10. For example, James Schlesinger, "Fragmentation and Hubris: A Shaky Basis for American Leadership," *The National Interest* (Fall 1997), p. 5.

11. ILSA provided that the minimum sanctioned investment was $40 million during the act's first year, after which time the minimum fell to $20 million except for investors whose government had taken steps to reduce the threats from Iran. Washington did not judge any government as having fulfilled this requirement.

12. Sec. 2(1) of Public Law 104–172 (50 USC 1701).

13. Cf. Zbigniew Brezinski, Brent Scowcroft, and Richard Murphy, "Differentiated Containment," *Foreign Affairs* 76, no. 3 (May/June 1997), pp. 20–30.

14. The U.S. government action, announced by Assistant Secretary of State Alan Larsen, was erroneously characterized in Dan Morgan and David Ottoway, "U.S. Won't Bar Pipeline Across Iran," *Washington Post,* July 27, 1997, pp. A1, A27. Contrary to that article, the decision was reached before Khatemi's election, it was openly announced (by Assistant Secretary of State Alan Larsen before the House International Relations Committee on July 23), and it did not involve a $1.6 billion pipeline across Iran (it concerned a pair of short connector pipelines linking up to Iran's gas lines on the east to Turkmenistan gas fields and on the west to the Turkish gas distribution network).

15. For example, Stephan-Götz Richter, "America's Iran Policy Rethinks Itself," *New York Times,* August 18, 1997, p. A21.

16. Executive Order 13059, issued August 19, 1997, which also brings together in one place all the existing restrictions on trade with Iran. The accompanying letter to the House Speaker and Senate President highlights the reexport issue.

17. On Russia, see John Hannah, "Evolving Russian Attitudes Towards Iran," in Patrick Clawson (ed.), *Iran's Strategic Intentions and Capabilities* (Washington, DC: National Defense University Press, 1994), pp. 55–60.

18. "Three Political Torpedoes Sink Conoco's Ship," *Iran Times*, March 24, 1995, p. 1.

19. Chris Hedges, "A Vast Smuggling Network Gets Advanced Arms to Iran," *New York Times*, March 15, 1995, p. A8.

20. Quoted in a Deutsche Presse-Agentur release cited in *Iran Times*, December 23, 1994, " Germany Warns its Firms About Iran," p. 15.

21. Chancellor Kohl, at his joint press conference with President Clinton in Washington, February 9, 1995.

22. For example, Peter Guilford, spokesman for the European Union's Trade Commissioner, stated, "We remain firmly opposed to the extraterritorial nature of both pieces of legislation [D'Amato and Helms-Burton]." See Youssef Ibrahim, "Planned U.S. Sanctions Anger Europeans," *New York Times*, July 25, 1996, p. A14.

23. Cf. "U.S. Government Policy with Respect to the Arab Secondary Boycott of Israel," prepared by Patton Boggs for the European Energy Coalition, September 4, 1996 (graciously provided by Bruno Cova of Agip).

24. "EU Settles on Sanctions with U.S. (maybe)," *Iran Times*, April 25, 1997, p. 14, which reviews the history of the actions.

25. As reported by various articles in *Financial Times*, September 29 and 30, 1997, including David Owen, "Total to Defy US with $2bn Deal to Develop Iran Gas," September 29, 1997, p. 1, and "Total Chief Defies US Threats," September 30, 1997, p. 9.

26. "Iran can't sell its oil," *Iran Times*, August 18, 1990, p. 15, and Donald Southerland, "2-Month-Old Trade Embargo Begins to Take Toll on Iran," *Washington Post*, August 9, 1995, p. F1.

27. International Monetary Fund, "Statistical Appendix—Islamic Republic of Iran," IMF Staff Country Report 96/108. (Washington, DC: IMF, October 1996). Unless otherwise noted, this report is the source used for all further economic data about Iran.

28. Michael Eisenstadt, *Iranian Military Power* (Washington, DC: The Washington Institute for Near East Policy), pp. 36–37.

29. International Monetary Fund, "Islamic Republic of Iran—Statistical Appendix," IMF Staff Country Report No. 96/108, p. 23, converted at the offshore market exchange rate given on pp. 54–55.

30. "New Sub Arrives in Bandar Abbas; Will Be Named Jonah," *Iran Times*, January 24, 1997, p. 14.

31. For instance, in opposing the sale in Iran of Coca-Cola bottled locally, Mohsen Rafiqdoost, supervisor of the powerful Janbazan and Mostazafan Foundation, argued, "We shall not permit the return of Western culture even in its weak form under the cover of economic prosperity" (*Resalaat*, December 14, 1993).

32. John Diamond, "Replacing Iran Regime Advocated by Gingrich," *Washington Post*, February 9, 1995, p. A24. Gingrich held up the intelligence community funding for fiscal year 1996 to insist on covert operations against Iran; in the end, $18 million was approved for a program to promote democracy in Iran. On retaliation over Khobar and Iranian concern about this, see Thomas Lippman and Bradley Graham, "U.S. Mulls Possible Response to Iran in Saudi Bombing," *Washington Post*, December 22, 1996, p. A30, and Robin Wright, "Iran Braces to Get Blamed for Bombing of U.S. Site," *Los Angeles Times*, December 25, 1996, p. A4.

33. International Monetary Fund, *Direction of Trade Statistics Yearbook 1987–1993* (Washington DC: IMF, 1988), p. 421.

34. Reexports to Iran from the United Arab Emirates in the first half of 1996 were $523 million, according to the UAE central bank, as reported in *Hamshahri* (Tehran), January 11, 1997. The proportion of those goods coming from the United States is from personal interviews with traders active in the Iran trade, Dubai, 1996 and 1997. The next sentence is based on personal interviews with European diplomats, 1997.

35. Article IV, section 2, of the treaty reads in its entirety, "All the Parties to the Treaty undertake to facilitate, and have the right to participate in, the fullest possible exchange of equipment, materials and scientific and technological information for the peaceful uses of nuclear energy. Parties to the Treaty in a position to do so shall also cooperate alone or together with other States or international organizations to the further development of the applications of nuclear energy for peaceful purposes, especially in the territories of non-nuclear-weapon States Party to the Treaty, with due consideration for the needs of the developing areas of the world."

36. Patrick Clawson, *Business as Usual? Western Policy Options Towards Iran* (New York: American Jewish Committee, 1995), pp. 43–48.

37. George Brock, "Britain Saves EU from Shameful Compromise on Rushdie," *London Times*, July 8, 1996.

38. Agence France Presse (AFP), March 19, 1997.

39. President Ali Akbar Rafsanjani described Rabin's assassination as "a clear case of the materialization of the divine revenge on the oppressors in history" (Radio Iran as transcribed in *Akhbaar Ruz*, November 5, 1995, p. 13.) The largest-circulation Iranian newspaper wrote, "The assassination of Yitzhak Rabin . . . sent a wave of joy and exhilaration among our country's people. In some districts, newspaper offices, and establishments, people passed around sweets and cakes." ("People Rejoice over Killing of Israeli Terrorist Premier," *Keyhan*, as translated in *Akhbaar Ruz*, November 5, 1995, p. 14.)

40. The Islamic Republic News Agency dispatch continued, "The Islamic revolutionaries should pay no heed to the outcry of the hypocritical West . . . Muslims are obliged to obey only God's command in the holy Koran to wage jihad against the occupiers of Muslim lands until final victory and liberation." ["Iran: IRNA Sees Israeli Bombings as 'Divine Retribution,'" Foreign Broadcast Information Service (FBIS)–Near East and South Asia, March 5, 1996, p. 87, citing IRNA, March 4, 1996.]

41. Michael Lindemann. "German Warrant for Iran Minister," *Financial Times*, March 16, 1996, p. 2.

42. Michael Melke, "The Men Pulling the Strings Were in Tehran," *Die Welt* as printed in FBIS, November 13, 1996, and "Iran Adopts Harsher Tone Toward Germany," *Die Welt* as printed in FBIS, November 16, 1996.

43. "The Mykonos Trial: Excerpts from the Opinion of the Berlin Court." *Frankfurter Runschau*, April 12, 1997, as printed in FBIS, April 21, 1997, p. 9.

44. Lionel Barber, "Brussels Fires Shot Across Iran's Bows," *Financial Times*, April 30, 1997, p. 8; and Ian Black, "Response to Iran Divides Europe," *Washington Times*, April 28, 1997, pp. A1, A10.

45. Tehran Radio, "President on Critical Dialogue" April 30, 1997, which is also the source for the Rafsanjani quote in two sentences. The Foreign Minister Ali Velayati quote in the following sentence is from "It is not important for Iran whether European Ambassadors come to Tehran or not," *Keyhan* of the same date. All these are as translated in *Akhbaar Ruz*, April 30, 1997, pp. 11, 12.

46. Both editorials appeared April 30, 1997.

47. Dieter Rulff, "Looking Like Damned Fools," *Die Tageszeitung*, May 2, 1997, as translated in FBIS of the same date.

48. "EU Official: Iran Dialogue Dead in Water, Beyond Repair" *Iran Times*, May 16, 1997, p. 3.

49. Sec. 8(a) Public Law 104-172 (50 USC 1701).

50. For one example of such an approach, see Robin Wright and Shaul Bakhash, "The U.S. and Iran: An Offer They Can't Refuse?" *Foreign Policy*, no. 108 (Fall 1997), pp. 124–37.

51. Estimating the borrowing during 1989 to 1992 is complicated by systematic misreporting of Iran's debt. Iran's debt at end-1992 was at least $40 billion. That was at least $30 billion higher than its debt at end-1988, which was no more than $10 billion. In fact, debt at end-1992 may have been higher and debt at end-1988 may have been lower, in which case the increase in debt between 1988 and 1992 would have been more than $30 billion.

52. For details, see Clawson, *Business as Usual?* pp. 19–23.

5

Iraq

Eric D. K. Melby

IRAQ IS AMONG the most dramatic cases involving economic sanctions in the twentieth century. The case divides into two distinct phases: the period from August 1990 to March 1991—that is, before the Desert Storm cease-fire—and April 1991 to the present. Iraq is the first case since the collapse of the Soviet empire in 1989 of a multilateral effort to discipline a country that sought to redress its regional grievances by overt military means. It is also the first attempt by the United States to provide crisis leadership in a global environment not defined principally by the struggle against communism. As a result, the Iraq sanctions case is likely to be examined for possible lessons for the application of economic sanctions elsewhere. How the United States handled this crisis *could* have created a precedent for other crises. However, as important as Iraq is for the lessons it provides, the Iraq case is close to unique. It is likely to be replicated only in the most extreme of circumstances.

Prior to Iraq's Invasion of Kuwait

It is useful to outline briefly the situation prior to Iraq's invasion of Kuwait. When President George Bush took office in 1989, the Persian Gulf, while a strategically important region for U.S. interests, did not command as much attention as the evolving situation in the Soviet Union and Eastern Europe. However, the region was the focus of a national security review (NSR-10) and a presidential decision (NSD-26) that broadly supported the Reagan administration's policy toward Iraq.[1] The objective was to try to encourage minimally acceptable behavior while at the same time not ignore Saddam Hussein's activities, which were of serious concern. The inducements included credit guarantees for the import of U.S. grain.[2]

American diplomatic and economic overtures did not have the desired effect on Saddam. In early 1990 he began accusing the United States of leading a conspiracy against his country. He escalated his rhetoric against Israel, threatening in April to incinerate half of Israel if it attacked Iraq again.[3] U.S. intelligence sources gathered disquieting information on Iraq's efforts to build weapons of mass destruction, including a long-barreled "supergun."

Although U.S.-Iraqi relations worsened significantly, other countries in the region cautioned the United States not to escalate tensions by taking an overtly confrontational stance; they continued to believe that the best way to deal with Saddam was to engage him. In part as a result, the United States sent Saddam a message that it wanted regional stability and a constructive relationship but that this was very difficult given Iraqi behavior.[4]

Also in spring 1990 Saddam's grievances with Kuwait and the United Arab Emirates mounted. There were financial, territorial, and oil-related disputes.[5] Saddam, needing large sums of money to rebuild Iraq after the 1980 to 1988 war with Iran and in order to pursue his military ambitions, had little desire to repay loans to his Arab neighbors.

In mid-July Saddam sharply escalated tensions in the region by accusing Kuwait and the United Arab Emirates of ignoring quotas by the Organization of Petroleum Exporting Countries (OPEC) by over-producing oil and consequently driving down the price of oil on international markets. He threatened to take action if production were not cut voluntarily. While few expected Iraq to take military action against Kuwait, Saddam's remarks led to a flurry of diplomatic activity. Egyptian President Hosni Mubarak, Saudi King Fahd, and Jordanian King Hussein tried mediation between Iraq and Kuwait. They also urged restraint on the United States, again concerned that U.S. government action might precipitate Saddam to respond rashly. OPEC ministers also met to consider Iraq's complaints.

Wanting to avoid either taking sides regarding the particulars of Iraq's dispute with Kuwait or to upset apparently successful diplomatic efforts to resolve the crisis, President Bush nevertheless sent Saddam Hussein a message on July 28 warning him against any belligerent actions and reiterating that the United States had vital national security interests in the area.[6] U.S. intelligence indicated that Saddam had around 100,000 troops on the border with Kuwait by the end of July. However, there were few, if any, indications he intended to invade. In fact, OPEC ministers had just met and agreed to try to increase oil prices and monitor compliance with OPEC production quotas (primarily to benefit Iraq). President Mubarak believed he had assurances from Saddam that there would be no military action against Kuwait, and had relayed these assurances to President Bush. There also appeared to be progress on providing Iraq with some debt relief from its neighbors. These events suggested that some of the steam had gone out of the situation, if only temporarily.

The Invasion of Kuwait
and Its Immediate Aftermath

The assessment by the United States and other governments (including Egypt, Saudi Arabia, and Jordan) that an explosion was not imminent proved incorrect and then some. On August 2, 1990, Iraq invaded Kuwait. Within hours Iraqi military forces had conquered the country and had advanced toward the Saudi Arabian border, threatening the political stability and oil resources of the entire Persian Gulf region. Worldwide condemnation, led by the United States, was immediate and forceful.

The immediate U.S. reaction was to impose strong bilateral economic sanctions on Iraq and Kuwait. Within hours of news of the Iraqi invasion reaching the White House on August 2, the United States took steps to freeze all Kuwait's assets under U.S. control anywhere in the world to prevent their use or acquisition by Iraq. At the same time, the United States also froze Iraq's assets in this country and imposed a comprehensive economic embargo on both Iraq and Kuwait. To implement the sanctions, President Bush invoked his authority under the International Emergency Economic Powers Act (IEEPA), the National Emergencies Act, the Export Administration Act (EAA), and the Arms Export Control Act. These various laws provided the president with broad authority over exports, imports, and financial transactions. The president issued a series of executive orders under the relevant laws, which were followed by various implementing regulations issued by the Department of the Treasury's Office of Foreign Assets Control.[7]

The economic sanctions were imposed in an environment of substantial uncertainty about the situation on the ground in Kuwait and about Saddam's ultimate intentions (e.g., Did he intend to seize the oil fields in Saudi Arabia's Eastern Province?). Time was of the essence, both to freeze assets that Saddam otherwise could acquire and to send an unambiguous message, to Saddam and others, that the United States would not accept a fait accompli in Kuwait and that it also intended to protect Saudi Arabia and the other Gulf countries. Apart from any impact economic sanctions might have had on Saddam's immediate calculations, imposing economic sanctions sent an important political signal that Washington was poised to respond forcefully to the crisis and was contemplating next steps. At this point, military action seemed premature and, in any event, was impractical as it would take time to organize, given the size of American and other military forces in the region. However, economic sanctions could be imposed quickly through presidential action. In addition, they bought time to assess what other steps were needed.

The principal objectives of the economic sanctions program were to prevent Iraq from benefiting from Kuwait's substantial oil and financial resources and to provide Saddam Hussein a strong incentive to withdraw from Kuwait by attempting to impose substantial economic pain on Iraq. Senior officials in Washington quickly realized that Iraq's invasion of Kuwait was more than just a regional crisis. It was the first test of how states would behave in the post–Cold War era following the collapse of communism. President Bush and his senior advisors felt strongly that if Saddam succeeded in Kuwait, others would be encouraged to flaunt international norms of behavior. A potentially unstable world would evolve, with the United States appearing ineffectual and unable to exert leadership and influence. The sanctions were meant to underline and, if possible, realize economic and political objectives including:

- Sending an unambiguous signal of U.S. (and, a few days later, of global) condemnation of Iraq's military aggression against Kuwait;

- Encouraging Iraq's immediate and unconditional withdrawal from Kuwait;

- Preserving Kuwait as an entity by preventing the looting of its financial assets;

- Restoring the legitimate government of Kuwait to power; and

- Buying time to assess further Saddam's intentions and to design additional strategies as necessary (such as deploying military forces to the Gulf).

Gaining Multilateral Support

From the start, President Bush realized that although the United States would have to act unilaterally at the outset, multilateral support would be essential for the actions to have significant impact. Because of the coincidence of the end of the Cold War with the Soviet Union, a unique opportunity presented itself to use the U.N. Security Council as its founders had intended in 1945. Thus Kuwait became the first test of the ability of the United Nations to deal with a post–Cold War crisis.

At the urging of the United States, the Security Council on August 2 unanimously condemned Iraq's invasion of Kuwait (Resolution 660), demanding the immediate and unconditional withdrawal of all Iraqi forces to their preinvasion position and calling upon both countries to negotiate their differences. The Arab League and the Gulf Cooperation Council also condemned the invasion. When Iraq announced Kuwait's incorporation as an Iraqi province on August 8, the Security Council adopted Resolution 662 declaring the annexation illegal.

The European Community and its individual members enacted measures similar to those of the United States. The United Kingdom took steps on August 4; other countries, including Japan, Canada, Australia, and Norway, did so as well. The Soviet Union and China supported these measures and also suspended all military aid to Iraq (although it took some time before all Soviet military advisers left Iraq). Turkey and Saudi Arabia played critical roles by closing oil pipelines crossing their territories.[8] On August 6, the individual efforts of the United States and other countries were transformed into a multilateral embargo by a vote of the Security Council (Resolution 661).[9] On August 25 the Security Council adopted Resolution 665 authorizing all appropriate measures to enforce Resolution 661. This was a critical vote as it put teeth in the blockade of Iraq and Kuwait.[10]

Early in the crisis, it became evident to President Bush and many of his senior advisors that economic sanctions alone would not persuade Saddam Hussein to withdraw from Kuwait.[11] There was no experience with a sanctions program of this magnitude and hence little solid evidence on which to base an assessment of how long it might take for the sanctions to have sufficient impact to convince Saddam to give up. Would it take six months, a year, or longer? If it took this long, it was highly doubtful there would be a Kuwait or a Kuwaiti people left to save. The passage of time also would make it harder to hold the multilateral sanctions regime together. Over time, there would be more leakage in the sanctions and attempts at profiteering, a natural occurrence in all embargos given the enormous profit potential.

The sanctions program could not, and did not, operate in a vacuum. There were numerous diplomatic efforts, principally by the United States but also by the Soviet Union, France, and China, to achieve the U.N. Security Council's objectives. In the end, all failed to convince

Saddam to meet the U.N. demands.[12] Most important, the United States and its coalition partners (principally the United Kingdom, France, Saudi Arabia, and Egypt) undertook a massive deployment of military forces in Saudi Arabia and elsewhere in the Persian Gulf to create a defensive and, subsequently, an offensive capability. Military units (mostly naval) were also used to enforce the economic blockade. The so-called Multilateral Interception Force (MIF), composed principally of naval ships from the United States, the United Kingdom, and France, patrolled sea lanes in the Persian Gulf and the Gulf of Aqaba, challenging vessels suspected of carrying sanctioned goods to or from Iraq. The sanctions effort was a critical element in building support, in the United States and elsewhere, for the military deployment to the Gulf. The sanctions not only bought the time necessary to deploy the forces, they also persuaded most people that military action would be undertaken only as a last resort, after nonmilitary options had run their course.

Impact on Iraq

Most countries followed the U.N. sanctions regime against Iraq. Out of 159 members of the United Nations, 122 supported the Security Council resolutions directly or adopted measures in support.[13] Of major significance was the support of the embargo by the Soviet Union, which had been a key supporter of Iraq during the Cold War. U.S. estimates at the time were that 90 percent of Iraq's imports and more than 97 percent of its exports (principally oil) were cut off. The embargo deprived Iraq of $1.5 billion in monthly foreign exchange earnings, equivalent to one-third of its total gross national product (GNP). Moreover, due to the freeze on its assets, as well as those of Kuwait, Iraq did not have access to international financial markets, thus virtually eliminating its ability to do business anywhere in the world.

Iraq, whose only access to the sea was through Umm Qasr on the Persian Gulf, was highly vulnerable to the naval blockade instituted by the coalition forces. In addition, Iraq's borders were tightly controlled by the participation of Syria, Saudi Arabia, Turkey, and Iran in the sanctions effort. The main uncertainty was the border with Jordan, the only other route into and out of Iraq. Because of long-standing economic ties with Iraq, Jordan was a reluctant and often incomplete participant in the U.N. sanctions program. However, the naval blockade of Jordan's ports (which was aimed at Iraq, not Jordan) and intense pressure from the United States ensured that relatively little merchandise reached Iraq through Jordan.

While Iraq's commerce dropped to negligible levels, this did not lead Saddam Hussein to change his strategic objectives. Western intelligence analysts underestimated the resiliency of the Iraqi economy and the ability of the Iraqi people to withstand economic deprivation. More important, they underestimated Saddam Hussein's total lack of regard for any economic suffering of his people. Thus imposing severe hardship on the Iraqi people failed to make a significant impression on Saddam and did not convince him to withdraw from Kuwait. In Saddam, the United States and others faced a leader so committed to his strategic objectives in the region, and so convinced he could not be thwarted, that only decisive military force was likely to achieve the objective laid out in U.N. Security Council Resolution 660.

Impact on Other Countries

The cutoff of Iraqi oil exports in August 1990 reduced world oil supply just as the Western Hemisphere was beginning to build up stocks for the winter heating season. However, several factors contributed to a muted price response. First, with the experience of the 1973–74 and 1979 oil price shocks in mind, major oil-consuming governments and oil companies made a concerted effort through the International Energy Agency (IEA) to supply all market participants with accurate information on oil supplies and demand. Consequently, there was little of the panic buying (and resulting price spikes) that characterized the earlier periods. Members of the IEA, which included the main oil-consuming countries, met regularly in late summer and fall of 1990 to assess the oil market and refine plans for the possible release of government-owned or controlled oil stocks.[14] Second, key oil producers in OPEC, including principally Saudi Arabia, agreed to increase their oil production, thereby relieving pressures on prices.[15] Increased OPEC production accounted for approximately 75 percent of the output lost from Iraq and Kuwait. Third, oil companies refrained from building up oil stocks unnecessarily, thus contributing to a measured response to the cutoff of oil supplies from Iraq and Kuwait.

Nevertheless, a number of countries, principally developing ones, were adversely affected by the war and the U.N. sanctions regime. Increases in oil prices particularly affected those developing countries that imported all their oil, which had to be paid in dollars. This reduced foreign currency holdings and made foreign debt servicing more difficult. Foreign reserves were further depleted by the loss of billions of dollars in foreign worker remittances from Kuwait and Iraq.

The so-called front-line states of Jordan, Turkey, and Egypt were most affected by their participation in the sanctions regime. Jordan was a major trading partner of Iraq, and its port of Aqaba was a key transit point for goods entering and leaving Iraq. Many of its nationals worked in Iraq and Kuwait (and thus were a source of important remittances home). Iraq was also a major oil supplier to Jordan and, along with Kuwait, an important source of foreign aid (approximately $190 million annually before the invasion). The International Monetary Fund estimated that Jordan lost around 55 percent of its GNP as a result of the embargo on economic activities with Iraq and Kuwait. However, Jordan continued to receive free oil from Iraq, with the tacit approval of coalition partners.

Turkey was an important trading partner of Iraq and a key transit partner for Iraq's oil, which provided Turkey with $400 million in annual transit fees and 60 percent of its imported oil.[16] Before the embargo, Turkey's export trade with Iraq amounted to $8 billion; all of this was now cut off. In addition, Iraq owed Turkey $800 million on which payment was suspended.

Egypt lost several billion dollars in revenues from a decline in tourism, Suez Canal transit fees, and worker remittances. Egyptian workers in Iraq and Kuwait, an important source of foreign exchange remittances, returned home to an economy already suffering from high unemployment and limited social services. In addition, Egypt lost bank deposits in Iraq and Kuwait and foreign aid from Kuwait. Egypt estimated that its losses from all these sources amounted to $9 billion annually.[17]

Yemen was also hard hit by the sanctions regime, largely because of its decision to maintain friendly relations with Iraq. Saudi Arabia canceled working and residence privileges for over 1 million Yemenis and halted financial assistance of over $600 million per year. Worker remittances were estimated at $2 billion per year.[18]

Lebanon also was affected seriously by the sanctions regime. Approximately 40 percent of its exports went to and many of its nationals were employed in Iraq, in the Gulf area, or in Jordan. Lebanon lost access to about $500 million in bank deposits in Kuwait in addition to the loss of over $150 million in worker remittances.[19]

Economic losses due to sanctions were not limited to the Middle East. All countries that traded with Iraq or Kuwait were affected as commerce stopped. Companies with outstanding contracts in Iraq and Kuwait were not paid. An indication of the magnitude of these contracts can be obtained from claims filed by U.S. companies with the Department of the Treasury's Office of Foreign Assets Control (OFAC). OFAC received claims of $5 billion, which included $2 billion for Credit Commodity Corporation agricultural loan guarantees and $700 million for oil on the high seas.[20] International tourism, particularly to the Middle East and Europe, was adversely affected because of fears of terrorism. Airlines and travel agents reported sharp drops in bookings. In addition, the economic costs of imposing sanctions escalates sharply if one includes the cost of military enforcement.

To specific contract losses claimed by individual companies must be added the opportunity cost due to the political instability in the Middle East and the resulting lack of business confidence in the region. While this cost is impossible to quantify with any degree of accuracy, it is reasonable to assume it has been high (although doubtless some of the forgone investment in the Middle East went elsewhere).

As the United States worked to ensure a solid multilateral coalition to support the U.N. sanctions regime, it soon realized that something would have to be done to alleviate the economic and financial losses suffered by the front-line states (which would have to play a critical role in implementing the sanctions). The United States proposed an Economic Action Plan (EAP) designed to encourage support of the sanctions regime by those most affected—Egypt, Jordan, and Turkey. The EAP provided about $20 billion in financial assistance (contributed by the United States, the European Community, Japan, Saudi Arabia, and Kuwait).[21] To ensure solid Egyptian support, the United States forgave $7.1 billion in Egyptian debt to the United States. While the front-line states were the main concern, the Soviet Union also benefited. Saudi Arabia gave the Soviets an unprecedented $4 billion line of credit in response to an urgent request for help from President Mikhail Gorbachev.[22]

Impact of Phase I Sanctions on Iraq

The expulsion of Iraq from Kuwait by the multilateral military coalition in January and February 1991 marked the end of the first phase in the Iraq sanctions regime. The success or failure of the sanctions must be addressed on several levels. On a simplistic level, economic sanctions did not succeed. Saddam did not withdraw from Kuwait because of the impact of the sanctions; he had to be thrown out.

At first glance, Iraq looked like a textbook case, one in which sanctions reasonably could be expected to have the desired impact on Iraqi conduct. Iraq depended on imports for 60 to 80 percent of its food; oil revenues amounted to 95 percent of foreign exchange receipts. Iraqi industry depended largely on imports for raw materials and spare parts. Foreign debt was high, partly as a result of the obligations incurred during the 1980–88 war with Iran. The local economy was in difficult straits with inflation high and the Iraqi dinar heavily discounted on the black market. However, Saddam is not a textbook leader. He does not care about the misery imposed on his people, and he has the means (and has demonstrated the will) to put down brutally any opposition. In addition, the ability of the Iraqi people to withstand economic hardship passively was probably greater than most realized. Thus Iraq's economic situation was unlikely to convince Saddam to withdraw from Kuwait, especially given the role he had defined for Iraq in the Arab world.

Of course, it is conceivable that over a long period, a rigidly enforced and universally supported sanctions program could have convinced Saddam to withdraw from Kuwait. However, given that the economic sanctions remained in place seven years after Saddam's defeat and he still refused to comply with relevant United Nations resolutions, this would be very tough to argue convincingly. In any case, all that would remain would be a skeleton of Kuwait, thus defeating the objective of preserving Kuwait as a country. Moreover, it is unlikely that the United States would have been able to maintain coalition solidarity for an unlimited period. On the contrary, the longer the sanctions continued without adequate evidence that they were having the desired effect, the greater the likelihood there would have been significant leakage in the embargo and the harder it would have been to maintain unity, particularly among Arab countries. In the best of circumstances, multilateral sanctions are hard to put together and difficult to enforce. The circumstances with the Iraq sanctions were unique in that formerly antagonistic states (e.g., the United States and the Soviet Union; the Soviet Union and Saudi Arabia) were working together closely. The chances of this continuing without an end in sight were slim.

Military realities were not conducive to an unlimited wait for sanctions to have the desired impact. Foreign forces in Saudi Arabia reached 500,000 by January 1991. It was logistically and operationally difficult, if not impossible, to keep them there for an extended period without engagement. Saudi Arabia, already very nervous about the size of the foreign forces, would not have tolerated an extended deployment. Sitting in the very hot Saudi desert indefinitely would have eroded the effectiveness of the force. The coalition force also faced practical problems, such as the Muslim holy month of Ramadan, which could have severely restricted any military action during March 1991.

But while the economic sanctions did not force Saddam out of Kuwait, they were an essential precondition for building public support, in the United States and among other members of the coalition, for escalating from sanctions to military action. The sanctions thus served an important political purpose and were a key element in the overall strategy of ejecting Iraq from Kuwait. It is highly improbable that Congress would have voted to support the use of force in the Gulf had the

United States and others not vigorously pursued sanctions first and thereby exhausted peaceful options for responding to the crisis.[23] Key allies also wanted to see if sanctions had a reasonable chance of succeeding in the short term. When it was clear that they did not, most allies were fully supportive of military action. The sanctions prevented Saddam from obtaining economic resources to improve his military position and bought time while the coalition put its forces together in the Gulf.

In sum, it is difficult to give the Phase I sanctions a simple "pass" or "fail" assessment. Sanctions did not succeed in expelling Saddam from Kuwait, but few of the senior policymakers in Washington thought they would. However, they did succeed in preventing Saddam from benefiting from Kuwait's financial and oil assets, critical ingredients in Kuwait's identity as a country. Moreover, the experience of going through the Phase I economic sanctions and failing to expel Saddam as a result was essential in preparing the United States and its allies for the only option that was likely to succeed given Saddam's personality and intentions: military force.

Phase II: The Post–Desert Storm Sanctions

The expulsion of Iraq from Kuwait by the end of February 1991 and the cease-fire in April marked the end of one phase in the sanctions regime and the opening of another. The objective changed from getting Saddam to withdraw from Kuwait (accomplished ultimately by the military campaign) to getting Iraq to comply with provisions of U.N. Security Council Resolutions 686, adopted March 2, 1991, and 687, adopted April 3, which set the terms for a formal end to the hostilities. The economic sanctions imposed on Kuwait by Resolution 661 were lifted, while those imposed on Iraq have remained in effect with certain important exceptions.

The principal objective of U.N. Security Council Resolution 687 has been to prevent Iraq from once again becoming a military threat to its neighbors or the region. Although decisively defeated on the battlefield, Iraq remains the most powerful military force in the region and thus a clear threat to regional stability.[24] The United Nations called for the destruction, removal, or rendering harmless, under international supervision, of all of Iraq's chemical and biological weapons as well as related research and development (R&D) and support and manufacturing facilities; and all its ballistic missiles with a range of greater than 150 kilometers together with repair and production facilities. A U.N. Special Commission (UNSCOM) was created to carry out on-site inspections and to take responsibility for carrying out the provisions of Resolution 687 related to Iraq's weapons of mass destruction. Iraq further was required not to acquire or develop nuclear weapons or to undertake any nuclear weapons R&D, support, or manufacturing, actions to be monitored by the International Atomic Energy Agency (IAEA).

Iraq also committed to return all seized Kuwaiti property, return prisoners of war, honor its international debts and obligations (which it had renounced in August 1990), and pay compensation for various claims lodged against it.[25] Resolution 687 loosened only somewhat the economic sanctions against Iraq by permitting the sale or supply of foodstuffs (and relevant financial transactions) with the approval of the U.N. Sanctions Committee.[26] Materials and supplies for essential civilian needs as identified by the U.N. Secretary General were also permitted with the approval of the Sanctions Committee. A secondary, though unofficial, expectation—one not shared by the entire coalition—of the sanctions in Phase II was that continued tight restrictions on dealings with Iraq *might* encourage Iraqis, particularly in the army, to depose Saddam. There was ample precedent for replacing a leader humiliated on the battlefield.

Iraq's Reactions

Iraq's situation in April 1991 was dire. It had been thrashed on the battlefield with the rapid collapse of its large military machine. A large proportion of its military capability was destroyed or inoperable; its military had thousands dead or wounded (against few coalition casualties). Damage to its infrastructure and industrial capability was conservatively estimated at $20 billion to $30 billion. The economic embargo was causing severe economic dislocation and discomfort among the Iraqi people. As a result of these factors, some observers thought it reasonable that a popular uprising, led or supported by elements within the Iraqi military, would result in Saddam Hussein's removal from power. Even if this were not to materialize, the general feeling was that Saddam would be willing to comply with the provisions of Resolution 687 in order to get permission to resume exporting oil.[27]

Few of these expectations have been met. More than seven years since the end of the war, Saddam Hussein remains in power, pursuing his own agenda. While he has recognized Kuwait's independence, he periodically has moved troops into positions threatening to Kuwait (i.e., in October 1994). He also has launched missiles at his neighbors and has continued to suppress the Kurds in northern Iraq and the Shiites in southern Iraq.

His actions have forced the allied coalition to devote substantial resources to Operations Northern Watch in the north and Southern Watch in the south and as well as to keep substantial military assets in the Persian Gulf region.[28] Saddam gives little indication that the economic suffering of the Iraqi people has any impact on his policies or objectives.

Iraqi officials, operating under clear instructions from Saddam, go to great lengths to impede and block the UNSCOM mission, cooperating only when all avenues of resistance have been exposed.[29] The defection of Hussein Kamel, Saddam's son-in-law and head of the weapons of mass destruction program, to Jordan in August 1995 provided authoritative evidence of the extent of prohibited activity under way or concealed in Iraq. UNSCOM has seen its original verification mandate changed into an enforcement agency to "confront blockage, cheating, denials, and threats, as well as to attend to a complex political and security agenda."[30]

In October 1997, Saddam dramatically escalated tensions by expelling American members of the UNSCOM inspection teams, prohibiting inspection of so-called sensitive sites, and demanding an end to the inspection regime by a date certain. UNSCOM withdrew its inspectors in protest. Intensive diplomatic negotiations, in which Russia played a large role for the first time since the Gulf War, accompanied by a significant increase in U.S. military forces in the region, resulted in Saddam accepting the return of the inspectors. However, in early 1998, Saddam again attempted to control UNSCOM operations in Iraq. In the face of probable U.S. military strikes designed to punish Saddam, U.N. Secretary General Kofi Annan persuaded Saddam to accept a slightly modified inspection regime. The Security Council, deeply divided over the wisdom of military action, approved Annan's compromise. Inspections resumed without apparent obstruction by the Iraqis.

Impact of Phase II Sanctions

The economic sanctions in place since the April 1991 cease-fire are part of a broader strategy to contain Saddam Hussein's ambition to dominate the Middle East. Saddam is unlikely to change his ways, and there is little evidence that the Iraqi opposition, as currently constituted, can mount an effective challenge to his rule. As Saddam is likely be in charge in Iraq for the foreseeable future, the challenge is to shape his behavior within Iraq where possible and prevent him from exerting coercive influence outside the country.

The economic sanctions have prevented Iraq from rebuilding its weapons of mass destruction capability by enabling the United Nations to maintain an intrusive inspection regime there, destroying prohibited military equipment, and preventing Iraq from restocking equipment lost in the war. However, Iraqi authorities seek to frustrate and challenge the mission of the Special Commission whenever and wherever possible. They cooperate only when they have no other choice. Saddam is prepared to take strong, even dramatic, action (as he did in November 1997 and again in January 1998) to block UNSCOM inspectors and to attempt to divide the coalition. It is unlikely that the head of the Special Commission will be in a position any time soon to assert that the committee has completed its mission as outlined in 687. Just before stepping down as its head, Rolf Ekeus said the Special Commission had "documentary evidence about orders from the [Iraqi] leadership to preserve a strategic capability. That means to keep the production equipment ready to produce at any given moment."[31]

The sanctions have not changed Saddam's repressive treatment of the Iraqi people nor his aggressive behavior toward countries in the region, Kuwait in particular. Thus either as a punishment on Saddam or as an inducement for him to adopt different behavior, the economic sanctions have yet to produce a convincing result. However, the sanctions have prevented him from significant rebuilding of Iraqi military capability, something he doubtless would have done in the absence of the sanctions. This is an important achievement. Removing the economic sanctions, and thus permitting unrestricted export of Iraqi oil, would yield Saddam $12 to 15 billion in oil revenues at current production capabilities.[32] This revenue stream would remove any incentive Iraq has for even minimal cooperation with UNSCOM and, in all likelihood, would result once again in significant Iraqi expenditures for offensive military weapons.

The Sanctions in 1998

On December 9, 1996, Iraq finally agreed to the terms of Resolution 986, which provided for limited sales of Iraqi oil for humanitarian purposes.[33] This permitted Iraqi oil to flow for the first time since August 1990. Of the initial $2 billion of oil revenues, nearly 30 percent is allocated to pay war claims and for U.N. operations in Iraq. Of the remainder, $805 million is allocated to food imports and $210 million for medicine. As with UNSCOM, Saddam has sought to control tightly the activities of the U.N. observers, restricting the United Nations from seeing if the terms of Resolution 986 are being complied with fully. Nevertheless, in an effort to calm Arab concerns over the humanitarian impact of the sanctions amidst U.S. preparations to strike Iraq in early 1998, the Security Council at U.S. instigation approved Resolution 1153. This new resolution which supercedes Resolution 986, increases the value of Iraqi oil exports from $2 billion to $5.256 billion every six months. It also expands permissible imports beyond food and humanitarian relief to include rehabilitation of basic services (e.g. water, electricity, education).[34]

With the passage of time, there are indications that sanctions "fatigue" has begun to set in. There are increasing calls for easing up on aggressive implementation of the economic sanctions. Some Arab countries have become concerned that their impact is falling mainly on the average Iraqi and not on Saddam or his key supporters. This concern is shared by others, in Europe and the United States, as reports of malnutrition and poor health among Iraqis, particularly children, multiply. These reports, some of which are emotionally compelling but difficult to verify independently, raise difficult issues about whether the sanctions should be modified on humanitarian grounds. However, any substantial suffering that occurs is a result of Saddam's actions. There is nothing in the U.N. sanctions that necessarily would inflict undue hardship on innocent Iraqis. So, while innocent Iraqis doubtlessly are suffering, it is because of Saddam's calculated refusal to comply with the sanctions, not because of the sanctions themselves.

In addition, the vast oil resources of Iraq are of significant interest to oil companies and oil service companies.[35] There are reports that some oil companies (possibly supported by their governments) are seeking special arrangements with Iraq, in preparation for the day when the sanctions may be lifted. Some members of the Security Council favor a phased lifting of sanctions as UNSCOM certifies Iraqi compliance with elements of Resolution 687 (e.g., nuclear and missile programs). It is also only a matter of time before calls emerge for more dramatic changes, something anticipated in paragraph 22 of Resolution 687 which calls for the complete lifting of limits on Iraq's ability to export once it has complied fully with all U.N. demands relating to its weapons of mass destruction programs.

Procedurally, these and the other sanctions cannot be lifted without a favorable vote by the Security Council. Thus it could not take place without the support (or at least abstention) of all the permanent members of the council. Accordingly, the United States technically can maintain the sanctions regime for as long as it believes necessary. However, politically and practically, it would be very difficult to continue the current sanctions regime if the United States and the United Kingdom were its only supporters. Open disregard for enforcement would be damaging to the United Nations' authority. It would create a bad precedent should another situation develop whereby the United States, or any other country, would seek a U.N.-sanctioned multinational embargo.

Conclusions

Some argue that every sanctions case is unique. Iraq certainly *is*. Some lessons of the Iraq case have general relevance; others do not. The United Nations imposed economic sanctions in highly unusual circumstances, ones not likely to be replicated easily. With only a few exceptions, every country branded Saddam an international outlaw for the invasion of Kuwait. His action threatened the flow of oil out of the world's main producing region. The United States and the Soviet Union were in the first glow of cooperation in the post–Cold War era; there were excellent relations between Presidents Bush and Gorbachev and their respective senior aides. President Bush, the undisputed leader in marshaling international forces to confront Saddam, had remarkably strong, personal relations with the leaders of the allied coalition.

Still, President Bush and his senior advisors believed it unlikely that economic sanctions alone could force Saddam to retreat fully from Kuwait, certainly not within a period they considered acceptable. The sanctions were the best tool available on August 2, 1990, to signal outrage and determination to resist Saddam and also to preserve Kuwait as an entity by protecting its assets abroad while preventing sale of its oil. They bought the time necessary to build an effective multilateral coalition, to build public support for additional measures, and to position the necessary military forces in the region. As such, the sanctions during Phase I should not be considered a complete failure even though they did not achieve their fundamental objectives.

The assessment of the sanctions in Phase II is, on balance, that they have been a success to date. The sanctions have prevented Saddam from significantly rebuilding his military machine, which he doubtless would have done otherwise. The sanctions are essential to enabling UNSCOM to pursue its mission in Iraq, albeit under very difficult conditions. Without the sanctions, Saddam probably would cease permanently any cooperation with UNSCOM. It is reasonable to assume that he would be acting far worse in the absence of sanctions. Saddam has publicly recognized the legitimacy of Kuwait as a state. From these perspectives, the economic sanctions continue to be a success.

Both Phases I and II provide useful lessons for applying sanctions. Broad multilateral support, preferably endorsed by the U.N. Security Council, significantly improves the chances for success. From the beginning, President Bush and his senior advisors were determined to use the U.N. Security Council to gather international support. Through skillful diplomacy and a common assessment of the problem among its permanent members, the Security Council for the first time functioned as its founders had envisioned in dealing with a major threat to global peace.

Multilateral support is easier to obtain, and keep, if those affected (as opposed to targeted) by the sanctions receive help to mitigate the impact of sanctions. Thus the Economic Assistance Program for the front-line states was very helpful in preventing significant leakage through countries that had had strong economic ties with Iraq. Sanctions enforcement is greatly facilitated through the use of military force, such as the Multilateral Interception Force in the Persian Gulf and the Mediterranean Sea.

The experience of the Iraq sanctions, particularly in Phase II, also holds useful lessons on their limitations. Strongly held beliefs of ruthless, authoritarian leaders are very difficult to change by sanctions alone. Iraq has foregone more than $100 billion in oil export earnings since the end of the Gulf War; its yearly loss has been approximately $12–15 billion. This indicates the high value Saddam attaches to possessing prohibited weapons. It is also a good indication that sanctions alone would *not* have forced him out of Kuwait. The result is that sanctions have put constraints on Saddam but have not changed him or his objectives. In addition, the sanctions have not created conditions enabling forces within Iraq to depose him. (However, this was a desire rather than an explicit objective of the sanctions.) Furthermore, with the passage of time and in the face of a stalemate with no clear path to resolution, sanctions fatigue can develop. Over time, concern is likely to mount that innocent people are bearing the brunt of the sanctions, while the targeted leaders find ways to cope. Consequently, coalition solidarity can weaken over time and be exploited by a determined opponent (as Saddam has attempted since the fall of 1997). In addition, international support for sanctions can be adversely affected by developments on other issues, such as the stalemated Middle East peace process which has made it difficult for some Arab leaders to justify to their peoples continued support for sanctions on Iraq while Israel is seen as ignoring its obligations under the Oslo Accords.

Perhaps the clearest lesson that the case of Iraq provides is that sanctions cannot be measured by a simple "success" or "failure" label. Sanctions inevitably have a range of impacts that vary over time. Thus lack of clear success in one area does not necessarily mean sanctions have failed. In this, sanctions closely resemble other foreign policy instruments.

Notes

The author would like to thank Timothy Deal, Richard N. Haass, Kenneth Juster, Richard Newcomb, Bruce Riedel, Brent Scowcroft, and Robert Zoellick for their advice and comments.

1. NSD-26, issued October 2, 1989, stated that "normal relations between the United States and Iraq would serve our longer-term interests and promote stability in both the Gulf and the Middle East." See Secretary of State James A. Baker's account in his book, *The Politics of Diplomacy: Revolution, War, and Peace, 1989–1992* (New York: G.P. Putnam's Sons, 1995), p. 263.

2. In 1989 the Bush administration allocated $1 billion in Credit Commodity Corporation (CCC) credits guarantees, with $500 million immediately available. Under the CCC program, U.S. banks provided money to U.S. farmers shipping grain to Iraq, with the CCC guaranteeing payments to the U.S. banks by Iraq over a three-year period. For the definitive discussion of this much-misunderstood issue, see Kenneth I. Juster, "The Myth of Iraqgate," *Foreign Policy* 94 (Spring 1994), pp. 105–119. In January 1990 President Bush also approved a $200 million Exim line of credit for grain purchases.

3. On June 7, 1981, Israeli air force planes attacked and destroyed an Iraqi nuclear facility, claiming it was being built to develop nuclear weapons that threatened Israel's security.

4. The same message was delivered by a bipartisan congressional mission, led by Senators Dole and Metzenbaum, that visited Saddam Hussein in April 1990 as part of a Middle East tour. The senators returned to Washington with the impression that the United States should keep the relationship open. See Baker, *Politics of Diplomacy*, p. 269.

5. Kuwait was pressing Iraq for repayment of $30 billion lent to Iraq during the 1980 to 1988 Iran-Iraq war. During that war, Kuwait and Saudi Arabia lent Iraq the proceeds of the sale of oil from the Neutral Zone to compensate Iraq for lost oil revenues from its own shut-in production. Iran had destroyed Iraq's offshore loading platforms in the northern part of the Persian Gulf, thus preventing Iraq from exporting oil through the Gulf. In addition, Iraq and Kuwait had territorial disputes, along the northern border of Kuwait and over Bubiyan and Al-Wadah islands, which controlled access to the Iraqi port of Umm Qasr. Iraq and Kuwait also disputed production from the Rumailah field, which straddles their border.

6. President Bush's message followed on the heels of a July 25 meeting between Saddam and Ambassador Glaspie. At this meeting, Saddam acknowledged that the United States had legitimate interests in the region and indicated that various mediation efforts might be able to resolve his grievances with Kuwait and Iraq. While some have argued that Glaspie did not warn Saddam adequately about the consequences of military aggression against Kuwait, the record suggests that she faithfully articulated U.S. policy. Moreover, at the time, there was no consensus within the executive branch or Congress as to what specific steps the United States would—or should—take if Iraq crossed the northern border of Kuwait.

7. U.S. sanctions were covered by four key executive orders signed by the president. The first two were issued on the day of the invasion; the others were designed to conform with U.N. Resolution 661.

- Executive Order 12722, issued August 2, 1990, blocked the property and interests of Iraq held in the United States or by U.S. persons worldwide. The order prohibited the import of any Iraqi goods and services, and the export of any U.S. goods, services, technology, and technical data or other export-controlled information to Iraq; all transport and travel to Iraq (except to depart from Iraq or by professional journalists); the reexport of Iraqi goods to any country; and the grant or extension of credits, loans, or guarantees to the government of Iraq or any institution or entity affiliated with it.

- Executive Order 12723, also issued August 2, blocked all assets of the government of Kuwait held in the United States or by a U.S. person worldwide.

- Executive Order 12724, issued August 9, prohibited the performance of any contract, including financial contracts, in support of industrial, commercial, public utility, or Iraqi government contracts. It also prohibited any financial or economic transaction with the Iraqi government or its representatives.

- Executive Order 12725, issued August 9, prohibited any import of Kuwaiti origin; any export of goods, services, or technology to Kuwait; any financial transaction with Kuwait, and any travel to Kuwait (with exceptions for humanitarian, official, and media travel).

In addition, on September 1 the United States denied developing country status to Iraq; ended any foreign aid, Exim bank guarantees, and the sale of items on the Munitions List. U.S. executive directors at multilateral financial institutions were directed to vote against any loan or program for Iraq. The executive orders and other actions were strengthened by the Iraq Sanctions Act of 1990 (Public Law 101–513), which continued the sweeping embargo against trade, economic, or financial transactions with Iraq or Iraqi-occupied Kuwait and strengthened enforcement by increasing civil and criminal penalties.

For a comprehensive view of how the U.S. Department of Treasury implemented the economic sanctions, see "Economic Resistance to Iraqi Aggression," presentation by R. Richard Newcomb, director of the Office of Foreign Assets Control, Department of the Treasury, before the Kuwait Economic Society, Kuwait City, Kuwait, February 24, 1992.

8. Turkey halted operation of the Kirkuk-Yumurtalik pipeline carrying Iraqi crude across Turkey to the Mediterranean; Saudi Arabia closed the pipeline bringing Iraqi crude across Saudi Arabia to Yanbu. With the closure of these two pipelines (Iraq's only land outlets) and the naval blockade of the Persian Gulf, Iraq lost over 95 percent of its oil exports. A small amount of oil was shipped overland to Jordan, which depended on Iraqi oil for most of its supply.

9. The vote was 13–0, with Cuba and Yemen abstaining. The resolution did allow shipment of medicine and *humanitarian* food supplies to Iraq.

10. Resolution 665 was approved by the same vote as Resolution 661. While the emir of Kuwait had asked for help on August 11 to enforce Article 51 of the U.N. Charter (individual and collective self-defense), a number of countries had disagreed with the U.S. interpretation that this was sufficient authority to enforce Resolution 661. Hence the importance of getting Resolution 665 approved.

11. Interview on May 27, 1997, with Brent Scowcroft, National Security Adviser to President Bush. In addition, during August and early September 1990, an interagency group led by Deputy Secretary of the Treasury John Robson and Assistant Secretary of State for Economic and Business Affairs Eugene McAllister carried out a detailed study of the likely impact of sanctions on Iraq. The group concluded that sanctions would not have any significant effect on Iraq for at least six to 12 months under the best of circumstances. The study's conclusions were too controversial, given the pressures in Congress and elsewhere to give primacy to sanctions over a military response, and the study was quietly shelved.

12. For a detailed discussion of the various diplomatic initiatives, see Baker, *Politics of Diplomacy*, especially chapters 14–19.

13. Libya and Cuba were notable in their refusal to support the United Nations sanctions.

14. When the air war began on January 17, 1991, the United States and Japan immediately announced the release of government oil stocks in an effort to convince oil markets (which were open in Asia) that sufficient supplies would be available regardless of whether the Iraqis attacked Saudi oil facilities. The same day in Paris, the IEA announced that its members had activated a stock drawdown and demand restraint plan agreed upon on January 9, 1991. Because of the quick success of the air war, crude oil prices actually fell and few government oil stocks ultimately were released. However, the political determination to release stocks clearly had a calming effect on oil markets.

15. King Fahd told Secretary of Defense Dick Cheney on his first visit to Saudi Arabia after the invasion that Saudi Arabia would increase production to help calm oil markets. Venezuela also informed the United States it would increase crude oil production.

16. Miyagawa Makio, *Do Economic Sanctions Work?* (New York: St. Martins Press, 1992), pp. 55–56.

17. See the *Economist Intelligence Unit* country reports on Egypt from 1990 to 1991.

18. Allison Sample, "Caught in the Middle," *Middle East*, no. 199 (May 1991), p. 26.

19. D. L. Bethlehem and E. Lauterpacht (eds.), *The Kuwait Crisis: Sanctions and Their Economic Consequences* (Cambridge: Cambridge University Press 1991), pp. 665–67.

20. U.S. companies were requested to file claims with OFAC for outstanding claims with Iraq. These claims have not yet been adjudicated. Compensation, when finally established, will be paid out of the U.N. Compensation Fund and the Iraq Claims Act.

21. In September 1990 Secretary of State James Baker and Secretary of the Treasury Nicholas Brady separately visited all the key players in the coalition, seeking—and obtaining—multibillion dollar commitments, both for the EAP and to reimburse the United States for the substantial sums it was spending to deploy forces to the Gulf. The key participants quickly named the effort the "Tin Cup" exercise. It resulted in a gold-plated response from those asked, raising $54 billion for the U.S. military deployment in addition to funds for the front-line states. The United Kingdom also obtained moderate financial support abroad for its military efforts. The fund-raising effort first covered Desert Shield and then Desert Storm.

22. Baker, *Politics of Diplomacy*, p. 295.

23. On January 12, 1991, the House of Representatives voted 250–183 in favor of the Solarz-Michel resolution authorizing the use of force in the Gulf. The Senate voted 52–47 in favor of a similar resolution put forward by Senators John Warner (R-Va.) and Joseph Lieberman (D-Conn.). Both resolutions supported U.N. Security Council Resolution 678 of November 19, 1990, which authorized all necessary means to expel Iraq from Kuwait, if Iraq had not retreated by January 15, 1991. It should be noted that right up to the vote, sentiment in both the House of Representatives and in the Senate was strongly in favor of sticking to economic sanctions.

24. The United States and the other coalition partners rapidly drew down their military forces in Saudi Arabia in the spring of 1991. While some equipment was left behind for use in an emergency, Saudi Arabia is extremely reluctant, for political and cultural reasons, about having foreign troops on its soil.

    Iraq has the largest military in the Gulf with 400,000 men under arms, 2,500 tanks, and 300 combat aircraft. See remarks by Bruce Riedel, special assistant to the president and senior director, Near East and South Asian Affairs, National Security Council, before the Middle East Institute Conference on Iraq, Washington, DC, May 27, 1997.

25. These commitments have yet to be fulfilled. However, some of the receipts from oil sales under U.N. Resolution 986 are being allocated for compensation claims.

26. The U.N. Sanctions Commission was established in August 1990 under Resolution 661.

27. See remarks by Ambassador Rolf Ekeus, executive chairman of the U.N. Special Commission to the National Committee on American Foreign Policy, February 11, 1997, New York City.

28. Before December 1996, Operation Northern Watch was called Operation Provide Comfort. While the air mission remains the same, France no longer participates.

29. For a list of incidents between the Iraqis and UNSCOM from June 1991 to April 1997, see *Research Notes,* June 3, 1997, no. 1, published by the Washington Institute for Near East Policy.

30. Ibid, p. 4. Rolf Ekeus ended his term as executive chairman of the U.N. Special Commission on Iraq on June 30, 1997, and was Sweden's ambassador to the United States. His successor is Richard Butler, an Australian diplomat.

31. "Iraqis Still Defying Arms Ban, Departing U.N. Official Says," *New York Times,* June 25, 1997, p. 1.

32. Iraq today has production capacity of 2.5 million barrels a day (MBD). With adequate investment, it could be producing 4.5 to 5.5 MBD within a few years.

33. Since October 1991, in response to increasing signs of hardship imposed by a deteriorating economic situation, the United Nations passed several resolutions to permit Iraq to sell up to $1 billion in oil every 90 days to pay for humanitarian supplies, reparations, and operating expenses of various U.N. oversight bodies involved in the country. It took five years of negotiations for Saddam Hussein to agree to the strict monitoring conditions set forth in the various resolutions (which culminated in Resolution 986 of April 1995). These conditions are intended to prevent the Iraqi government from diverting any humanitarian supplies, or funds generated by the oil sales, to other purposes. Payment for the oil goes into an escrow account established by the U.N. secretary general. The sale of Iraqi crude for humanitarian purposes is limited and strictly controlled.

34. For a critical analysis of the potential impact of Resolution 1153, see Patrick Clawson, " 'Oil for Food?' or the End of Sanctions?" *Policywatch,* no. 303 (Washington, DC: Washington Institute for Near East Policy, February 26, 1998).

35. Iraq's proven oil reserves are conservatively estimated at 112 billion barrels. As little analysis and exploration has been done this decade, and exploration techniques have undergone enormous leaps in technology, it is reasonable to assume that its reserves are even higher.

6

Libya

GIDEON ROSE

AFTER SEIZING power in Libya in 1969, Muammar Qaddafi devoted a significant portion of his country's burgeoning oil revenues to harassing enemies and exporting his "revolution." These actions soon led him into conflict with the United States, which has tried now for over two decades to coerce Libya into changing its ways. U.S. officials periodically increase the pressure further, following a familiar pattern: Each tightening of the screws is enough to produce angry squeals from Libya and its business partners, but not enough to dislodge Qaddafi or compel Libya's full compliance with international norms.[1] Over time, a byzantine array of economic and legal measures has resulted that together keep Libya on the sidelines of regional and world politics but allow its oil to flow onto international markets.

The Libyan sanctions have come in three broad phases, with the latter two layered onto existing arrangements. The first phase ran from the 1970s to late 1991, during which time the United States waged a relatively lonely campaign to isolate Qaddafi, cutting off bilateral economic ties and trying to persuade other countries to do the same. The second phase ran from late 1991 to mid-1996 and saw the addition of limited U.N. sanctions against Libya in response to the bombings of Pan Am Flight 103 and UTA Flight 772. The third and present phase began in mid-1996 with the passage of the Iran-Libya Sanctions Act (ILSA) and has been marked by a U.S. attempt to use secondary sanctions as a weapon to coerce its allies into following a stiffer anti-Libya line.

Judging the desirability and even the impact of these various sanctions is clearly a subjective exercise, both because they involve so many stated and unstated goals and because the Qaddafi regime's decision-making is unusually opaque and bizarre. The issue, in a nutshell, is what the United States should do about a foreign state that engages in occasional criminal behavior but remains an attractive commercial partner for many American allies. Neither appeasement nor invasion seems appropriate, and the United States and other countries disagree strongly over measures in between. The pre-1996 U.S. policy toward Libya could hardly be called a major success, and was deplored both by those seeking justice and by those seeking commerce. Nevertheless, it served important U.S. interests without disrupting the Atlantic alliance or raising the Libyan issue above its proper level of importance for American foreign policy in general—and so, until the situation in Libya changes dramatically, that pre-1996 policy appears, on balance, to be the least bad of the alternatives realistically available.

Phase I: U.S. Sanctions Against Libya During the 1980s

The United States' troubles with Libya began with Qaddafi's rise to power and his decision to pursue a foreign policy based on radical activism. Challenging the West in both word and deed, Qaddafi supported numerous terrorist groups and revisionist causes (particularly those opposing Israel and its American patron) and was linked to atrocities such as the killing of Israeli athletes at the Munich Olympics in 1972 and the assassination of the U.S. ambassador to Sudan in 1973.[2] In the mid-1970s, accordingly, the United States declared a unilateral embargo against arms sales to Libya and in 1980 closed its Tripoli embassy (which had recently been torched by government-incited mobs).

In this area as in others, the Reagan administration took office determined to be more assertive than its predecessor. How to punish Libya for its various transgressions was a key topic on the agenda of the new administration's early National Security Council (NSC) meetings. In May 1981, citing Libyan support for terrorism and regional subversion, the United States ordered the Libyan mission in Washington closed; three months later U.S. Navy jets downed two Libyan warplanes after being fired on during an exercise over the Gulf of Sidra. That fall officials debated what else could be done, considering options ranging from harsher rhetoric up to a U.S. boycott of Libyan oil. In these discussions the chief argument against an oil embargo was that it would not do much to pressure Libya unless the Europeans joined, and confidential soundings revealed they would refuse to do so. As Ronald Reagan said in September, "No one country could affect the Libyans by having a boycott."[3]

In December reports circulated about Libyan "hit squads" sent to assassinate U.S. officials,[4] and in response the administration banned U.S. citizens from using American passports and money for travel to Libya and asked those citizens there to leave. Secretary of State Alexander Haig presented the U.S. case against Libya to the North Atlantic Treaty Organization (NATO), but the Europeans refused to take similar measures. On March 10, 1982, nevertheless, the administration imposed a unilateral U.S. boycott of Libyan crude oil and established export controls for goods and technology; the rationale given for these actions was that they would curtail revenues used by Qaddafi to finance terrorist groups.

Because of changes in the international oil market, the American boycott was far less significant than it would have been even two years earlier. In 1980 the United States had been Libya's largest single crude oil customer, with purchases accounting for nearly 40 percent of Libya's total production and 11 percent of U.S. crude oil imports. As the United States increased its purchases of North Sea oil from the United Kingdom and crude oil from Mexico, however, U.S. imports of Libyan oil decreased rapidly. In 1981 Libya accounted for only 7 percent of total U.S. crude oil imports, and U.S. purchases were plummeting still further when the boycott was imposed.[5]

Several U.S. companies, including Exxon and Mobil, ceased operations in Libya once the boycott was announced, but others remained and continued production (although not exploration) over the next few years; estimates placed the number of Americans working in Libya during this period at between 400 and 1,000. Libya's revenues from oil exports dropped by more than half in the early 1980s, but the chief reason was not the U.S. boycott but rather a worldwide oil glut. In 1984 Britain cut off diplomatic relations after a policewoman was killed by fire from within the Libyan embassy in London, but the Europeans still generally refused to join the Americans in a tougher anti-Libya line.

The Reagan administration's frustration continued to mount, however, as Qaddafi's radicalism and foreign meddling continued. Libya's actions, primarily within the Middle East and North Africa, contributed to a general rise in international terrorism during the 1980s—although Iran and Syria played an even greater role than did Libya. In June 1984 a "Vulnerability Assessment" prepared by the Central Intelligence Agency (CIA) concluded that "no course of action short of stimulating Qaddafi's fall will bring any significant and enduring change in Libyan policies." The only way to exploit the regime's weaknesses, the report argued, was "through a broad program in cooperation with key countries combining political, economic, and paramilitary action. . . .

[Libyan] exile groups, if supported to a substantial degree, could soon begin an intermittent campaign of sabotage and violence which could prompt further challenges to Qaddafi's authority."[6] By late 1994 existing restrictions appeared to have had few, if any, effects on Libyan behavior, and the administration's exasperation was growing. During the following year, accordingly, President Reagan authorized a covert operation designed to undermine the Libyan regime.[7] Following the discovery of some Libyan oil sales within the United States, moreover, the administration extended the ban on the importation of Libyan crude oil to cover refined products as well.

At the end of 1985 dramatic terrorist attacks took place at the Rome and Vienna airports. When evidence emerged pointing to Libyan involvement, the Reagan administration stepped up its campaign to get its allies involved in strict anti-Libya measures, but still the Europeans refused. The administration again decided to move forward unilaterally, and in January 1986 it announced the imposition of a new set of sanctions designed "to stop all American economic activity with Libya and bring all Americans home." The actions, officials said, were "necessary to make the [Libyan] regime. . . pay a price for its support of international terrorism and render it 'a pariah' among nations."[8] The administration soon announced, however, that foreign subsidiaries of American firms would not be affected and that the embargo was being modified to permit certain firms to retain their assets in Libya temporarily and to continue certain operations (so that the companies would not be forced to terminate their Libyan involvement at a huge loss or with windfall profits accruing to the Libyan government).[9] In addition to the embargo, Reagan ordered Libyan government assets in the United States frozen.[10] These measures were accompanied by threats of further action should Libyan behavior not change.

Reagan opted for increased sanctions at this point rather than a military response, aides said, because he felt the latter would raise unacceptable risks—including potential harm to American citizens still in Libya, an outbreak of anti-Americanism in Arab countries, and the possibility that American planes might be downed in an attack. The president also had insisted that any target for retaliation be clearly connected with the relevant terrorists, and available intelligence could not satisfy that requirement. Foreign subsidiaries of U.S. firms were not included in the embargo because Secretary of State George Shultz "wanted to avoid a direct clash with the Europeans reminiscent of the feud in 1981–82 over the American efforts to block subsidiaries in Europe from helping to build the Soviet natural gas pipeline."[11] According to administration officials, as important as the new measures' expected economic impact was the extent to which they would exhaust all U.S. options short of future military action, as well as perhaps provoke Qaddafi into a response that could serve as a pretext for such action.[12] Days after the sanctions were imposed, in fact, U.S. contingency planning was stepped up for future naval maneuvers in the Gulf of Sidra and air strikes against Libya by American planes based in England.[13]

With its various exemptions and modifications, the U.S. embargo really represented an economic nuisance for both countries rather than a heavy blow for either. According to the most up-to-date figures available to American decision-makers at the time, U.S. exports to Libya had dropped from $860 million in 1979 to less than $200 million in 1984, while imports from Libya had dropped from $5 billion in 1979 to $9 million in 1984; U.S. direct investment in Libya at the end of 1984 was valued at $446 *million* (90 percent of it in oil production) out of a total U.S. overseas investment of $223 *billion*. U.S. companies were the main operators of Libyan oil fields and accounted for roughly three-quarters of the country's total production of 1.1 million barrels per day; U.S. firms also marketed at least one-third of Libya's production to customers in Europe and elsewhere. Practically all U.S. business in Libya, however, in both the energy and construction industries, operated through subsidiaries based in London or Rome.[14]

After the embargo was announced, Qaddafi maintained his challenging posture, and at the end of March 1986 the U.S. Sixth Fleet deliberately crossed Libya's self-proclaimed "line of death" (32°30' north latitude) in the Gulf of Sidra. The Libyans responded by firing some missiles at U.S. planes, and the American forces retaliated by silencing the air-defense battery and sinking some Libyan patrol boats. Then in early April a bomb exploded at a Berlin disco favored by American servicemen, and evidence pointed to Libyan involvement. The American response was to launch a bombing raid on various Libyan targets including Qaddafi's residence, trying simultaneously to punish him for supporting terrorism, to incite a coup, and ideally to remove him from the scene completely.[15] The raid killed a number of Libyans and damaged Qaddafi's quarters, but the Libyan leader survived and his rule was not seriously challenged. The impact of the strike on later Libyan terrorism is uncertain. Some observers claim that it chastened Qaddafi, others that it spurred him on to acts of revenge including Lockerbie.

In the wake of the bombing—which only Britain had supported and which other U.S. European allies had opposed, refusing overflight permission and thus seriously complicating the mission—European Community (EC) members imposed a modest set of diplomatic sanctions on Libya and banned arms sales. Buoyed by this change in attitude as well as by the agreement of a Group of Seven (G-7) summit to condemn Libyan terrorism, the Reagan administration launched a broad effort to get the Europeans to join in a variety of further sanctions.[16] None was adopted. The administration and Congress then decided to impose a deadline for the cessation of all direct involvement in Libya by U.S. firms. Eventually the companies managed to negotiate three-year "standstill agreements" with Qaddafi, which suspended the companies' operations without prejudice to their interests or concessions while allowing the Libyan government to sell the companies' share of Libyan oil.[17]

After a year in place, the American embargo had neither made a significant impact on Libya's economy nor prevented some trade from taking place there by U.S. firms, mostly legally through their foreign subsidiaries.[18] In May 1987 the General Accounting Office (GAO) reported that "the practical impact of the U.S. trade sanctions on Libyan oil production is minimal because of the extensive foreign availability of oilfield equipment, services and supplies. . . . The short-term effect of the sanctions on the U.S. oil companies has been a loss of revenue while Libya continues to reap the full benefit of their oilfield operations."[19]

By the beginning of 1988 the Reagan administration had resigned itself to the fact of Qaddafi's existence and moved away from attempts to overthrow or intimidate him. As a White House official put it, "If one characterizes our earlier policy as one of active destabilization, one could say we're now trying to further isolate him." Another official was more blunt: "We finally decided we cannot remove the man from the outside by military means." Hallmarks of the new policy included lowered rhetorical attacks, an end to U.S. Navy maneuvers in the Gulf of Sidra, and a decline in funding for Libyan exile groups. Among the reasons for the shift were Qaddafi's persistence in power despite U.S. actions; his diminished momentum and external activities; and a change in Reagan administration personnel—notably the death of CIA Director William Casey and the departure, after the Iran-Contra affair, of National Security Adviser John Poindexter and NSC staffer Oliver North.[20]

As one of its final acts, in January 1989 the Reagan administration granted permission for major U.S. oil companies to resume operations in Libya through their European subsidiaries. The standstill agreements they had negotiated with Libya in mid-1986 were set to expire, and the companies had lobbied the administration passionately so as to avoid once again any situation that would force them to sell off their Libyan assets, collectively estimated to be worth at least $2 billion and possibly twice that.[21] The administration kept a number of restrictions in place, however, with the result that Qaddafi was not fully satisfied and would not permit the companies to return.[22]

During 1989 Qaddafi set out on a new foreign policy tack designed to reduce his isolation. He played down his links with terrorism, made peace with some regional governments he had earlier tried to subvert, and sought wider diplomatic contacts and alliances. These moves brought better relations with Europe but were soon offset by Qaddafi's support for Saddam Hussein following the Iraqi invasion of Kuwait and his continued radical rhetoric and opposition to the Middle East peace process.[23] As far as Libya-watchers could tell, for Qaddafi the continuing U.S. sanctions were, on balance, "a headache." "It is very difficult to build anything [in Libya] in the sector without U.S. technology and equipment. In addition, some major European firms have shied away from Libya, not only for fear of treading on American assets, but also because the sanctions prohibit companies prospecting in the United States to offset exploration costs against Libyan equity production."[24] At this point, however, a new crisis emerged, sparked by fresh developments in an old investigation.

Phase II: Lockerbie and the 1992 U.N. Sanctions

Back on December 21, 1988, Pan Am Flight 103 had exploded in the air over Lockerbie, Scotland, killing all 259 passengers and crew on board and 11 people on the ground. Of the passengers, 189 were American citizens. And on September 19, 1989, the French airliner UTA Flight 772 had exploded in the air over Niger, killing all 171 passengers and crew. Investigators in the Lockerbie case focused initially on the possibility that the bombing had been the work of Ahmad Jibril's Popular Front for the Liberation of Palestine–General Command (PFLP-GC), with help from Syria and Iran. Evidence emerged later on, however, that appeared to establish that the explosion had been the work of two Libyan intelligence agents operating out of Malta. French authorities investigating the UTA bombing, meanwhile, uncovered evidence that it too was the handiwork of Libyan agents. In October 1991 a Parisian judge issued a warrant for the arrest of four Libyan intelligence officers charged with complicity in the UTA bombing, including Abdallah Senoussi, Qaddafi's brother-in-law; two weeks later the United States and Britain jointly announced the indictment of two Libyan security officials, Abdelbaset Ali Mohamed Al Mehgrahi and Al-Amin Khalifa Fhimah, for the Lockerbie attack.[25]

In November the three Western nations issued a joint declaration on the two cases. Regarding Lockerbie, the Americans and British declared that the Libyan government had to "surrender for trial all those charged with the crime; accept responsibility for the actions of Libyan officials; disclose all it knows of this crime, including the names of all those responsible, and allow full access to all witnesses, documents, and other material evidence, including all the remaining timers [of the type used in the attack]; [and] pay appropriate compensation." The three countries together declared that Libya had to comply with their demands regarding the two cases and prove by concrete actions that it renounced support for terrorism.[26]

On December 2 the European Community called on Libya to comply with the U.S.-U.K.-French demands and raised the possibility of imposing economic sanctions if it did not. By early December, according to bankers, Libya began transferring its liquid holdings out of Europe (particularly away from Britain and France, toward Switzerland and the Gulf) in order to avoid having them frozen by any EC measures.[27] The United States, United Kingdom, and France sought international support for U.N.-mandated sanctions or for sanctions mandated by the European Community or G-7 should the United Nations be cool to the idea. Officials said they had not ruled out military action as a last resort but were not trying to drum up support for it internationally.[28]

In January 1992 Britain, taking advantage of its chairmanship of the Security Council and of the recent departure of Cuba and Yemen from its ranks, shepherded the unanimous adoption of Resolution 731, which essentially endorsed the U.S.-U.K.-French statement of the previous November. Attempting to stave off the imposition of sanctions, Qaddafi offered to hand over the Lockerbie suspects to an international tribunal and allow the UTA suspects to appear before a French court, but this response was deemed insufficient. At the end of March the Security Council passed Resolution 748, calling for sanctions on Libya unless it complied with Resolution 731 and handed over the Lockerbie suspects within two weeks. The measures specified were a ban on all air links with Libya, a ban on arms sales, and a reduction in personnel at Libyan embassies abroad.[29]

The goal of the sanctions was to get Libya to turn over the two Lockerbie suspects, who would then be prosecuted, fulfilling the demands of the Western governments and publics for judgment and punishment in the bombing cases. The suspects presumably would be convicted and/or implicate Qaddafi directly, thus also providing grounds for further anti-Libya measures. More speculatively, U.S. and other Western officials hoped that the sanctions would undermine Qaddafi's regime by resulting in either a humiliating loss of face (if he complied) or the ratcheting up of domestic discontent one more notch (if he did not). These outcomes were not considered especially likely, but the sanctions still were expected to isolate Qaddafi further and restrain his ability and will to make trouble for others. According to local and foreign businessmen, the Libyans used the six-month interval between the announcement of the indictments and the imposition of sanctions to stockpile food, spare parts, and medicine.[30]

Over the next several years the sanctions were renewed continually at three-month intervals, with occasional battles between countries trying to tighten them (led by the United States) and countries trying to limit or ease them (led by Italy, Germany, and Spain, which depend on Libyan oil supplies, and Russia and China, which generally oppose U.S. attempts to sanction "rogue" states). Before the November 1992 renewal the United States, the United Kingdom, and France issued a statement saying that they would press for stronger sanctions unless Libya handed over the suspects, but no changes followed. In August 1993 Libya's opponents again tried to strengthen the sanctions regime and failed; nevertheless, the United States, the United Kingdom, and France issued yet another statement, promising that if Libya continued its noncompliance, they would propose a new resolution "strengthening the sanctions in key oil-related, financial, and technological areas."[31]

This threat was followed up with action, and resulted in the adoption of Security Council Resolution 883 in November 1993. The resolution provided for a further tightening of restrictions on the Libyan aviation industry; a ban on exports to Libya of selected equipment for "downstream" oil and gas sectors (e.g., refineries and distribution); a further reduction in staff levels at Libyan missions abroad; and a freezing of existing Libyan funds and financial resources overseas.[32] The tightening of sanctions was designed primarily for psychological impact and to create further annoyances and uncertainty for the Libyans; the new measures were not designed to cripple the Libyan economy (for which a ban on oil sales would be required), nor were they expected to have real economic impact for a number of months—both because they were modest incremental measures and because the Libyans had been given ample time to prepare for them by stockpiling material and shifting liquid assets around.[33] Qaddafi remained obstinate and soon renewed his violent rhetoric and announced that his war on exiled Libyan opponents would continue.[34]

The Causes and Consequences of the U.N. Sanctions

The most interesting question surrounding the imposition of the U.N. sanctions against Libya is what made the Lockerbie case different from its predecessors. The United States had sought cooperation on anti-

Libyan measures from its European allies and the international community numerous times before; why this time did they go along?

Five factors were crucial. First, the scale of the Lockerbie and UTA attacks was dramatically higher than that of previous cases of Libyan troublemaking. Together more than 400 people were killed, creating a deep sense of popular outrage in the West and a real constituency pressing for redress. Second, the victims included scores of British and French citizens in addition to Americans, ensuring that these countries would join the United States in demanding a response of some sort. Third, evidence of Libyan complicity in these attacks was much more damning than it had been in the past (the 1986 Berlin disco bombing being a case in point). Fourth, because of the demonstrated willingness of the United States to use force in the region during previous crises (such as the 1986 raid and the 1991 Gulf War), the Europeans realized that agreeing to sanctions actually might be the best way to keep the crisis from escalating further, one of their perpetual goals. Fifth, the end of the Cold War made it easier for major Western nations to use the U.N. Security Council for their own purposes. If the first four factors had been present without the fifth, it is still likely that multilateral sanctions would have been imposed, but under different institutional auspices.

While less critical, two additional factors also played a role. From the mid-1980s onward a change had taken place in the general Western attitude toward terrorism. The international community grew more disposed to regard it as a legal (as opposed to a political) issue and recognized that it should be combated through collective international action. This shift made it easier for U.S. officials in the early 1990s to move logically from evidence of Libyan complicity to the imposition of multilateral sanctions under U.N. auspices. It also accounts for the sanctions' narrow focus—the fact that they were imposed not in response to a perceived Libyan strategic threat but rather as (at least overtly) a lever designed to pry loose two defendants for trial.

Finally, during the late 1980s and early 1990s the demise of the Soviet bloc, the Gulf War, and progress in the Middle East peace process all had worked to isolate the Arab rejectionist bloc from the mainstream of world and even regional politics, making collective action against Libya less controversial than it would have been even a few years earlier. (This last factor, to be sure, also made it more difficult to portray Libyan activities as part of a broader, larger threat.)

In practice, the entire international community has participated in the sanctioning, including (to the surprise of some) Iran and the Arab world.[35] Kuwait, however, was the only Arab nation to expel Libyan diplomats at the start of the crisis—an exception due more to Gulf War resentments than to finer sensibilities regarding terrorism. The sanctions, moreover, have not had to be enforced militarily. On April 15, 1992, the day they came into effect, Libyan planes were turned away from airports in Italy, Tunisia, and Switzerland; afterward, no foreign airliner was allowed to depart for Libya nor was any Libyan Arab Airline plane given permission to land abroad.[36]

The particular U.N. sanctions adopted were selected because the governments involved wanted to do something to demonstrate their outrage, but the European countries that consumed Libyan oil were opposed to more stringent measures which would have had a much greater expected impact but also much higher costs. Foreign exchange receipts from hydrocarbon exports accounted for more than 95 percent of Libya's total hard-currency earnings during the period in question; all parties involved knew that these were the truly important potential target for any sanctions. But since roughly three-quarters of Libyan oil is purchased by European customers (chiefly Italy and Germany), any comprehensive oil embargo of Libya would impose serious costs on Europe as well—something European leaders are naturally loath to do. By exempting oil sales and purchases of basic oil drilling equipment from the measures, therefore, the sanctioners deliberately chose sanctions that would, at best, merely harass and humiliate the Libyan regime rather than cripple it.[37]

The question of why the United States opted to pursue a multilateral economic response in 1991–92 instead of the unilateral military response it had selected in 1986 is more interesting. The answer relates to the timing of the Lockerbie and UTA revelations. The crucial links between Libya and the bombings emerged years after the tragedies occurred, when public passions had cooled significantly and the issue had lost its urgency. Had the Libyan connection come to light in the immediate wake of the explosion, in other words, a military response might well have followed. By late 1991, moreover, the Bush administration had its hands full in the Middle East maintaining support for the containment and isolation of Iraq as well as managing the emerging Arab-Israeli peace process. U.S. officials deemed these higher priorities than striking out at Libya and decided not to risk overloading the circuits of the Arab world by launching another attack on Qaddafi.

An important interest group during this second phase of the Libyan sanctions has been the families of the Lockerbie victims. As soon as the evidence emerged relating to Libyan involvement, they pressed the U.S. government to impose stiffer penalties.[38] At the same time, many family members were upset that the official Lockerbie investigation had come to concentrate solely on Libya; they still felt that Iran and Syria were respon-

sible and believed the United States was downplaying those other countries' involvement for political reasons. Over time, many family members became frustrated at the lack of progress in the case and criticized
the U.S. government for not doing more to resolve it. Family representatives met repeatedly with senior officials in both the Bush and Clinton
administrations. While their pressure did not result in the imposition of
new measures (at least until 1996), it did keep the issue in play and
reminded officials that backsliding would carry public relations costs.[39]

As far as their practical consequences, the U.N. sanctions further isolated Libya and produced some minor changes in its behavior, but they
did not result in the handing over of the Lockerbie or UTA suspects. Nor
did they significantly undermine the Libyan regime or economy. A reputable December 1994 study of the sanctions' effects found them to be
real but limited, and argued that the arms embargo in particular actually had had a beneficial impact on the Libyan economy, preventing
Qaddafi from wasting resources in that area.[40] (The Libyan government,
on the other hand, claims that the U.N. sanctions have cost the country
$19 billion and over 21,000 lives—primarily from sick people being
denied transport to foreign medical facilities—but no one believes such
figures.)[41] Libya's general economic performance continues to depend
primarily on oil exports, which earned the country $7 billion in 1994,
$8 billion in 1995, and $8.5 billion in 1996; it has remained by far the
richest country in Africa on a per capita basis, with its current and
future resources entirely at the regime's disposal.

One reason why the U.N. sanctions have had only a limited effect is
that previous sanctions already had driven out all businesses except
those with deep roots and/or incentives to continue operating. By the
time the new measures were imposed:

> Business activity [was] dominated by firms that, in some cases, [could]
> boast up to 20 years of experience in avoiding the more obvious practical
> and financial pitfalls. Everyone [had] become well accustomed to shocks,
> having weathered the idiosyncrasies of Qaddafi's economic policy, the
> 1986 bombing of Tripoli and the. . . U.S. sanctions. . . . A company [was]
> therefore not going to relinquish its market share purely because the U.N.
> [was] threatening to make travel arrangements more problematic.

Libyan arrears in payments, moreover, gave firms a sunk cost difficult
to walk away from: "Companies believe[d] that the only way to stand
any chance of retrieving outstanding payments [was] to continue operating, even in the most trying circumstances."[42] The Libyan regime also
has offered powerful incentives for individual businesses to remain or
invest, largely offsetting pressures on those firms to stay out.[43]

Uncertainty over future U.N. moves did not deter Western firms from carrying out existing contracts but dramatically curtailed the signing of new ones. Because gas contracts are long term and place a premium on stability, they were hit harder by the uncertainty than oil contracts. The ban on external flights doubled the time it took to get in and out of the country; still, by late 1993 only one Western firm, Royal/Dutch Shell, was known to have stopped doing business in Libya because of the new difficulties. The rest stayed put because they were reliant on Libyan business, they did not want to forfeit debts owed by the Libyan government, and they believed that they could wait out the crisis and profit from Libyan business in the future.[44]

Imports to Libya, like travelers there, now "go along two main routes: either via Malta and then by boat to Tripoli, or overland via Tunisia. The result has been that transport and distribution difficulties have pushed up costs, while strong demand for limited goods has pushed up prices."[45] This has effectively devalued the currency; by late 1994 the Libyan dinar's black market value had plummeted to one-tenth the official exchange rate.[46] Nevertheless, according to visitors, there are "few obvious signs of hardship in the Libyan capital. The shops are well stocked and there are satellite dishes on the rooftops."[47] Foreign firms find working under sanctions to be "an inconvenience rather than a serious hindrance."[48] The main difficulties they encounter "are related to their work conditions. The air embargo. . . complicate[s] travel, delay[s] the delivery of equipment and spare parts and make[s] it difficult to transfer savings home."[49]

There have been continual small-scale breaches of the unilateral U.S. economic embargo from 1986 onward; the details of the cases and the penalties levied are contained in the president's semiannual letters to Congress reporting on the sanctions' implementation. There also have been repeated minor breaches of the U.N. sanctions.[50] By 1995 Libya's oil sector was able to avoid some potential damage "since oil equipment, including items banned by the U.N. sanctions, [was] reported to be reaching Libya, although at a high cost."[51]

The arms embargo also has been violated on a number of occasions, but more on the margins than at its core. In November 1995 Italian police seized ten tons of goods worth several million dollars en route to Libya from manufacturers in Britain, Canada, and the United States, including wing components for MiG planes and sophisticated electronic weaponry as well as parts from an American-built tanker aircraft being sent by the Libyan Air Force for repairs abroad.[52] In August 1996 a Russian transport plane crashed outside of Belgrade and was quickly cordoned off to all prying eyes (including the Russian ambassador), highlighting the arms trade between Serbia and Libya. "We think what is being shipped is primarily spare parts for weapons, for planes, military vehicles, and some small arms," commented a European military official, "but our intelligence on this is not as good as it should be."[53]

The U.N. sanctions also have had an interesting range of side effects and unintended consequences. The Libyan government's use of income from oil production to stock up on food, medical supplies, and other goods, for example, froze plans for developments in infrastructure and industry and further increased the arrears of payments to Western firms. From the 1970s onward Libya has sought to soften the U.S. government's attitude through various means, including enlisting well-connected Americans to press its case—including, in one memorable example, President Carter's brother Billy. This behavior intensified in the 1990s, and although the efforts did not succeed their revelation created a minor scandal.[54] Libyan road accidents have increased because of the increased traffic due to the aviation ban, while taxi and bus services do well ferrying people to the Tunisian and Egyptian borders for flights.

Last but not least, some observers feel the U.N. sanctions have allowed Qaddafi to divert blame for economic hardship in Libya onto foreigners and away from the regime's own mismanagement— although other observers believe the opposite, and the difficulty of assessing Libyan domestic political currents from the outside makes it impossible to know for certain which view is correct. Fierce domestic repression, meanwhile, has ensured that anti-Qaddafi coup attempts have been unsuccessful,[55] while the recent rise of an indigenous radical Islamic opposition has led some to ask whether Qaddafi himself might represent a lesser evil compared to the available alternatives.

Phase III: The Iran-Libya Sanctions Act of 1996

With Lockerbie now almost a decade in the past, most of the international community thinks the U.N. sanctions against Libya are too stringent and probably would ease them if given the chance. The opposite is true in the United States, where domestic political incentives have led politicians of all stripes to ever-increasing paroxysms of outrage against rogue states. The result has been a third phase of the Libyan sanctions, this time directed less against Libya itself than against its European business partners.

In February 1993 Senator Edward M. Kennedy (D-Mass.), who has Lockerbie victim family members among his constituents, introduced a bill calling for a tightening of sanctions. That summer Kennedy and

New York Senator Alfonse D'Amato, along with more than 50 colleagues, sent a letter to the president calling for stronger action against Libya, and later in the year the Senate urged the administration to seek a full international oil embargo.

With the Republican takeover of Congress in 1994, the campaign to step up pressure on rogue states increased, as D'Amato became an influential figure and Iran his chief target. By the end of 1995, thanks indirectly to the efforts of D'Amato and the American Israel Public Affairs Committee (AIPAC, the pro-Israel lobby in Washington), the Clinton administration had announced a unilateral commercial embargo on Iran, and Congress was mulling over D'Amato-sponsored legislation that would impose a secondary boycott on Iran's European trading partners. To D'Amato's surprise and discomfiture, when his bill was on the Senate floor, Senator Kennedy intervened to insert Libya as an additional target—as a gesture to the families of the Lockerbie victims on the seventh anniversary of the bombing. Kennedy refused to hold back even after being asked to do so by D'Amato, AIPAC, and the White House; once he acted, however, the others decided to go along rather than appear soft on terrorism.[56]

In an unrelated event during early 1996, a similar piece of legislation dealing with Cuba—the so-called Helms-Burton bill—passed Congress and was signed into law, thus setting a precedent for the enactment of extraterritorial sanctions by the United States against foreign business partners of regimes it dislikes. By the summer of 1996, therefore, the Clinton administration had little principled ground to stand on when opposing what had now become known as the Iran-Libya Sanctions Act (ILSA), even had it wanted to, and chose to focus instead on moderating its provisions. As Acting Assistant Secretary of State for Near East Affairs David Welch testified before Congress, the administration supported the D'Amato legislation subject to various modifications, which it believed would "permit us to succeed in imposing additional economic pressure on Iran and Libya without causing a boomerang effect that unnecessarily hurts other American interests."[57]

As signed on August 5, 1996—in the wake of the TWA Flight 100 explosion—the Libya-related sections of ILSA force the president to impose at least two out of six possible sanctions on any foreign company that invests more than $40 million in any year for the development of Libyan petroleum resources or on any company that violates the U.N. sanctions.[58] President Clinton invited family members of the Lockerbie victims to the signing ceremony and declared that the measure "will help to deny [Iran and Libya] the money they need to finance international terrorism. It will limit the flow of resources necessary to obtain weapons of mass destruction. It will heighten pressure on Libya to extradite the suspects in the bombing of Pan Am Flight 103."[59]

Even in its modified form, which gives the president some leeway to blunt its impact, ILSA has been strongly opposed by Europeans, who are motivated by pride (they resent being bullied), by economic interest (they see Iran and Libya as important commercial partners), and to a lesser extent by principle (they see secondary sanctions as unjustified restrictions on international trade). In November 1996 the European Union (EU) passed a blocking statute making it illegal for European companies to comply with extraterritorial measures like ILSA, and have vowed to challenge their legality through the World Trade Organization (WTO) if the United States does not back down.

Since Helms-Burton was passed first, it rather than ILSA has become the principal object of transatlantic legal skirmishing and negotiations. Deadlines for resolving the dispute passed unheeded during 1997, as the Europeans held off pressing their suit in apparent return for the Clinton administration's agreement to waive certain of Helms-Burton's more objectionable provisions. In the fall, however, the announcement of a $2 billion investment deal in Iran by French, Russian, and Malaysian companies seemed to flout ILSA directly and thus brought the extraterritoriality question to a head once again. The Clinton administration seemed caught in an impossible position, drawing fire from both a U.S. Congress demanding that penalties be levied and European allies vowing a trade war if they were; as of this writing the issue was still unresolved.[60]

Gauging the practical impact of this third phase of sanctions is difficult, because much depends on how the United States responds to its bluff being called. The ILSA provision that punishes those who violate the U.N. sanctions against Libya is uncontroversial but also trivial; the key Libya-related issues surround future development of Libyan oil and gas resources by European firms—whether there will be any and, if so, how the United States will react. The *Economist Intelligence Unit* noted that the law "will almost certainly hurt the medium- to long-term development of Libya's oil sector. In the short term, however, most international oil companies are waiting to see how the law is interpreted in practice."[61] Developments on the Iranian front will in all likelihood precipitate a resolution of the ILSA debate before major Libyan issues rise to the surface, but if not there is likely to be some controversy over whether a $3 billion deal with Agip to build a pipeline taking natural gas from Libya to Italy falls under the law's provisions. (The original contract for the deal was signed in 1993, but its execution will involve substantial Italian investment in Libya for many years into the future.)

Conclusion

To judge the wisdom of employing sanctions in any particular case, one must answer two separate questions: How effective particular sanctions are likely to be in the circumstances at hand and how they compare to other potential policy options. The sanctions against Libya fare poorly on the first count but well on the second.

Because of his proven hostility to the West, penchant for violence, and erratic behavior, Qaddafi has always represented a real but low-level threat to American and Western interests. U.S. policymakers might have responded to his radicalism in three basic ways: by appeasing him, by moving decisively to oust him, or by trying to punish and isolate him until his behavior changed. The first course—followed by some European countries—would have been easy to implement (although perhaps difficult to sell domestically). But since Qaddafi's terrorism and regional ambitions threatened American lives and interests, appeasement would have involved a significant moral hazard, and might have exacerbated the problem rather than ended it. The second course, in turn, was always problematic, and whatever promise it seemed to hold evaporated in the mid-1980s when it became clear that overthrowing Qaddafi might well require a full-scale foreign invasion— an alternative so obviously difficult, costly, and provocative that few if any favored it.

For more than a decade and a half, accordingly, U.S. policymakers have followed the third course, using limited sanctions to isolate and contain the Libyan threat.[62] Critics are correct to point out that the U.S. sanctions (Phase I) and the U.N. sanctions (Phase II) have not toppled Qaddafi, have not produced the Lockerbie suspects for trial, and have cost some American and other firms real economic opportunities. Yet the sanctions *have* helped keep Qaddafi on the margins of world politics and prevented him from causing too much trouble beyond his borders, without requiring the United States and its allies to spend vast amounts of blood, treasure, or effort. Because of their very limitations, moreover, the sanctions have proven sustainable. In the special circumstances of the Libyan case, therefore, limited sanctions have represented an acceptable middle course, one yielding modest benefits for a modest price. They have helped to *manage* a difficult foreign policy challenge if not to *master* it.

The years of sanctions have hobbled Libya's conventional military capability, grounded its air force, and crimped its weapons of mass destruction (WMD) programs.[63] All this has substantially reduced the threat Qaddafi poses to his neighbors and the world at large, at least compared to what would have been the case had he been allowed to carry on business as usual. The U.N. sanctions, moreover, have put a giant question mark over Libya's future: Long-term contracts and exploration remain in limbo, and over time sectors of the Libyan economy will begin to crumble, so the current situation probably cannot persist indefinitely. The tough stance taken by the United States on Libya over the years, furthermore, has contributed in important ways to the stigmatization of terrorism as an illegitimate activity and to the partial isolation of its state sponsors. These results justify the price paid for them.

The U.S. shift to extraterritorial sanctions against foreigners doing business in Libya, on the other hand—the hallmark of the Iran-Libya Sanctions Act—violates this prudent calculus by needlessly picking a potentially major fight with important allies. There was no new provocation by Libya during 1996,[64] nor any increase in the threat Libya poses to U.S. interests, nor any increased Libyan vulnerability that might merit such a move. However the transatlantic dispute over Helms-Burton and ILSA is resolved, the latter Act's Libyan-related sections are wrong-headed simply because they raise the priority and costs of Libya policy far above what is appropriate, given the full range of American global foreign policy interests.

A variety of other generalizable conclusions can be drawn from this case about sanctions as a tool of statecraft. First, the Libyan case confirms what one would expect about the ineffectiveness of *limited* sanctions in producing major changes of behavior by the target country. Whatever we think the consequences of a comprehensive, sustained multilateral embargo might have been,[65] we know that the limited sanctions actually employed have neither brought Qaddafi down nor dramatically changed Libya's foreign policy orientation.

Second, the Libyan case confirms the ineffectiveness of *slow, publicly signaled, and incremental* sanctions in producing behavioral change by the target country. Threats to impose or increase sanctions have had practically zero effect over the years—except to spur anticipatory, offsetting Libyan countermeasures—and the gradualness of the pressure on Libya has made it easier to bear, not more excruciating.[66] As for whether threats of secondary sanctions will be effective in halting European activity in Libya, as of this writing it is too soon to tell—although not too soon for them to have created controversy between the United States and Europe.

Third, the Libyan case suggests that no sanctioning country is likely to adopt truly painful economic measures except in extraordinary circumstances. The United States enacted its boycott of Libyan crude oil in

1982 only after changes in the international oil market made such a boycott relatively easy to bear, and it enacted its full economic embargo in 1986 only after carving out exceptions ensuring that the impact on American firms would not be too dramatic. The Europeans, for their part—particularly the Italians and the Germans—have never been willing even to consider jeopardizing their oil links to Libya, no matter what the provocation.

Fourth, the Libyan example provides interesting evidence that choosing a legalistic or criminal justice rationale for sanctions offers both advantages and disadvantages. The driving factor behind the U.N. sanctions was not any current or future perceived strategic threat from Libya, but rather a desire to exact punishment and legal redress for its role in the Lockerbie and UTA bombings. This led, in light of the special circumstances detailed earlier, to multilateral cooperation and international support in the campaign to isolate Libya on a scale that the Reagan administration could only dream of during the 1980s. It also has led, however, to an unhelpful distortion of American public debate about Libyan policy.

Because they focus so narrowly on the question of legal guilt for past actions and implacably demand such a specific response from Libya, the U.N. sanctions have essentially been severed from their foreign policy moorings and have taken on a life of their own. This conveniently removes the need for U.S. officials to persuade others that Libya is a continuing foreign policy threat deserving general isolation. But it inconveniently fosters unrealistic and imprudent demands at home for actions that may run counter to other American foreign policy interests. The extraterritorial sanctions characteristic of ILSA, in other words— which have no real strategic justification—stem in part from certain constituencies' taking the stated rationale behind the U.N. sanctions too seriously. These constituencies now see the task at hand as a crusade for justice rather than a search for the best way to keep Qaddafi contained at reasonable cost. From this one can learn that officials who accept a significant gap between the stated and unstated goals of their policy are playing with fire and should think carefully about how not to get burned.

Fifth and finally, the Libyan case suggests that decisions on sanctions, like other foreign policy issues, often are driven by inertia: It is easier to stay on course, whatever that course may be, than to change it. It was a big decision for the Reagan administration to institute a unilateral embargo against Libya in 1986, but now it would take a big decision (at least in terms of its domestic political consequences) for any subsequent administration to return to the pre-1986 status quo, at least as long as

Qaddafi remains in power. Like the Spartans fighting the Helots, there-fore, the United States solemnly redeclares the existence of a foreign pol-icy "emergency" regarding Libya every year. So too with the U.N. sanctions: Once set in place, relatively little effort is required to get them renewed three times a year, but it also has been difficult to muster votes in favor of modifying them. Backing down a ladder of escalation involv-ing sanctions seems particularly hard: As both Phase I and Phase II demonstrate, when sanctions "fail" calls emerge to increase rather than decrease the pressure. This pattern, unfortunately, is the chief factor bod-ing ill for the coming struggle over ILSA; it suggests that a country may end up paying more for bad choices than officials realize at the time.

Notes

1. Given Qaddafi's internal control and ideological intransigence, achieving either of these goals probably would take at least a sustained, comprehen-sive multilateral oil embargo, if not a full-scale military intervention. (See note 37 below.) Such an embargo would impose high costs on Libya's European customers, however, and so it has always been rejected.

2. Jeffrey P. Bialos and Kenneth I. Juster, "The Libyan Sanctions: A Rational Response to State-Sponsored Terrorism?" *Virginia Journal of International Law* 26, no. 4 (Summer 1986), pp. 802–3.

3. Michael Getler, "U.S. Officials Differ on Sanctions Against Libya," *Washington Post,* November 10, 1981, p. A8.

4. While widely believed at the time, these reports are now considered by U.S. intelligence officials to have been almost certainly greatly exagger-ated, and perhaps entirely inaccurate.

5. Bialos and Juster, *Libyan Sanctions,* pp. 803–4.

6. Bob Woodward, "CIA Anti-Qaddafi Plan Backed," *Washington Post,* November 3, 1985, p. A1. The assessment was prepared by NIO/NESA; a State/INR dissent argued that it "rests too heavily on fragmentary, unsub-stantiated reporting and fails to give sufficient weight to Qaddafi's endur-ing popularity. . . ."

7. Ibid. Apparently a similar plan had been blocked a year earlier by CIA Deputy Director John McMahon because it was unlikely to succeed. The operation proved unsuccessful, as had been the prior small-scale support for Libyan dissidents in exile.

8. Don Oberdorfer and David B. Ottaway, "President Imposes Boycott on Business with Libya," *Washington Post,* January 8, 1986, p. A1. U.S. firms were not permitted to perform any contract in support of an industrial, other commercial, or governmental project in Libya after February 1 and

were not allowed to avoid the ban by transferring the contracts to their foreign subsidiaries. The legal basis for the embargo, stemming chiefly from the 1977 International Emergency Economic Powers Act, was a determination that Libya's policies and actions "constitute[d] an unusual and extraordinary threat to the national security and foreign policy of the United States" and a declaration of a "national emergency" to deal with it. These sanctions have remained in effect ever since.

9. "U.S. Eases Libyan Oil Curb Rules," *New York Times*, February 8, 1986, pp. 1, 33. See also *EIU Libya Country Report* 2 (1986), pp. 14–15, 17.

10. The Libyans might have begun withdrawing some liquid assets from the United States as the freeze was in preparation. *EIU Quarterly Economic Review of Libya* 1 (1986), p. 9.

11. Bernard Gwertzman, "Why Reagan Shuns Attack," *New York Times*, January 8, 1986, p. A1. For a definitive discussion of the 1986 sanctions, see Bialos and Juster, *Libyan Sanctions*, pp. 807–39. For the factors behind the U.S. decision, see Bernard Weinraub, "Response to Terrorism: How President Decided," *New York Times*, January 12, 1986, p. 1; Russell Watson, "A Warning to Libya," *Newsweek*, January 13, 1986, p. 20; and James Wallace, "Ruling Out Force," *U.S. News and World Report*, January 20, 1986, p. 16.

12. Harry Anderson, "Get Tough: The Reagan Plan," *Newsweek*, January 20, 1986, p. 16.

13. Charles C. Cogan, "The Response of the Strong to the Weak: The American Raid on Libya, 1986," *Intelligence and National Security* 6, no. 3 (1991), pp. 608–20.

14. Barnaby J. Feder, "Libya Trade Was Low Before Ban," *New York Times*, January 8, 1986, p. A7, and Bernard Gwertzman, "U.S. Puts Pressure on Allies to Join Libyan Sanctions," *New York Times*, January 3, 1986, p. A1.

15. For various perspectives on this attack, see Brian L. Davis, *Qaddafi, Terrorism, and the Origins of the U.S. Attack on Libya* (New York: Praeger, 1990); Seymour Hersh, "Target Qaddafi," *New York Times Sunday Magazine*, February 22, 1987, p. 17; and Cogan, "The Response of the Strong to the Weak."

16. Specifically, the administration favored a crackdown on Libyan airlines, withdrawal of European assets from Libyan-controlled financial institutions, and withdrawal of European companies from Libyan operations. David B. Ottaway, "U.S. Drafts New Libya Sanctions," *Washington Post*, May 8, 1986, p. A1.

17. "Oil Companies in Libya Pressed," *New York Times*, June 10, 1986, p. A10; David B. Ottaway, "Reagan Lets 5 Oil Firms Resume Business in Libya," *Washington Post*, January 20, 1989, p. A33; and *EIU Libya Country Report* 4 (1988), pp. 11–12. In mid-June 1986 OFAC also moved to prohibit the export of petroleum or petrochemical industry equipment to Libya by way of third parties; see "U.S. Imposes New Sanctions on Libya," *Washington Post*, June

21, 1986, p. G1. During the fall of 1986, it emerged that the administration was continuing to pressure Libya covertly, through a disinformation campaign designed to unnerve Qaddafi and ratchet up tensions. One consequence of this revelation was the resignation of State Department spokesman Bernard Kalb. See Leslie H. Gelb, "Administration Is Accused of Deceiving Press on Libya," *New York Times,* October 3, 1986, p. A1.

18. Libyan imports from the United States in 1986 had dropped to $46.2 million, one-sixth the 1985 total, while Libyan exports to the United States had plunged from $47.1 million to $1.6 million. See Robert D. Hershey Jr., "U.S. Trade with Libya Continues," *New York Times,* December 9, 1986, p. D1; *EIU Libya Country Report* 1 (1987), pp. 10–11; and *EIU Libya Country Report* 2 (1987), p. 15.

19. *EIU Libya Country Report* 3 (1987), pp. 21–22. The Libyan trade of foreign subsidiaries of U.S. firms had also declined, meanwhile, falling by 73.6 percent between mid-1986 and mid-1987, from $1.006 billion to $265 million.

20. Elaine Sciolino, "U.S. Sees Qaddafi as Being Weaker," *New York Times,* January 10, 1988, section 1, p. 9. Figures regarding the funding of Libyan exile groups during this era remain classified, so the degree of the decline of this funding is uncertain. The earlier departure of Secretary of State Alexander Haig also may have facilitated the change of policy.

21. David B. Ottaway, "Reagan Lets 5 Oil Firms Resume Business in Libya," and *EIU Libya Country Report* 2 (1989), pp. 11–12. Under the sanctions and standstill agreements, the companies collectively were losing earnings of $100 to $120 million annually. The sanctions also prevented the sale of oil drilling equipment and spare parts to other companies in Libya, which market was taken over by British and European firms. *EIU Libya Country Report* 4 (1988), p. 11.

22. Over the next few years this situation continued to fester, with the future of the U.S. oil companies' Libyan holdings in perpetual limbo. The result has been that they have lost ground there to competitors: "European firms have benefited greatly from the absence of U.S. oil majors since 1987. . . . Italian and French firms have used their wide influence in the Libyan oil sector to position themselves for a greater role in Libyan development if restrictions are relaxed in the future." *EIU Libya Country Report* 4 (1995), p. 19. See Roger Vielvoye, "A Hard Line on Libya," *Oil & Gas Journal,* March 25, 1991, p. 33; "U.S. Company Return Prevented," *Petroleum Economist* (October 1991), p. 27; and *EIU Libya Country Report* 4 (1989), pp. 11–12; and 3 (1990), p. 14.

23. During the fall of 1989, Italian Foreign Minister Gianni De Michelis and lower-level French and Belgian representatives visited Libya, and in April 1990 France decided to normalize its relations following Qaddafi's help in securing the release of three French hostages held by the Abu Nidal group. Germany resumed diplomatic relations in the winter of 1988–89. In late 1990 Italy and France were prepared to partially lift the EC sanctions against Libya that embargoed modern technology for its oil and petrochemical industries, but the move was blocked by the United Kingdom. In

April 1991 French Foreign Minister Roland Dumas visited, followed in June by Italian Prime Minister Giulio Andreotti. One reason for continuing sanctions on high technology and military sales to Libya after mid-1990 was fear that such goods would make their way to Iraq.

24. Angus Hindley, "Qaddafi Aims for Respectability," *MEED Middle East Business Weekly,* June 28, 1991, p. 4.

25. Accurately parceling out responsibility for these attacks is extremely difficult, not only because of the scarcity of information about them but also because of the close contact and cooperation during the 1980s among the Iranian, Syrian, and Libyan intelligence agencies, together with various Palestinian groups. Many U.S. intelligence officials familiar with all the evidence, for example, feel that Lockerbie might have been the product of Iran's desire to strike back at the United States in retaliation for the downing of Iran Air 655. In this scenario the Iranians, with fairly limited ability to mount such an operation themselves, turned to the Libyans for help because of their extensive foreign operational network. Syrian operatives, furthermore, might have played some role in the attack without that country's leadership specifically authorizing it; some officials feel that Syria also might have had a role in the UTA 772 attack. For the status of French views on the UTA case, see Craig R. Whitney, "France Charges 6 Libyans with '89 Sahara Jet Bombing," *New York Times,* May 8, 1997, p. A5.

26. "Statement Announcing Joint Declarations on the Libyan Indictments," *Weekly Compilation of Presidential Documents* 27, no. 48, November 27, 1991, p. 1735.

27. Libya did not, however, attempt to liquidate its fixed European assets. As of June 1991, Libyan entities held more than $6 billion worth of government and private deposits in Western financial markets. See "Tripoli Starts Moving Deposits Out of Europe," *MEED Middle East Business Weekly,* December 13, 1991, p. 18.

28. Options considered included a ban on all international flights in and out of Libya and on all aviation-related goods and services; a ban on the sale of military equipment and dual use technology; stricter limits on diplomatic representation; a freeze on Libyan assets in foreign banks; and a ban on Libyan oil exports. Elaine Sciolino, "U.S. and Its Allies to Move on Libya over Air Bombings," *New York Times,* December 19, 1991, p. A1.

29. The resolution was cosponsored by the United States, the United Kingdom, and France, and it passed 10–0, with the abstainers including China and India. China's abstention required substantial arm-twisting and may have been procured by threats that a veto would jeopardize its MFN trading status with the United States. Angus Hindley, "Qaddafi's Battle for Survival," *MEED Middle East Business Weekly,* April 17, 1992, p. 4. In a final attempt to avoid or at least postpone the implementation of sanctions, Libya took the case to the International Court of Justice, arguing that it had the right to try the Lockerbie suspects under a previous international protocol (the Montreal Convention on terrorism), which had prior legal status

compared to the Security Council resolution. Rendering the quickest decision in its history, however, the court refused to intervene, and the sanctions came into effect as scheduled. See George Joffe, "The New Libyan Crisis," *Jane's Intelligence Review,* June 1, 1992, p. 261, and *EIU Libya Country Report* 3 (1992), p. 9. In the United States, Executive Order 12801 of April 15, 1992, established the U.S. section of the aviation ban, the only part of the sanctions new for the United States.

30. "Sanctions Are Biting, Libyan Official Says," *MEED Middle East Business Weekly,* May 8, 1992, p. 22. A month after the sanctions were introduced, the Libyans announced that they had cut their links with terrorist groups and banished all terrorist training camps from Libyan territory and had passed on to Britain some information about their prior dealings with the Irish Republican Army. These measures were dismissed by the United States and United Kingdom as insufficient, and the sanctions were not removed or lightened.

31. Angus Hindley, "The Lockerbie Conundrum," *MEED Middle East Business Weekly,* September 10, 1993, p. 2.

32. The resolution stipulated that special accounts were to be set up from the sale of Libyan hydrocarbons and agricultural products, which would then be used to pay firms doing business with Libya. "Council Widens Air, Arms Embargo," *U.N. Chronicle* (March 1994), p. 60, and Angus Hindley, "The Sanctions Time-Bomb," *MEED Middle East Business Weekly,* November 26, 1993, p. 6. A draft resolution strengthening the sanctions had circulated during the fall of 1993; voting on it was postponed, however, because of Russian fears that new measures would interfere with Libyan repayments of debts to Moscow. This difficulty was resolved by adding a clause stipulating that "Nothing in the resolution affects Libya's duty scrupulously to adhere to all its obligations concerning the servicing or repayment of foreign debt." Moscow estimates the debt in question at $4 billion; Libya, at $1.8 billion. See "Libya: The Draft Security Council Resolution," *MEED Middle East Business Weekly,* October 29, 1993, p. 27, and *EIU Libya Country Report* 1 (1994), p. 9.

33. Hindley, "The Sanctions Time Bomb." For a description of Libyan ingenuity in evading the restrictions, see Edward T. Pound, "Sanctions: The Pluses and Minuses," *U.S. News & World Report,* October 31, 1994, p. 58.

34. Angus Hindley, "Contractors Face Hard Times in Libya," *MEED Middle East Business Weekly,* January 28, 1994, p. 2. Of some importance for future relations with the United States, the former Libyan Foreign Minister Mansour Kikhiya was abducted from Egypt in mid-December 1993, not to be heard from afterward. Mrs. Kikhiya, an American citizen, would press the Clinton administration vigorously for action in his case from this point on, meeting often with senior officials. For the status of the case, see Jim Hoagland, "Egypt, Libya Linked to Abduction," *Washington Post,* September 28, 1997, p. A1.

35. Syria, Sudan, and Iran promised to defy the sanctions, but in the event did not. Certain leaders, such as Egypt's Hosni Mubarak, have tried repeatedly to find some resolution to the crisis, appealing to both the United States and Libya to soften their positions somewhat, and the Arab League also has tried to act as a go-between, but to no avail. The OAU and the Conference of Ministers for Foreign Affairs of the Islamic States have both urged the Security Council to reconsider the resolutions and lift the embargo, but their members have generally complied with most provisions. *EIU Libya Country Report* 3 (1992), pp. 8, and 4 (1992), p. 8.

36. Every year or two, however, Qaddafi thumbs his nose at the air ban by sending a Libyan plane somewhere, to (or over) Egypt, say, with pilgrims bound for the Haj. The planes are allowed to land, Qaddafi revels in his audacity, the United Nations issues a stern warning, and the Egyptians sheepishly apologize. For an example, see Douglas Jehl, "It's a Bird, It's a Plane, It's the U.N. Flouted," *New York Times*, June 23, 1996, p. A8. For recent developments in this area, see Douglas Jehl, "Arab Countries Vote to Defy U.N. Sanctions Against Libya," *New York Times*, September 22, 1997, p. A12.

37. The most reputable study of the subject suggests that a full-scale international oil embargo would force the Libyan economy to collapse within a year, because the country has neither an independent industrial base nor sufficient agricultural production to feed its population. See *EIU Libya Country Report* 2 (1995), p. 16.

38. George Lardner Jr., "Flight 103 Relatives Push for Sanctions," *Washington Post*, November 21, 1991, p. A36. The families specifically suggested a cut-off of air links with Libya, decertification of Libyan Arab Airline, freezing of Libyan overseas assets, and an oil embargo. Most families opposed military options.

39. During the 1992 campaign, Clinton promised the families that he would not relent until the two suspects were turned over; he reiterated his determination not to back down at the ground-breaking of a memorial for the Lockerbie victims in December 1993 and then again at the dedication of the monument in November 1995.

40. The study is summarized in the *EIU Libya Country Report* 2 (1995), p. 16.

41. Almost a third of the $19 billion, for example, supposedly has been lost because of forgone exports of Libyan fruits and vegetables—yet before the sanctions such exports were minuscule. "Libya Says Sanctions Cost $19 Billion," *Reuter European Business Report*, October 12, 1996.

42. Hindley, "Qaddafi's Battle for Survival."

43. "Embargo Remains Tight in Libya," *EIU Business Middle East*, March 16, 1995. Libyan wealth also had provided incentives for firms to find ways around earlier sanctions. As one observer wrote in early 1992: "Those Western companies which continue working in Libya keep a very low pro-

file, charging twice the world market rate for supplies and services. . . . Libya uses joint ventures with foreign oil companies to place orders for equipment and services on the market, often using a number of interme-diaries, each receiving his cut from the agreed price. Such is the money which can be made in Libya that the imposition of an embargo would appear to make the country a more attractive business project with high profits." *EIU Libya Country Report* 2 (1992), p. 15.

44. Hindley, "The Lockerbie Conundrum."

45. "Libya: Country Update," *EIU Views Wire,* July 12, 1995.

46. "Stalemate in Libya," *EIU Business Middle East,* December 1, 1994, and "Embargo Remains Tight in Libya," March 16, 1995. The Libyan infla-tion rate was 50 percent in 1994; 30 percent in 1995; and perhaps 35 to 40 percent annually in 1996–97. See "Libya: Country Update," *EIU ViewsWire,* November 30, 1995; "Libya Economy," *EIU ViewsWire,* July 30, 1996.

47. Edmund Blair, "Qaddafi Remains Defiant," *MEED Middle East Business Weekly,* September 16, 1994, p. 5.

48. "Libya: Life in Qadhafi's Shadow," *EIU Business Middle East,* October 1, 1994.

49. "Libya: Country Update," *EIU ViewsWire,* November 9, 1995.

50. Embargoed aircraft parts have been shipped repeatedly from Malta to Libya, and some other violations have come through Egypt, according to the State Department. Some U.S. officials feel that European governments are not enforcing the sanctions aggressively, by permitting banks and trading companies with some Libyan connections to continue to operate: "We would like [the allies] to enforce not just the letter but the spirit of the existing sanctions." Edward T. Pound, "Sanctions: The Pluses and Minuses," *U.S. News & World Report,* October 31, 1994, p. 58. See also Ray-mond Bonner, "Libya Is Said to Evade Sanctions by Buying U. S. Goods in Europe," *New York Times,* October 4, 1997, p. A1.

51. "Libya: Country Update," *EIU ViewsWire,* May 10, 1995. For further details on violations, see *EIU Libya Country Report* 4 (1993), p. 20; essentially, the arms embargo and the flight embargo have been followed generally, but some other goods are transshipped through Libya's neighbors, primarily by German, Swiss, and Maltese firms.

52. "Arms Bound for Libya Seized in Italian Raid," *New York Times,* Decem-ber 1, 1995, p. A4.

53. Chris Hedges, "Serbs Said to Ship Arms to Libya in Effort to Evade U.N. Sanctions," *New York Times,* November 7, 1996, p. A1. In December 1996 reports emerged of an alleged deal between Libya and Ukraine in which the latter would sell the former $500 million worth of SRBMs and help maintain Libya's four Soviet-made submarines.

54. Edward T. Pound, "Qadhafi's Big Adventure," *U.S. News & World Report,* December 20, 1993, p. 36. At one point Libya even hired Abraham Sofaer, the former State Department counsel who had written the legal justification for the 1986 U.S. air strike, to represent it. (Sofaer resigned shortly after accepting.) *EIU Libya Country Report* 4 (1993), pp. 8–9. The outcomes of two of the lobbying cases are detailed in Toni Locy, "21 Months for Lobbying for Libya," *Washington Post,* March 29, 1996, p. F3, and "Smuggler Sentenced to Halfway House," *Washington Post,* September 18, 1996, p. A6.

55. *EIU Libya Country Report* 2 (1992), pp. 5, 9, and "Libya: Qadhafi's Debt to Sanctions," *EIU Business Middle East,* March 16, 1994.

56. "D'Amato and AIPAC preferred to focus on Iran but could not afford to be seen to be somehow supporting. . . Qaddafi." Vahe Petrossian, "A Winning Alliance," *MEED Middle East Economic Digest,* August 19, 1996, p. 23. See also R. Jeffrey Smith, "White House Agrees to Bill Allowing Covert Operations Against Iran," *Washington Post,* December 22, 1995, p. A27.

57. David Welch's testimony before the House Ways and Means Committee, Subcommittee on Trade, May 22, 1996.

58. The six possible sanctions include a ban on U.S. Export-Import Bank assistance; a ban on U.S. export licenses to receive goods; a ban on eligibility for loans totaling more than $10 million a year from U.S. financial institutions; a denial of the right to be a primary dealer in U.S. government bonds; a denial of the right to bid on U.S. government contracts; and a denial of the right to export goods to the United States. For a clear discussion of ILSA and its legal context, see Bruno Cova, "Extra-Territorial Reach of the US Iran and Libya Sanctions Act of 1996," *Oil & Gas Law and Taxation Review* 14, no. 11 (November 1996), pp. 449–58; see also the chapter by Patrick Clawson in this volume.

59. "Remarks by President Bill Clinton at Signing Ceremony for the Iran and Libya Sanctions Act," *Federal News Service,* August 5, 1996.

60. For the status at time of writing of the debate over whether to impose ILSA sanctions, see "Officials Take Steps to Delay Iran Sanctions," *EIU ViewsWire,* December 15, 1997, citing the *Journal of Commerce.* For views about the efficacy of ILSA, see "Iran-Libya Sanctions Act," Hearing of the Senate Banking, Housing and Urban Affairs Committee, October 30, 1997, and "Effects of Sanctions on Iran and Libya," Hearing of the House International Relations Committee, July 23, 1997. For a summary of the Helms-Burton dispute, see "USA Trade: EU Stand-Off," *EIU ViewsWire,* October 20, 1997.

61. "Libya Industry," *EIU ViewsWire,* December 5, 1996.

62. The U.S. sanctions, Phase I, were limited because they cut off only bilateral trade; the U.N. sanctions, Phase II, were limited because they exempted oil and oil-related sales.

63. Robert Waller, "The Libyan Threat to the Mediterranean," *Jane's Intelligence Review,* May 1, 1996, and James Wyllie, "Libya—Regime Stress," *Jane's Intelligence Review,* December 1, 1995, pp. 554–55.

64. Except perhaps the continuation of the chemical weapons plant at Tarhuna, a separate issue that calls for its own discussion; see Robert Waller, "Libyan CW Raises the Issue of Preemption," *Jane's Intelligence Review,* November 1, 1996. For a general discussion of the threat posed by missile and WMD proliferation around the Mediterranean, see Ian O. Lesser and Ashley J. Tellis, *Strategic Exposure: Proliferation Around the Mediterreanean* (Washington, DC: RAND, 1996).

65. See note 37 above.

66. One of many examples that could be cited here comes from the tightening of the U.N. sanctions in late 1993: "The delay [between when the tougher sanctions were announced on August 15 and imposed on November 11]. . . gave the Libyan procurement companies. . . ample time to stockpile equipment listed to fall under the embargo by the resolution." As for the freeze on financial assets, there were none "to be frozen in British and French banks. Libya reportedly moved $6.5 billion to safe accounts in other countries, including Italy." To circumvent the tightening of sanctions on its downstream activities, Libya transferred majority control in its holding company, Oilinvest, and its subsidiaries to friendly European businessmen (chiefly Italians). *EIU Libya Country Report* 1 (1994), pp. 19, 23.

7

Pakistan

DENNIS KUX

THE STORY begins in January 1972, when Pakistan had just emerged, psychologically savaged, from the Bangladesh crisis and the loss of East Pakistan. Zulfikar Ali Bhutto had become president, replacing discredited military dictator Yahya Khan. In his 1969 book *The Myth of Independence*, Bhutto made no secret of his desire that Pakistan acquire nuclear weapons.[1] Once in power, he set out to realize this aim. At a gathering in Multan in 1972, Bhutto informed top scientists that Pakistan needed the bomb to ensure its security against India.[2] He felt certain that India, with its active nuclear program, would soon achieve a weapons capability. Two years later he was proven correct when India exploded an underground nuclear device.

The Indian test shattered the calm that followed the negotiation of the Nonproliferation Treaty (NPT) in 1968. The fact that a poor developing country could explode a device shocked NPT supporters, who then pressed for a tougher policy. A few months later, in October 1974, Pakistan signed a contract with France for a plutonium reprocessing plant that was supposed to produce fuel for a string of nuclear power plants. The contract raised eyebrows since the plans seemed far beyond Pakistan's financial reach and nuclear fuel needs. U.S. specialists suspected that Pakistan wanted the reprocessing plant as part of an independent nuclear fuel cycle "that would make the nuclear explosion option feasible."[3]

The Ford Administration Fails to Sway Bhutto

During this same period, German-Brazilian and French-Argentine nuclear proposals—as well as intelligence that South Korea and Taiwan were covertly pursuing a nuclear weapons option—set off alarm bells. Unless drastic action were taken, U.S. experts in and out of government feared the proliferation dam would collapse. Although at first slow to react to the Indian test, the administration of Gerald Ford moved toward a more rigorous nonproliferation policy. The United States employed its full diplomatic muscle in a bruising and largely success-ful effort to derail suspect projects; still, Washington failed to budge the Pakistanis or the French. After Bhutto spurned appeals by Secretary of State Henry Kissinger and President Ford,[4] Kissinger made a special trip to Pakistan in August 1976 to urge Bhutto to conclude a deal with the Republicans or face far harsher treatment should Jimmy Carter win the election. The secretary dangled significant carrots, offering to ease U.S. arms supply restrictions to provide 100 A-7 attack bombers, a capability that the Pakistan military badly wanted against India.[5]

Despite the "tilt" toward Pakistan during the 1971 Bangladesh crisis, U.S. influence was limited. After the cutoff of military and economic aid during the 1965 India-Pakistan war, neither Bhutto nor other senior Pakistani officials believed that their country could base its security against India on the Americans. From Pakistan, Kissinger traveled to France, where he got into a public row over the reprocessing plant. In so many words, France's prime minister, Gaullist Jacques Chirac, told the secretary of state to mind his own business.[6]

Unknown at the time in Washington, Pakistan was secretly embark-ing on a parallel and technically more difficult path toward a nuclear weapon. By chance, a well-qualified Pakistani metallurgist, Dr. Abdul Qadeer Khan, who worked for a Dutch company, gained detailed knowledge of the highly sensitive and complex ultracentrifuge ura-nium enrichment process. This technique offered an alternative route to reprocessing plutonium as a means of developing a nuclear device. At the end of 1975 Dr. Khan returned to Pakistan, where Bhutto put him in charge of a high-powered, covert effort to produce enriched uranium for nuclear weapons.[7]

Making use of plans that he brought back from Holland, Dr. Khan set about purchasing the necessary equipment from suppliers in Germany, Switzerland, France, Belgium, and Britain. At first, he made little effort to cover his tracks. Although the European countries and the United

States imposed tighter export controls after the Indian test, the Pakistanis evaded them by procuring individual components and parts of sensitive equipment rather than entire units.[8]

Carter Convinces the French and Sanctions Pakistan

After Jimmy Carter became president, Washington intensified efforts to block the French reprocessing plant. To provide the administration with greater leverage, Congress adopted amendments by Senators John Glenn (D-Ohio) and Stuart Symington (D-Mo.) to bar assistance to countries providing or receiving reprocessing (1976) or uranium enrichment plants (1977). Economic sanctions thus became a weapon in U.S. efforts to sway Pakistani policy.

There was, however, virtually no chance for success. When the Carter administration withdrew the A-7 offer and adopted a friendlier policy toward India, what little leverage America had with Pakistan was lost.[9] After winning February 1977 elections handily—too handily, in fact—Bhutto unexpectedly found himself in grave trouble. When the opposition took to the streets to protest vote-rigging, massive demonstrations shook his position. An increasingly cornered Bhutto shrilly charged that Washington was trying to undermine him because he would not give up Pakistan's nuclear option.[10]

During the night of July 4–5, 1977, the Pakistani military proclaimed martial law. The pro-democracy and pro–human rights Carter administration was even cooler toward military dictator Zia-ul-Haq than toward Bhutto. After State Department nuclear specialist Joseph Nye failed to convince Zia to drop the reprocessing plant, Washington imposed sanctions in September 1977 and suspended economic aid.[11]

The Carter administration had more success with French President Valéry Giscard d'Estaing, who agreed to revise the contract with Pakistan to eliminate the proliferation risk. The French unsuccessfully suggested a technically different approach called "coprocessing" that yielded fuel that could be used for nuclear reactors but not for bombs.[12] Finally, in June 1978, Giscard decided "to stop definitively" the contract with Pakistan.[13]

The State Department had hardly finished its celebration of the cancellation of the French contract and announced the resumption of economic aid to Pakistan when it learned about the parallel uranium enrichment track.[14] In July 1978 Western governments realized something was amiss after the British discovered that the Pakistanis were trying to purchase "inverters," a key element of the centrifuge process.[15] On April 6, 1979, the Carter administration once again suspended aid, this time pursuant to the Symington amendment against countries importing unsafeguarded enrichment technology.

When questioned about the nuclear program, the Pakistanis articulated what became their mantra. As then Foreign Affairs Adviser Agha Shahi told visiting Congressman Lester Wolff (D-N.Y.) in August 1979, Pakistan "has no intention to make a bomb" and has a peaceful program to gain knowledge of nuclear technology for power purposes.[16] Zia similarly responded to a *Newsweek* query, "Absolutely not. . . . It's pure fiction. We don't want to make a bomb. . . . Our oil bill has just gone over $1 billion a year. . . . By the end of this decade, we must have nuclear energy."[17]

U.S.-Pakistani relations reached their all-time low on November 21. Agitated by reports that the United States and Israel were responsible for an attack by gunmen on the Grand Mosque in Mecca, an angry mob set fire to the U. S. Embassy in Islamabad. Two Americans died and some 137 employees, caught inside, nearly suffocated before the mob dispersed.[18] When Pakistani authorities were slow to protect the beleaguered embassy, the Americans were furious, and an angry Jimmy Carter had "a very impassioned" telephone conversation with Zia.[19]

Pakistan Becomes a Front-Line State

Five weeks later, on December 29, 1979, Soviet troops invaded Afghanistan. The U.S. attitude toward Pakistan fundamentally changed. When Jimmy Carter telephoned Zia-ul-Haq this time, his tone and message were dramatically altered. The United States, the president stated, reaffirmed the 1959 bilateral security agreement to help Pakistan against a Communist attack.[20] Pakistan had become a "front-line" state. Although restraining the nuclear program remained a goal, it was subordinated to gaining Pakistan's cooperation against the Soviet occupation of Afghanistan. Carter and Congress signaled willingness to waive Glenn-Symington sanctions so that the United States could provide economic and military aid. National Security Adviser Zbigniew Brzezinski flew to Islamabad, where he unsuccessfully tried to woo the Pakistani dictator with $400 million worth of assistance.[21] "Peanuts" was Zia's undiplomatic response. According to Agha Shahi, the Pakistanis judged the U.S. offer insufficient to offset the risk of further antagonizing the Soviet bear.[22]

After Ronald Reagan became president, working out an assistance arrangement with Pakistan stood near the top of his foreign policy agenda. Ambassador to Pakistan Arthur Hummel and State and Defense Department colleagues quickly put together an aid program that Zia did not spurn as "peanuts"—a five-year, $3.2 billion package, half military and half economic assistance. The administration also sought a six-year waiver of Symington-Glenn sanctions.[23] In April 1981, after meetings in Washington, a smiling Foreign Minister Agha Shahi declared, "I believe we have moved forward in developing a Pakistan-U.S. relationship on a durable basis."[24]

In the talks, Shahi and General K. M. Arif, Zia's chief of staff, recalled Secretary of State Alexander Haig's saying that the nuclear issue would not become the centerpiece of U.S.-Pakistan relations. Haig, however, warned that if Pakistan exploded a device, the congressional reaction would make it difficult to cooperate in the way the Reagan administration hoped.[25] In effect, there seemed to be an unstated understanding that as long as Pakistan desisted from exploding a device, the United States could live with the nuclear program.[26] Senators John Glenn, Alan Cranston (D-Calif.) and others continued to press for a tougher stance, but the majority in Congress agreed with the administration, which won congressional approval for the arms package and the six-year waiver. Senior officials asserted that arms aid to Pakistan would, in fact, promote nonproliferation aims. Under Secretary of State James Buckley declared: "In place of the ineffective sanctions on Pakistan's nuclear program imposed by the past administration, we hope to address through conventional means (i.e., through conventional arms supply) the sources of insecurity that prompt a nation like Pakistan to seek a nuclear capability in the first place."[27]

This set the stage for an eight-year minuet during which top American officials regularly would raise the nuclear issue and senior Pakistanis regularly would deny they were building a bomb. In response to a personal warning from President Ronald Reagan when he met Zia in December 1982,[28] the Pakistani president offered "assurances . . . that Pakistan will not develop a nuclear explosive device."[29] Six months later, in May 1983, during Secretary of State George Shultz's visit to Islamabad, Zia volunteered that Pakistan has "neither the capability nor the intention of acquiring or developing a nuclear explosive device of any kind."[30] In May 1984, when Vice President George Bush traveled to Pakistan, Zia reiterated his assurances and said that Pakistan would not embarrass the United States.[31]

The trouble was that U.S. intelligence reports kept colliding with what Zia was telling his American interlocutors. Drawing on information leaked by disgruntled U.S. officials, Senator Alan Cranston alleged in June 1984 that Pakistan was charging ahead with a weapons program capable of producing "several nuclear weapons per year."[32] A month later in Houston, Texas, three Pakistanis were indicted for trying illegally to export items that could be used in a nuclear weapons program. The indictment came on the heels of the conviction in Canada of two other Pakistanis for illegally exporting U.S.-made nuclear-related equipment.[33]

Congress Adopts the Pressler Amendment

Worried about the progress of Pakistan's nuclear program, President Reagan sent Zia a September 12, 1984, letter that warned of "serious consequences" if Pakistan enriched uranium beyond 5 percent.[34] (This level of enrichment could produce nuclear reactor fuel but was insufficient for an explosive device.) In 1985, when the administration sought another long-term congressional waiver of Symington-Glenn sanctions and was gearing up for a second multiyear aid package, it ran into congressional trouble. As a substitute for a waiver, the White House had to settle for a new formula that permitted aid if the president certified annually that Pakistan did not possess a nuclear weapon. The provision seemed safe enough given Zia's assurances and, more important, what U.S. intelligence knew of the state of Pakistan's program. The White House got Senator Larry Pressler (R-S. Dak.), who had little prior involvement with the nuclear issue, to sponsor the amendment.

In November 1985 President Reagan met Zia during U.N. General Assembly meetings but apparently did not raise the nuclear issue. Zia discussed nuclear matters in a session with Robert (Bud) McFarlane, Reagan's national security adviser. Although McFarlane said that he could understand Pakistan's need for a nuclear deterrent, he told Zia that congressional pressures for sanctions were growing, hence the Pressler amendment. Whatever Pakistan did, McFarlane urged Zia that it not achieve a nuclear weapon or carry out a test.[35] Zia responded that Pakistan had a minimum nuclear program necessitated by its security environment. No leader of Pakistan could afford to shut that program down without compromising the country's security, but, Zia stressed, the program would not reach the stage where it would embarrass U.S.-Pakistan relations.[36]

In July 1986, when Pakistan's Prime Minister Mohammed Khan Junejo visited Washington, he declared that Pakistan's program was "purely for peaceful purposes" and "we have no intention of going for nuclear weapons."[37] Junejo publicly affirmed that Pakistan had pledged not to enrich uranium higher than 5 percent in response to Reagan's 1984 letter.[38] In October 1986 President Reagan certified under the Pressler amendment that Pakistan did not possess a nuclear explosive device. A few days later, however, leaked intelligence information indicated that Pakistan recently had tested a nuclear weapon–triggering device and that the Kahuta facility had enriched uranium to 93.5 percent—weapons grade. Anonymous U.S. officials told the press that the Pakistanis were moving ahead aggressively—one source spoke of their being only "two screwdriver turns" away from having a fully assembled weapon.[39]

A shrewd judge of how far he could push the Americans, Zia correctly calculated that occasional trouble over clandestine procurement from abroad—any link with the Pakistan government was denied routinely—and even enriching uranium to a weapons grade would not breach the "embarrassment" barrier. Underlying this assumption was his belief (shared by most in Washington) that the war in Afghanistan would continue for the foreseeable future, and, if trouble arose over the nuclear program, the Reagan administration would find a way to avoid imposing sanctions.[40]

On March 1, 1987, Dr. A. Q. Khan lifted the veil of secrecy about the program in an interview with Indian journalist Kuldip Nayir. Dr. Khan declared, "They told us Pakistan could never produce the bomb, and they doubted my capabilities, but they know we have done it."[41] Although Dr. Khan subsequently claimed he was misquoted,[42] the March 30 edition of *Time* magazine cited Zia as saying "You can write today that Pakistan can build a bomb whenever it wishes."[43] As tensions mounted sharply over India's threatening "Brasstacks" military maneuvers, the two statements seemed designed to warn New Delhi that Pakistan had a nuclear deterrent but to be sufficiently ambiguous to skirt the sanctions that Washington would have had to impose if the Pakistanis had flatly declared they had a nuclear weapon.

Meanwhile, Pakistani efforts to export sensitive equipment from abroad, including the United States, continued. In July 1987 Arshad Pervez, a Canadian citizen of Pakistani origin, was arrested in Philadelphia for trying illegally to export a special steel alloy used in nuclear casings.[44] When Under Secretary of State Michael Armacost visited Islamabad in August 1 of that year, the Pakistanis promised to cooperate in investigating the Pervez affair, which they termed a "rogue operation," but refused to permit inspection of Pakistan's nuclear facilities.[45]

Despite mounting evidence about Pakistan's nuclear progress, President Reagan issued the Pressler certification on December 17, 1987. His letter to House Speaker Jim Wright (D-Tex.) explained that the finding rested on the question of whether Pakistan "possesses a nuclear device," not whether it was trying to develop one.[46] On December 22,

1987, Congress approved further military and economic assistance as well as a waiver of Glenn-Symington sanctions. This was only for two and a half years, however, not the six years the administration initially sought.[47]

Soviets Withdraw from Afghanistan: Zia Dies in Crash

As 1988 began, Washington's attention increasingly focused on U.N. negotiations about Afghanistan. On April 15, 1988, Pakistan, Afghanistan, the United States, and the Soviet Union signed the milestone Geneva Accords, which provided a timetable for the departure of Soviet troops. Although the Communist regime retained power in Kabul until 1991, the departure of the Red Army (completed in February 1989) significantly altered the policy dynamic in Washington on the nuclear issue. As intelligence reports mounted that Pakistan—despite its assurances to the contrary—was developing a nuclear weapon, the pressure to look the other way diminished.

In August 1988 President Zia-ul-Haq died in a still-unexplained airplane crash. Although this created an opening for elections and the return of democracy to Pakistan, his sudden death removed from the scene a leader who had adroitly managed the nuclear issue with the Americans. Benazir Bhutto, the daughter of Zulfikar Ali Bhutto, whom Zia had deposed and hanged, became prime minister following her election victory. In lieu of one-man rule, an unsteady trio of Prime Minister Bhutto, President Ghulam Ishaq Khan, and Army Chief of Staff General Mirza Aslam Beg—popularly dubbed the troika—collectively governed Pakistan. The army chief and the president controlled the nuclear program.

In the fall of 1988 President Reagan certified again that Pakistan did not possess a nuclear weapon. He nonetheless signaled that the string might be running out in his letter to Speaker Jim Wright.[48] When General Beg visited Washington in early 1989, General Colin Powell, Reagan's outgoing national security adviser, and General Brent Scowcroft, Powell's successor under George Bush, both warned that if Pakistan advanced the nuclear program, it stood to lose U.S. military and economic assistance as well as any close political and security relationship with the United States. After Beg returned to Pakistan, U.S. intelligence gained the impression that parts of the program that troubled the United States, such as the high level of enrichment, were frozen.[49]

A highly successful visit by Prime Minister Benazir Bhutto to Washington in June 1989 further eased matters. Addressing a joint session of

Congress, she stated unequivocally, "I can declare that we do not possess, or do we intend to make, a nuclear device. That is our policy."[50] An articulate Harvard graduate and the first elected female leader of a Muslim country, Benazir Bhutto generated much goodwill for Pakistan while in the United States.

In the wake of her fresh assurances, intelligence that suggested the entire nuclear program was frozen, and desirous of bolstering Pakistan's fledgling democracy, Bush issued the 1989 Pressler certification. It was not, however, an easy decision,[51] and Ambassador Robert Oakley stressed to the troika in Islamabad that "If you take any action on the nuclear program and you go past that line . . . [H]e [Bush] will blow the whistle and invoke Pressler."[52]

While eloquent abroad, Benazir proved maladroit in her political dealings at home. After she fell out with Khan and Beg, they set about undermining her position. Domestic instability coincided with a war scare with India. As tensions rose in early 1990, U.S. intelligence concluded that the Pakistanis had taken the final step toward possession of a nuclear device, machining uranium metal into bomb cores and assembling one or more complete weapons.[53] Worried about the war threat, President Bush dispatched Robert Gates, his deputy national security adviser, to South Asia to urge Indian and Pakistani leaders to avoid any action that might trigger a conflict. In Islamabad, Gates also hit hard on the nuclear issue, warning Khan and Beg that the United States would impose Pressler sanctions unless Pakistan rolled the program back. Prime Minister Bhutto, off on one of her frequent foreign trips, went out of her way to avoid meeting Gates.[54]

Tensions between India and Pakistan eased, but the Pakistanis failed to heed Gates's warning regarding the nuclear program. Although Oakley emphasized to the troika that they were "committing suicide" as far as Pakistan's relations with the United States were concerned, the squabbling trio was unable to respond and did nothing, hoping that once again Washington would not invoke sanctions.[55] In August 1990 President Khan dismissed Benazir Bhutto and called for new elections in October. About the same time, President George Bush decided that he could not issue the Pressler certification. When Oakley returned from home leave on September 19, he informed the Pakistanis of this decision.[56]

Bush Imposes Pressler Sanctions

October 1, 1990, passed with no presidential certification, and Pressler amendment sanctions went into effect. U.S. economic and military aid to Pakistan, slated to be $564 million during fiscal year 1991, stopped.

At the time, Pakistan ranked third among aid recipients, after Israel and Egypt. When Foreign Minister Yaqub Khan met Secretary of State James Baker on October 9, the latter said that he could not recommend certification unless Pakistan destroyed existing cores and ceased to enrich uranium to weapons grade. Yaqub replied that Pakistan was willing to freeze the program but would not give up its existing capability.[57]

The reaction in Pakistan to Pressler sanctions was angry. The now-free press bitterly denounced the action as unfair, anti-Islamic, and discriminatory. There was particular bitterness that Washington was penalizing only Pakistan and not India, which actually had exploded a nuclear device. Pakistanis acidly commented, "Now that the Afghan War is over, the United States no longer needs Pakistan. You Americans have discarded us like a piece of used Kleenex."[58]

Although shocked, the Nawaz Sharif government, which won the October 1990 elections, reacted in a more subdued manner, hoping that the United States, still a partner against the Communist regime in Afghanistan, would find some way to resume assistance. When Nawaz Sharif sent senior diplomats to Washington in June 1991, they reiterated that Pakistan was willing to stop production of enriched uranium and weapon cores but would not agree to destroy the existing stock.[59] In November 1991 Under Secretary of State Reginald Bartholomew visited Islamabad. Both sides held to their previous positions. Sanctions continued.[60]

In January 1992 Sharyar Khan, Pakistan's foreign secretary, surprised the *Washington Post* by admitting that Pakistan had the components and the know-how to assemble at least one nuclear device. "The capability is there," the diplomat declared, dropping the claim that Pakistan neither possessed nor was developing a nuclear weapon. Sharyar Khan said he spoke candidly in order "to avoid credibility gaps" that past Pakistani statements had created.[61]

Clinton Tries a Different Tack

After Bill Clinton took office, his administration's first report on nonproliferation strategy in South Asia—a new congressional requirement—revealed a policy shift. Instead of seeking the immediate elimination of nuclear weapons, the revised objectives were "to cap, then reduce over time, and eventually to eliminate" nuclear weapons from the region. In effect, admitting that Pressler sanctions had been ineffective, the new administration sought to halt further nuclear weapons development rather than to abolish outright Pakistani (and Indian) capabilities.[62]

At the same time, fresh trouble arose over intelligence reports that China was supplying nuclear-capable M-11 missiles to Pakistan in violation of the Missile Technology Control Regime (MTCR), international ground rules to prevent the spread of missile technology. In accordance with U.S. law, the United States imposed sanctions affecting up to $1 billion worth of Chinese exports, but with negligible impact on Pakistan.[63] In October 1994, after the Chinese agreed to abide by the MTCR, Washington lifted the sanctions. In dealing with the sensitive M-11 missile issue, Washington once more subordinated nonproliferation concerns to a higher priority—in this case, U.S.-China relations. Meanwhile, the wheel of political fortune turned again in Pakistan. After Nawaz Sharif got into a messy struggle with President G. I. Khan, both resigned under pressure from the army. Pakistan voted in October 1993, the third time in five years. The winner was Benazir Bhutto.

Worried that South Asia represented the globe's highest risk of nuclear conflict, the Clinton administration launched a new initiative in early 1994. As a first step, the administration offered to release F-16 aircraft, which Pakistan had purchased but had not taken delivery of at the time Pressler sanctions were imposed. In return, Washington wanted Islamabad to cap its nuclear program and to permit "non-intrusive" inspection of nuclear facilities.[64] When Deputy Secretary of State Strobe Talbott traveled to Islamabad in April 1994, Bhutto turned him down. "If we are unilaterally pressed for the capping," she stated, "it will be discriminatory, and Pakistan will not agree . . . "[65] Since India already had refused to allow inspection of its nuclear facilities, the proposal died.

A year later, in 1995, when Bhutto visited Washington, she convinced President Clinton that Pakistan should either get the F-16s or its money back. "I don't think it's right for us to keep the money and the equipment," the president declared after meeting the prime minister.[66] In addition to trying to sell the F-16s to a third country and reimburse the Pakistanis with the proceeds, the administration joined forces with Senator Hank Brown (R-Colo.) to seek congressional approval to ease some Pressler restrictions to permit delivery of $368 million worth of Pakistan-owned military equipment and the resumption of economic aid, investment guarantees, and military training. New military assistance would, however, continue to be barred, and Pakistan would not receive the F-16s.

After heated debate that galvanized Indian American and Pakistani American ethnic lobbies, the Senate adopted the Brown amendment by a 55 to 45 vote. For tactical reasons, the administration did not seek a softening of Symington amendment sanctions, assuming this could be taken care of later. However, U.S. intelligence reports of Chinese exports to Pakistan of ring magnets, a component used in the enrichment process, retriggered Symington sanctions that barred investment guarantees, military training, and economic assistance. The question of fresh aid was, in any case, moot since the cash-strapped Agency for International Development (AID) had no plans to renew bilateral assistance. Because of U.S. campaign finance scandals, the proposed sale of F-16s to Indonesia also fell through. Congress eventually modified the Symington amendment to permit investment guarantees but refused to remove the bar to military training. As 1998 began, the only tangible benefit Pakistan received was the delivery of $368 million worth of military equipment, which it had paid for already, and the renewal of investment guarantees.

Despite its largely symbolic significance, the Brown amendment was still an important development, signaling the Clinton administration's desire to put relations with Pakistan on a friendlier footing. Officials in Islamabad took considerable satisfaction, perceiving developments as a vindication of Pakistan's complaints about the unfairness of Pressler sanctions. Nonofficial circles and the media in Pakistan were less impressed and saw the main benefit in that India had been bested in a congressional vote.

Consequences of Sanctions

The imposition of Pressler amendment sanctions in 1990 marked a major milestone in South Asia policy. As Generals Powell and Scowcroft warned, the action cost Pakistan U.S. economic and military aid and ruptured the security partnership that had flourished during the 1980s. After the end of the Cold War, security links with Pakistan would, in any case, have diminished, but almost certainly not in such an abrupt and sweeping fashion. Despite Pakistan's reduced strategic importance, U.S. aid programs, both economic and military, probably would have continued even if at lower budget levels.

Although public opinion in Pakistan has remained critical of the United States during the 1990s, the leadership, including both Bhutto and Nawaz Sharif, continued to seek friendly relations with Washington. Bilateral relations suffered less than might have been expected given the severity of the sanctions. Pakistan has not modified its foreign and security policies substantially. In view of Pakistan's shaky political scene and dire economic straits, neither Bhutto nor Nawaz Sharif has seen it in their country's interest to stir additional trouble with the sole remaining superpower. For example, despite domestic criticism, both prime ministers have cooperated with U.S. law enforcement agencies in extraditing Pakistani nationals charged with terrorist crimes.

The Pressler amendment also has had an important if unintended impact on U.S. relations with India. The sanctions have removed the source of New Delhi's most serious and longest-standing policy complaint against Washington—India's concern about U.S. arms aid to Pakistan. Despite the ruckus New Delhi made over the Brown amendment in 1995, the heart of Pressler sanctions remains in place and continues to bar American military assistance to Pakistan.

In terms of effectiveness, however, sanctions against Pakistan clearly have failed to achieve their principal goal—preventing the development of a nuclear weapons capability. Conceivably in the mid-1970s, the threat of sanctions combined with sufficient carrots might have worked. The nuclear program was just beginning and its prospects were uncertain. Yet given Pakistan's obsessive fear of India, the chances for success were never great unless Washington offered Islamabad an iron-clad security guarantee against India—something no American administration ever has been willing to do.

Again, in 1989–90, the deal that the Bush administration offered—freezing the nuclear program in return for continued U.S. aid—might have worked. For Pakistan, this would have been a good bargain, allowing Islamabad to keep both its nuclear capability and the security relationship with the United States. It is likely, however, that at some point the reality of the program would have triggered sanctions, especially if, as Pakistanis assert, they already "possessed" a weapons capability by 1989.

Have sanctions, nonetheless, provided some policy gains? U.S. willingness to damage relations with Pakistan has demonstrated to others that Washington is serious about nonproliferation—at least when some higher-priority interest, such as the war in Afghanistan, was not at risk. Although one can argue that sanctions deterred Pakistan from fielding an overt weapons capability, the fact that India had not done so until 1998 probably was more important. As long as India kept its capability undeclared, Pakistan could satisfy its deterrent requirement by nuclear ambiguity.

The threat of sanctions doubtless has helped keep Pakistan from actually testing a nuclear device. Technical computer modeling advances as well as help from China also have been factors. Now that India has again tested, it is possible that Pakistan will follow suit regardless of new U.S. penalties.

Pressler sanctions probably have had little direct impact on the Pakistan nuclear program. Having achieved its goal of developing a deterrent against India, Pakistan has had neither the desire nor the capability to engage in a genuine and expensive nuclear arms race. The more important military impact of sanctions has been to weaken Pakistan's conventional defense posture. The Pakistan Air Force, in particular, has been hit by U.S. refusal to deliver previously purchased F-16s and by problems in obtaining spare parts for its existing inventory.

The loss of economic aid also has hurt. Even though the growth of multilateral aid and the expansion of the Pakistan economy over the years cushioned the damage, the absence of U.S. AID funding and presence has had a negative psychological impact at a time when Pakistan faced grave economic difficulties. American companies have doubtless lost sales in Pakistan in the absence of U.S. military and economic aid procurement. Balancing off this loss has been the gain for the U.S. Treasury and the taxpayer in not having to pay for the aid.

Would alternative approaches have proven more effective? In retrospect, the United States would have been wiser to have targeted sanctions against Pakistan's defense sector, to have barred arms transfers and military cooperation. Having the "punishment" fit the "crime" would have made the policy point as emphatically while mitigating the damage to Pakistan's economic development, a long-term U.S. interest worth supporting despite Pakistan's nuclear weapons program.

Economic sanctions—quite apart from their advisability—would have been effective only if others had joined in cutting off assistance. Although Pakistan could get by without U.S. aid, its economy would have been badly hit had the European Community and Japan followed suit. Economic sanctions would have been crippling if the United States and others also had been willing to block World Bank multilateral economic aid. As there was scant chance that U.S. allies would join in imposing tough sanctions against Pakistan, Washington did not try to get them to agree and acted unilaterally.

Even if others did not follow the American lead in restricting assistance, they cooperated in barring sales of nuclear-related equipment to Pakistan as a country that did not accept the NPT or full-scope safeguards on its nuclear facilities. Focusing on stricter enforcement of export controls and imposition of penalties for illegal exports offered a plausible alternative approach to cutting off aid. Probably it would have had as much impact on the Pakistan nuclear program and done far less damage to bilateral relations. For example, the United States and others have employed the export control route with considerable success since 1974 to inhibit India's nuclear program.

Lessons Learned from the Pakistan Case

Several more general conclusions can be drawn from the Pakistan case. First, it illustrates the dramatic rise in the use of legislated sanctions since the Watergate-Vietnam years and the related reduction in executive branch flexibility in conducting foreign policy. In addition to nuclear and missile sanctions discussed in this study, Pakistan barely escaped the imposition of antiterrorist sanctions in 1992–93 over its covert help to the Kashmir uprising, and in 1996 and 1997 it required a presidential waiver to avoid sanctions for lack of cooperation in combatting drug trafficking.

In the 1960s and early 1970s Presidents Lyndon Johnson and Richard Nixon barred military and economic aid to Pakistan by executive action on several occasions. They nonetheless retained the authority to lift sanctions when they judged it in U.S. interest to do so. The chief executive does not have the freedom to lift legislated sanctions automatically and becomes the prisoner of the law's waiver authority, one that is broad in dealing with drugs but restrictive in nuclear and terrorist sanctions.

Second, the Pakistan experience strengthens the view that legislated sanctions are a blunt and inflexible national security instrument. Although their threat strongly underscored U.S. concern about proliferation, once imposed, the sanctions put Washington in a straitjacket. The difficulty that the Clinton administration had in winning a modest relaxation of Pressler restrictions through the Brown amendment illustrates how hard it can be to remove restrictions once they have become law.

Third, the Pakistan example shows how the process of deciding whether legislated sanctions should be imposed can transform a national security question into a quasi–law enforcement problem. In the mid-1980s the Pakistan nuclear issue became an internal U.S. battle between conflicting policy views while the Pakistanis were almost outside onlookers. And what made the whole business more bizarre was the reliance on highly classified clandestine intelligence as "proof" of whether Pakistan was in compliance with U.S. law.

The intelligence community focused on the narrow and subjective technical question of whether Pakistan was violating U.S. legislated standards. Acting more like police officers than intelligence analysts, they looked for the "gotcha" report. Fearing policymakers would ignore bad news, analysts leaked classified information to Congress and the media. For their part, policy-level officials and their congressional allies felt constrained to focus on managing the sanctions problem, at times shading or misrepresenting information received from intelligence sources. This was surely a messy and flawed way to deal with an important foreign policy issue.

Finally, the Pakistan experience points up how hard it is to achieve a fundamental change in the national security policy of another country unless, as in the case of Korea and Taiwan, that country is dependent on the United States for its survival—or thinks it is. This was not the case with Pakistan. Quite the contrary, Islamabad believed that the United States had "betrayed" Pakistan during the 1965 Kashmir War not only by refusing to come to its support but, even worse, by embargoing military and economic assistance. Ever since Bhutto launched the program in 1972, Pakistanis have been convinced that they need a nuclear capability to offset the superior strength of India. As Akram Zaki, the current chairman of the Foreign Relations Committee of the Pakistan Senate, put it: "Better the balance of terror than the terror of imbalance."[67]

Notes

1. Zulfikar Ali Bhutto, *The Myth of Independence* (London: Oxford University Press, 1969), p. 153.

2. Steve Weissman and Herbert Korsney, *The Islamic Bomb* (New York: Times Book, 1981), pp. 43–48.

3. State Department briefing memorandum for Secretary of State Henry Kissinger's February 5, 1975, meeting with Prime Minister Bhutto, undated.

4. State Department telegram to the U.S. Mission to the International Atomic Energy Agency in Vienna, April 9, 1976.

5. Weissman and Korsney, *Islamic Bomb*, p. 163.

6. Ibid.

7. Ibid., p. 175.

8. Ibid., pp. 181–87.

9. Shirin Tahir-Kheli, *The United States and Pakistan: The Evolution of an Influence Relationship* (New York: Praeger, 1982), p. 73.

10. "Bhutto Says Americans Aid Critics," *New York Times*, April 29, 1977, p. A12; James M. Markham, "Bhutto Arrests More Opposition and Imposes Curfew on 3 Cities," *New York Times*, May 6, 1977, p. A8; and Lewis Simons, "Bhutto Alleges U.S. Plot," *Washington Post*, April 29, 1977, p. A1.

11. Weissman and Korsney, *Islamic Bomb*, p. 168.

12. Ibid., pp. 168–69.

13. Ibid., p. 171.

14. Interview with former Deputy Assistant Secretary of State for South Asia Jane Coon, September 15, 1995.

15. Weissman and Korsney, *Islamic Bomb*, p. 172.

16. Embassy Islamabad telegram to the State Department, August 17, 1979.

17. Zia-ul-Haq interview with Arnaud de Borchgrave, *Newsweek*, January 14, 1980, p. 32.

18. Interview with Ambassador Arthur Hummel, June 15, 1995; See also Herbert Hagerty's "Attack on the U.S. Embassy in Pakistan," Joseph P. Sullivan (ed.), *Embassies Under Siege* (Washington: Brassey's, 1995), pp. 71–88.

19. Interview with Thomas P. Thornton, September 21, 1995. As an NSC staffer, Thornton monitored the phone calls between Carter and Zia.

20. Ibid.

21. Interviews with Jane Coon, December 5, 1990, and Thomas Thornton, December 10, 1990. Both were on the Pakistan trip.

22. Interview with former Foreign Minister Agha Shahi, December 31, 1995.

23. State Department talking points on the Pakistan nuclear issue, undated but presumably early 1981.

24. "Pakistan Reports U.S. Has Offered Five Year Aid Deal," *New York Times,* April 22, 1981, p. A1.

25. Interviews with General K. M. Arif, December 10, 1995, and Foreign Minister Shahi, December 31, 1995, and January 29, 1996.

26. Interviews with Jane Coon, September 15, 1995, and Howard Schaffer, October 27, 1995. Schaffer succeeded Coon as Deputy Assistant Secretary for South Asia in 1982.

27. Letter to the Editor of the *New York Times* from Under Secretary of State James Buckley, July 25, 1981. The letter appeared in the August 5, 1981, *New York Times.*

28. Cited in the State Department briefing paper for Vice President Bush's May 1984 visit to Pakistan.

29. Cited in State Department June 13, 1983, briefing memorandum for Secretary George Shultz's meeting with Zia.

30. Cited in undated State Department talking points for briefing Congress on the 1983 South Asia trip of Secretary Shultz.

31. Interview with General K. M. Arif, December 10, 1995.

32. "Cranston Says Pakistan Can Make A-Bomb," *New York Times,* June 21, 1984, p. A14, and Paul Houston, "Cranston Says Pakistan Has Nuclear Capability," *Washington Post,* June 21, 1984, p. A17.

33. Rick Atkinson, "Nuclear Parts Sought by Pakistanis," *Washington Post*, July 21, 1984, pp. A1, 12.

34. Gerald F. Seib, "Israel and 4 Other Nations Seen Most Likely to Start Testing Nuclear Arms," *Wall Street Journal*, October 25, 1984, p. 36; "Reagan Warned Pakistanis on Nuclear Project," *Washington Post*, October 26, 1984, p. A18.

35. Interview with Robert McFarlane, October 22, 1996.

36. Interview with Lt. General Ejaz Azim, November 30, 1995. Azim, Pakistan's ambassador in Washington in 1985, was briefed by Zia on the conversation. McFarlane told the author the account seemed "fair."

37. Embassy of Pakistan, "Pakistan Today: The Nuclear Program," advertisement supplement, pp. 4–5, *Washington Post*, July, 16, 1986; Don Oberdorfer, "Nuclear Issue Clouds Visit by Junejo," *Washington Post*, July 17, 1986, p. A21.

38. Don Oberdorfer, "Pakistan Spurns Soviets' Afghan Pullout Plan," *Washington Post*, July 18, 1986, p. A26.

39. Bob Woodward, "Pakistan Reported Near Atom Arms Production," *Washington Post*, November 4, 1986, pp. A1, 16.

40. Interviews with Sahibzada Yaqub Khan, January 12, 1996; General K. M. Arif, December 10, 1995; and Lt. Gen. Refaqat, April 17, 1996. (Refaqat succeeded Arif as Zia's chief aide in 1985.)

41. Quoted in Kuldip Nayar, "We Have the A-Bomb, Says Pakistan's Dr. Strangelove," *Observer* (London), March 1, 1987; Stephen Weisman, "Report of Pakistani A-Bomb Causes a Stir in the Region,"*New York Times*, March 2, 1987, p. A3.

42. Simon Henderson, "Row Possible over Pakistan Bomb Claim," *Financial Times*, March 2, 1987, p. 2.

43. Zia-ul-Haq interview with Ross Munro, *Time*, March 30, 1987, p. 42.

44. Michael Gordon, "Pakistani Seized in U.S. on Plot on A-Arms Alloy," *New York Times*, July 15, 1987, p. A1; Don Oberdorfer, "Three Indicted in Export of Electronics to Pakistan," *Washington Post*, July 18, 1987, p. A18.

45. Elaine Sciolino, "U.S. to Seek Pakistani Aid in Atom Case," *New York Times*, August 2, 1987, Sec. 1, p. 3; Michael Gordon, "Pakistan Rejects Atomic Inspection," *New York Times*, August 6, 1987, p. A5.

46. Letter from President Reagan to House Speaker Jim Wright, December 17, 1987. Earlier in 1987, the State Department's legal adviser found that a country could "possess" a nuclear device even if it had not assembled all the elements.

47. Neil Lewis, "Wide Range of Bills Would Affect Foreign Policy," *New York Times*, December 23, 1987, p. B9.

48. David Ottaway, "Pakistan May Lose U.S. Aid," *Washington Post*, January 28, 1989, p. A1.

49. Interview with Ambassador Oakley, June 14, 1995.

50. David Ottaway, "Addressing Congress, Bhutto Formally Renounces Nuclear Arms," *Washington Post*, June 8, 1989, p. A14.

51. Interview with Ambassador Teresita Schaffer, February 6, 1997. Mrs. Schaffer served as deputy assistant secretary for South Asia, 1989–92.

52. Interview with Ambassador Oakley, June 15, 1995.

53. Mitchell Reiss, *Bridled Ambition* (Washington, DC: Wilson Center Press, 1995), p. 188; interview with Ambassador Oakley, June 15, 1995. Pakistanis told the author a nuclear explosive capability was achieved before 1990, when U.S. intelligence reached a firm judgment that they had done so.

54. Seymour M. Hersh, "On the Nuclear Edge," *New Yorker* 69, no. 6, (March 29, 1993), pp. 66–68.

55. Interview with Ambassador Oakley, June 15, 1995.

56. Ibid.

57. Interview with former foreign minister Yaqub Khan, December 30, 1995.

58. The author often heard this view during a November 1995–April 1996 stay in Islamabad.

59. Steve Coll, "Pakistan Seeks Talks on Nuclear Weapons," *Washington Post*, June 7, 1991, p. A30; David Hoffman, "Pakistani Says Arms Plan Well Received," *Washington Post*, June 14, 1991, p. A23.

60. Maleeha Lodhi, "Effort to Halt Slide in Ties" (text of article in *The Nation* [Islamabad] November 25, 1991), *The External Dimension* (Lahore: Jang, 1994), pp. 93–97.

61. R. Jeffrey Smith, "Pakistan Official Affirms Capacity for Nuclear Device," *Washington Post*, February 7, 1992, p. A18.

62. Reiss, *Bridled Ambition*, p. 262.

63. John Goshko and William Branigan, "U.S. Warns China of Sanctions for Missile Exports to Pakistan," *Washington Post*, July 26, 1993, p. A10; Lally Weymouth, "Chinese Take-Out," *Washington Post*, August 12, 1993, p. A27; and Daniel Williams, "U.S. Punishes China over Missile Sales," *Washington Post*, August 26, 1993, pp. A1, 20; Steven Holmes, "U.S. Determines China Violated Pact on Missiles," *New York Times*, August 25, 1993, p. A1; Steven Greenhouse, "$1 Billion in Sales of Hi-Tech Items to China Blocked," *New York Times*, August 26, 1993, p. A1; and Steven Holmes, "High-Tech Exports Cut Off," *New York Times*, August 29, 1993, Sec. 4, p. 2. In October 1994, after the Chinese agreed to abide by the MTCR, Washington lifted the sanctions.

64. Erick Schmitt, "Lifting Aid Ban Is Proposed to Control Pakistan's Arms," *New York Times*, March 13, 1994, Sec. 1, p. 1; "Disarming the Sub-Continent," *New York Times*, March 29, 1994, p. A22; and R. Jeffrey Smith, "U.S. Proposes Sale of F-16s to Pakistan," *Washington Post*, March 23, 1994, p. A27.

65. John Ward Anderson, "Pakistan Rebuffs U.S. on A-Bomb," *Washington Post*, April 8, 1994, p. A30.

66. Todd S. Purdum, "Clinton Is Seeking to Pay Pakistanis for Blocked Arms," *New York Times*, April 12, 1995, p. A1.

67. Interview with Ambassador Akram Zaki, March 10, 1996.

8

The Former Yugoslavia

STEPHEN JOHN STEDMAN

ECONOMIC AND military sanctions were key instruments of American foreign policy toward the former Yugoslavia from 1991 through 1998. The purpose of the sanctions varied over time. Before war even came to Yugoslavia in 1991, Congress voted to threaten the country with sanctions in protest of Serbian persecution of ethnic Albanians in the province of Kosovo. In 1991, during the crises of Slovenian and Croatian secession, the United States, in conjunction with its European allies and the United Nations, applied sanctions and an arms embargo in the hope of preventing deadly conflict. When such measures failed and war spread to Bosnia in 1992, the United States labeled Serbia the aggressor and pushed for more intense sanctions as a means of weakening Serbian President Slobodan Milosevic in the hopes of removing him from power. At the same time mediators to the conflict promised to remove sanctions as an incentive to persuade him to terminate the war. In 1994 sanctions were extended to punish the Bosnian Serbs for their unwillingness to make peace. As late as March 1998 American policymakers threatened renewed economic penalties in order to push Milosevic to refrain from using force in Kosovo.

Little scholarly consensus exists concerning the effects or efficacy of the economic and military sanctions applied against the former Yugoslavia. The range of opinion is great. Some analysts suggest that while economic sanctions were ineffective as tools of conflict prevention, they forced Milosevic to negotiate an end to the war and therefore were successful.[1] Other experts argue that not only were the sanctions ineffective but that on almost every conceivable dimension they had unanticipated consequences directly opposite to those intended by the sanctioners.[2] Different scholars describe the effects of sanctions as weak or devastating; indeed, one can find different evaluations by the same author, sometimes within the space of several pages.[3] Two generalizations seem clear, however. First, one's evaluation of sanctions against the former Yugoslavia varies by publication date—before the Dayton peace accords one finds preponderantly negative assessments; after Dayton, preponderantly positive ones.[4] Second, area experts were much harsher in their evaluation of sanctions than policy generalists— a difference that reflects conflicting evaluations of the causes of the war and what was needed to stop it.

Further complicating analysis is the reality that sanctions were never applied in a coherent, strategic manner in the Balkans. Policymakers framed the decision to apply sanctions in contradictory logics. For some, sanctions were meant to punish Milosevic and to lead to his overthrow. For others, sanctions were a bargaining chip to persuade Milosevic to alter his policies and to support a negotiated settlement to the war in Bosnia. The former rationale was at odds with the latter; whereas the former policy was a punitive one aimed at destroying the leader seen as the war's primary instigator, the latter policy was a redemptive one aimed at persuading him to change his actions. Beyond the obvious contradictions at the core of policy, both rationales overestimated the ability of sanctions to produce desired effects. Sanctions never seriously threatened Milosevic's leadership in Serbia. On the other hand, they were inadequate as a tool to prevent the wars in the Balkans, and their contribution to bringing the war to a negotiated end was overrated. Although the sanctions succeeded in dissuading Milosevic from continuing his support for the Bosnian Serbs, they had little impact on Bosnian Serb willingness to sign a peace agreement. In the end game, sanctions were secondary to dramatic shifts in the battlefield balance of power and North Atlantic Treaty Organization (NATO) air strikes in persuading the Bosnian Serb leadership to end the war.

Historical Background

The Yugoslav crisis of 1991 resulted from three causes: a decade-long economic depression that differentially affected regions and ethnic groups; political institutions that failed to adapt to economic, societal, and international changes; and nationalist leaders who unscrupulously pursued policies of ethnic extremism for their own power and gain. A peaceful resolution of the crisis would have required heroic leadership from within the country and an attentive, coherent, and consistent approach from outside. Neither was forthcoming. Political leaders in

Serbia, Croatia, and Bosnia manipulated ethnic fears and hatred and fomented ethnic violence in order to consolidate their positions. International actors paid little attention to Yugoslavia and failed to reach consensus about the causes of the conflict, the issues at stake, possible solutions, and appropriate strategies to resolve the conflict.

After the death of Yugoslavian President Josip Broz Tito in 1980, his successors faced three major interrelated problems. First, Yugoslavia's economy required an overhaul; economic liberalization was needed to promote new sources of economic growth. Second, Yugoslavia's federal constitutional structure had to cope with new demands for greater regional autonomy. Third, any attempt to meet such demands had to do so in a way that ethnic nationalism would not become the guiding force in Yugoslav politics. With the exception of the republic of Slovenia, republics and provinces in Yugoslavia were ethnically mixed. Each attempt to appease an ethnic minority on a republican basis meant the likelihood of ethnic minorities within the republics demanding self-determination. Any rewriting of borders or meeting of demands for ethnic self-determination would raise the specter of violent confrontation over issues of membership and citizenship.

The 1980s were a decade of rapid economic decline in Yugoslavia, with different regions bearing the brunt of the crisis. One analyst described the situation or more accurately situations as follows: "Whereas Slovenia enjoyed full employment and Croatia experienced a single-digit unemployment rate, unemployment reached 50 percent in Kosovo, 27 percent in Macedonia, 23 percent in Bosnia-Herzegovina, and over 20 percent in Serbia. Inflation soared, climbing to 50 percent in the early 1980s and then sky-rocketing to 1,200 percent in the late 1980s. Per capita income dropped by almost 50 percent between 1979 and 1988."[5]

To combat Yugoslavia's economic depression, its economy required far-reaching reforms that would liberalize it and better position it to engage in Western markets. But any policy of economic liberalization in the early 1980s would benefit more prosperous regions in Yugoslavia that were better poised to enter Western markets and disadvantage regions where industries were enmeshed in trade with the Socialist bloc and Third World.[6] The unequal consequences of liberalization drove demands in Slovenia and Croatia for radical decentralization and weakened their commitment to Yugoslav federal institutions that were essential for containing pressures for ethnic nationalism and addressing regional economic inequities. At the same time, the International Monetary Fund and World Bank—crucial to the success of liberalization— also undermined federal institutions by insisting on government reforms that eliminated consensus rules of decision-making, thus further alienating the republics of Slovenia and Croatia.[7]

Economic liberalization and its concomitant generation of demands for greater regional political power threatened the republic of Serbia, because it stood to fall further behind other more successful economic regions. Although a faction within the Serbian Communist party advocated economic modernization and political pluralism, such a program threatened the status of conservative hard-liners in the party. These Serbian conservatives allied themselves with Serbian intellectuals to create a powerful voice for Serbian nationalism. An intellectual movement centered in the Serb Academy of Arts and Sciences expressed alleged slights to the Serb nation, questioned the federal compromises that had kept Yugoslavia intact, and stated that all minorities in Yugoslavia should be subservient to Serbs.

The critical issue for manipulating a Serbian sense of grievance was the situation of Serbs in Kosovo, where they composed only about 10 percent of the population but systematically discriminated against the ethnic Albanian majority. The Serbian Communist party responded violently to Albanian demands for self-determination—a policy that provided a convenient vehicle for Milosevic to consolidate his grip on power and to divert attention from the extreme economic and political conditions facing his constituents. But Milosevic's policy of promoting Serbian nationalism provoked ethnic counteractions by Slovenes and Croats. In Croatia, opposition leader Franjo Tudjman rode a wave of virulent nationalism to power. In important ways Milosevic and Tudjman were necessary for each other; Milosevic's Serbian nationalism provided fertile ground for Tudjman's ethnic national appeals, which in turn reinforced Milosevic's ethnic warnings and diatribes.[8]

The end of the Cold War provided further impetus to calls for greater regional autonomy and self-determination. The first wave of democratic elections in Yugoslavia in 1990 brought to power several antidemocratic leaders. Serbian ethnic nationalism further drove demands for Slovenian and Croatian independence. Ethnic violence against Serbs in Croatia further exacerbated Serbian fears and strengthened Milosevic's power. In 1990 Slovenia and Croatia secretly negotiated weapons deals in Eastern Europe and began organizing paramilitary organizations. The remaining hopes of the federal government declined as economic adjustment measures failed to bring recovery. In June of 1991 Slovenia and Croatia declared their independence, prompting the first two wars of the former Yugoslavia.

The European Community (EC) attempted to take the lead in managing the conflicts and chose mediation as its main tool to end the wars.

The first EC mediator, Lord Peter Carrington, labored under three crippling constraints. First, his political masters, the governments of the EC member states, disagreed about the optimal solution to the conflicts—sovereignty for the republics or a multinational Yugoslavia. Second, Carrington was limited in the carrots he could use to persuade the parties to pursue their goals peacefully. Diplomatic recognition was an obvious incentive at his disposal, but EC member states differed on when and under what conditions they would grant international recognition of Slovenia and Croatia. Moreover, little thought was given to the impact recognition of these republics would have for the other republics in Yugoslavia, especially Bosnia and Macedonia. Third, Carrington was constrained by a lack of coercive threat—no state in Europe was willing to risk its soldiers to intervene in a hot war to enforce peace.[9] Given these constraints, sanctions became the tool of choice for Western policymakers who sought a low-cost, low-risk punitive alternative to military force.

American Policy and Sanctions in the Balkans: What and When?

For the most part, American application of sanctions in the Yugoslav crisis followed European initiatives. The exception to this generalization was the first American attempt to use economic leverage to produce political change in Yugoslavia, when in 1990 Congress adopted the Nickles amendment (PL 101–513), which promised to suspend direct aid to the Federal Republic of Yugoslavia (FRY) if human rights violations by Serbs against ethnic Albanians in Kosovo did not cease within six months. The sanction came into effect automatically on May 5, 1991, but was rescinded on May 24, when Secretary of State James Baker granted a waiver by certifying that Yugoslavia was complying with its obligations under the Helsinki Accords. Notwithstanding the issuing of the waiver, the State Department voiced concern over serious human rights violations by Serbian authorities against ethnic Albanians in Kosovo and Croats in Croatia, warned that aid would be provided on a selective basis, and suspended Overseas Private Investment Corporation (OPIC) insurance for new foreign investment in Serbia because of human rights violations.[10]

At the time that the Nickles amendment came into effect, the crisis in the former Yugoslavia was at a make-or-break point. Although the issue of human rights in Kosovo was important, it was simply one of several conflicts in Yugoslavia and was secondary to the larger problem of Yugoslavian disintegration. The amendment was counterproductive in two ways. First, as Warren Zimmerman, U.S. ambassador to

Belgrade at the time, observes, "It was aimed at the wrong target. To get at Serbia, it attacked Yugoslavia. Even worse, the only one hurt was Markovic [the Yugoslavian prime minister], the last hope for a peaceful and democratic solution. Milosevic got off scot-free; in fact, he gained, because he could circle his wagons around a brave little Serbia being bullied by the United States."[11] Second, American policy incoherence contributed to international policy incoherence. As Susan Woodward notes, while the United States temporarily imposed sanctions and threatened economic punishment against the Yugoslavian government, its European allies were trying desperately to cobble together an economic incentive plan that would lead to a peaceful outcome of the immediate secession crisis.[12]

With violence escalating between Croats and Serbs in Croatia and armed conflict beginning between the Yugoslavian National Army and militias in Slovenia and Croatia, the Bush administration, by authority of the Arms Export Control Act, followed the European Union (EU) in suspending the sale and transfer of arms to Yugoslavia on July 11, 1991. This act was more symbolic than substantive as the United States supplied insignificant amounts of weaponry to Yugoslavia. On September 25, 1991, the United States supported U.N. Security Council Resolution 713, which widened the EU arms suspension into a mandatory arms embargo on Yugoslavia. Even though the United States blamed the government of Serbia and the federal military as the culprits in the escalation of violence, the arms embargo was put in place against the successor states of Slovenia and Croatia and was continued toward Bosnia-Herzegovina when it declared its independence.

In October 1991 Congress attempted to force the pace of applying sanctions. Senators Claiborne Pell (D-R.I.), Robert Dole (R-Kans.), Larry Pressler (R-S.Dak.), and Alfonse D'Amato (R-N.Y.) introduced legislation that sought to "impose an embargo on the import of products from Serbia until Serbia has ceased its armed conflict with the other republics of Yugoslavia."[13] The Bush administration opposed the legislation, arguing that it removed its flexibility in responding to ongoing negotiations led by Carrington, that American trade with Yugoslavia was insignificant compared to that of the European Union and therefore a unilateral embargo would be diluted in its effectiveness, and finally, that it was extraordinarily difficult to shape a trade embargo that would hurt Serbia and be benign to the other republics.[14] These arguments seem to have won the day, as the bill languished in committee. Nonetheless, two months later, on December 6, 1991, President George Bush by executive order suspended trade preferences and aid and ended a bilateral trade agreement with Yugoslavia.

In January 1992 mediators negotiated a cease-fire between Serbs and Croats in Croatia. To consolidate the cease-fire, U.N. peacekeepers, including large contingents of British and French soldiers, were deployed there. But just as the conflict in Croatia seemed to dampen, war spread to Bosnia. The effect of German and then European recognition of Slovenia and Croatia was to strengthen the desire of Bosnian Muslims for an independent Bosnian state. Such a state was opposed by Bosnian Serbs who feared minority status in a state dominated by Muslims. The result of this intersection of interests was a heavily boycotted referendum for independence that passed in March 1992 and a three-way civil war among Bosnian Muslims, Croats, and Serbs, with the latter two populations aided by their neighboring national states.

The outbreak of war in Bosnia set the stage for the next round of sanctions. In May 1992 the United States persuaded the U.N. Security Council that Serbia was an aggressor in the Bosnian war. In reaction to the failure of Serbia to remove the Yugoslavian National Army from Bosnia, the Bush administration (by presidential order) suspended aviation rights for Yugoslavia's national airline, JAT, on May 20 and blocked all Serbian property or interests in property under U.S. jurisdiction on May 30. These moves followed pressure by Congress, where the Senate Foreign Relations Committee had voted unanimously on May 19 for a bill that would have suspended aviation rights for JAT.

The United States pressed for U.N. Security Council Resolution 757, which was adopted on May 30, 1992, and imposed comprehensive sanctions on Serbia and Montenegro. The sanctions targeted the import of all goods from and export of all goods into Serbia and Montenegro; banned their representation at international sport and cultural events; suspended scientific, technical, and cultural exchanges; and prohibited any financial transactions with the FRY. In order to blunt the effects of sanctions on vulnerable populations within Serbia and on its neighbors, exceptions were allowed for humanitarian flights, the supply of medicines and foods for humanitarian purposes, and transshipments of goods through the FRY.[15]

Sanctions against Serbia were explicitly wedded to the attempt to mediate an end to the war in April 1993. Dismayed at the Bosnian Serbs' unwillingness to accept the Vance-Owen peace plan—a patchwork quilt that blended partition and multiethnic provinces and reflected some Bosnian-Serb military gains—the United States, again in conjunction with the United Nations (Security Council Resolution 820), tightened existing sanctions in April 1993. The effect was to close various loopholes that had watered down the May 1992 sanctions, including strict regulation of transshipments across Serbia and the use of sanctions monitoring units to patrol waterways and borders.

As mediators began to drive a wedge between Milosevic and the Bosnian Serbs, the United Nations looked for ways to punish the latter and reward the former. After the Bosnian Serbs rejected the Contact Group plan of August 1994, Milosevic signaled his willingness to enforce an embargo against Serbian-held territory in Bosnia. On October 25, 1994, the United Nations extended the trade embargo (Security Council Resolution 942) to encompass Bosnian Serb–controlled areas of Bosnia-Herzegovina. After Milosevic allowed U.N. sanctions monitors to deploy along Serbia's border with Bosnia and upon reports that Serbia was upholding the embargo against the Bosnian Serbs, the United Nations eased the sanction provisions against air traffic to and from Serbia and the prohibition against Serbian participation in international sporting and cultural events. Trade sanctions against Yugoslavia were lifted on December 27, 1995, as a reward to Milosevic for signing the Dayton accords in November 1995. Remaining in place as of April 1998 is an "outer wall of sanctions" against Yugoslavia that deprives Serbia and Montenegro from membership in the World Bank and the International Monetary Fund. This "outer wall" remains as a hedge against Serbian reneging on the Dayton accords.

The Arms Embargo: Rationale and Effect

There was no apparent causal theory among problem, action, and solution in the decision to impose an arms embargo on the former Yugoslavia in September 1991. At that time diplomats explained the adoption of the arms embargo as "an effort to prevent Croatia and other secessionist republics from buying arms from other countries."[16] This was problematic in two ways. First, it was well known at the time that both Slovenia and Croatia already had acquired arms from Eastern Europe. Second, the policy rationale would lead one to think that Croatia was the problem. Secretary of State James Baker, however, blamed Serbia and the Yugoslav army, saying "they had the major responsibility for the violence splitting the state."[17] Baker added: "Clearly, the Yugoslav federal military is not serving as an impartial guarantor of a cease-fire in Croatia. On the contrary, it has actively supported local Serbian forces in violating the cease-fire, causing death to the citizens it is constitutionally supposed to protect."[18]

The only possible theory behind the arms embargo is what Susan Woodward calls the "wildfire" approach to wars—that their ends can be hastened by depriving them of fuel.[19] This approach has many admirers at the United Nations and is applied almost automatically to each and every outbreak of war in the world; for example in Angola in 1993 and Rwanda in 1994. The approach rarely goes beyond a public display of disapproval of violence; rarely are there any provisions of monitoring or punishment for violators of the embargo. Indeed, in many conflicts, U.N. member states who vote for the embargo turn around and violate it with impunity; Russia was the largest supplier of weapons to Angola during the arms embargo in 1993, and France continued to supply weapons to the Rwandan army in 1994 in violation of a U.N. arms embargo.

In the specific case of Yugoslavia, the arms embargo was largely ineffective, except against the one party deemed to be the victim of international aggression—Bosnia. The arms embargo clearly advantaged the Serbs, for they largely controlled the Yugoslav army and its assets. In addition, Serbia had the capability to produce weapons, thus lessening the need for external arms, and by the time the arms embargo was in place, Croatia already had been able to acquire arms from Eastern European sources. Also, since the arms embargo was not policed by international actors, receiving arms continued to be easy for Croatia. The only party meaningfully affected by the embargo was the Bosnian government, which, eventually was able to overcome this handicap through its tenuous partnership with Croatia, the tacit approval of the United States, and willing suppliers such as Iran, Turkey, and Saudi Arabia.

Once the embargo was put into place, it became hard to dislodge. By the time that international recognition was afforded to Slovenia, Croatia, and Bosnia-Herzegovina, U.N. peacekeepers were deployed between Croats and Serbs in Croatia. The United Nations insisted, with British and French government support, that to lift the embargo so that it only applied to Serbia and Montenegro would discredit the peacekeepers' neutrality and put them at risk. Since France and Britain, unlike the United States, had troops on the ground in the former Yugoslavia, they had a veto on lifting the embargo. And although one cannot find a public statement of such a policy, it was also alleged that America's NATO allies were adamantly opposed to a well-armed Islamic regime in Europe. Thus, even though Serbia was deemed the aggressor in Bosnia, the embargo applied to Bosnia as well as Serbia.

The arms embargo did serve several functions in bringing the war to a close, but these were not foreseen at the time of its imposition. First, the arms embargo increased the Bosnian government's dependence on Croatia. This provided the United States with leverage against the Bosnian government during peace negotiations at Dayton in 1995; if it refused to sign a peace agreement, the Croats could reduce substantially the ability of the Bosnian government to defend itself.[20] Second, the embargo provided the Americans with leverage against its allies.

An American threat to lift the embargo unilaterally probably was helpful in maintaining alliance cohesion behind continued imposition of economic sanctions, which, according to David Owen, France and Russia wanted to remove as early as late 1992 or early 1993.[21] If the Europeans had been successful in easing economic sanctions, the Americans would have had a less potent hand to play as mediator in 1995. Third, the desire of the U.S. Congress to lift the embargo unilaterally provided the United States with a more credible threat to lift the embargo, which according to some accounts helped to persuade the European allies to use force in 1995.[22]

These unanticipated benefits have to be weighed against the negative consequences of the embargo. First, the policy was a stain on international morality. By international law, the recognition of Bosnia-Herzegovina as a sovereign state entitled it to pursue self-help measures to assure its survival. As international legal scholar Lori Damrosch argues, the extension of the embargo to Bosnia was not in and of itself immoral, but necessarily implied the international use of force to defend Bosnia—a policy that never materialized.[23] Second, the embargo strained the partnership between the United States and its European allies, especially when the United States encouraged surreptitious arming of the Bosnian government and announced that it would no longer participate in the naval monitoring of the embargo.[24] Third, by keeping up the pretense of the embargo to satisfy its allies, the United States provided Iran with an opening to exploit with the Bosnian government. Fourth, the arms embargo (and European and American prevarication) have left relations between Europe and the Bosnian government extremely chilly.[25]

Economic Sanctions: Rationale and Effects

The United States perceived Milosevic as the biggest threat to peace in the Balkans. Privately, U.S. government officials asserted that sanctions could hurt the Serbian economy and create a public groundswell in opposition to Milosevic.[26] For the United States, sanctions also had value apart from affecting political opposition in Serbia. In Warren Zimmerman's words, the mere imposition of sanctions against Serbia would "Saddamize" Milosevic: they "could humiliate a dictator, making clear that he wasn't fit to deal with the civilized world."[27] The Americans intended for sanctions to show disgust with Milosevic and provide a means to "help push the Serbian people to turn on their leader."[28]

On the other hand, the European states and the mediators of the war clearly saw sanctions as a lever to prompt Milosevic's cooperation with a negotiated settlement. At the same time that sanctions were applied against Milosevic, the mediators began to perceive him as a pragmatist who could be persuaded to strong-arm the more extreme radical nationalist Serbs in Bosnia.[29] While the mediators sought flexibility and well-timed removal or sharpening of sanctions as a potential tool in the Balkan bargaining game, U.S. policy demonized Milosevic, thereby creating a powerful practical, strategic, and ideological block against the deftness of the sanctions tool. After all, if Milosevic was a dictator unfit to deal with the civilized world, how could one remove the sanctions without appearing to reward him? This contradiction was not addressed until November 1994, when the United States embraced the strategy of rewarding Milosevic in order to pressure the Bosnian Serbs.[30]

Based on these policy rationales, sanctions failed to achieve their aims with one notable exception—they did prove a valuable bargaining chip to separate Milosevic from the Bosnian Serbs and to help deliver Milosevic to sign the Dayton agreements. They failed to create a mass opposition movement against Milosevic within Serbia. They had the exact opposite effect of making Milosevic a pariah unfit to deal with the civilized world; the strategy of sanctions against Serbia brought Milosevic center stage and made him the fulcrum for a negotiated peace in the Balkans.

Although the imposition of economic sanctions coincided with the collapse of the Serbian economy, it is difficult to assess their contribution to the collapse. Before the imposition of sanctions, Serbia's economy was in terrible condition and in need of drastic surgery. Moreover, the war itself drained the Serbian economy—by the end Serbia itself housed nearly 700,000 refugees—and destroyed normal trading relations between it and the former republics of Yugoslavia, which had accounted for 40 percent of Serbia's prewar trade.[31]

A RAND report written in 1994 also assessed the effects of the sanctions:

> By all accounts, the progressive tightening of the economic blockade has shattered the Serb economy. Gross national product and industrial production are a fraction of pre-crisis levels. Unemployment and inflation (perhaps 20,000 percent per month) have reached catastrophic rates. Shortages of basic commodities, including fuel and foodstuffs are now widespread. The civilian transport system has been crippled, with serious consequences for the distribution of critical commodities, including foodstuffs in which Serbia is normally self-sufficient. By technical measures, the economic sanctions are probably working as well as anyone could expect.[32]

Analysts disagree on how tightly the sanctions were applied. David Owen in his memoirs complained about the porousness of the sanctions; his complaints are echoed in a publication by the Carnegie Commission for the Prevention of Deadly Conflict.[33] U.N. monitors recorded numer-

ous violations between Macedonia and Serbia in 1994, and a story in the
Economist reported the gleeful statements of Serbia's minister of small
business about the ease of sanctions-busting.[34] This was despite the use
of NATO's Standing Naval Force Mediterranean and the innovative use
of sanctions assistance missions, coordinated through a central communications office in Brussels.[35] These missions each contained two or more
professional customs officers on secondment from Organization for
Security and Cooperation in Europe (OSCE) countries, who were
assigned to supervise river entries and border crossings into Serbia.[36]

Those who argue that the sanctions were inadequately policed miss
two points. First, sanctions-busting itself imposes a burden on the target, by raising transaction costs and adding layers of profits for those
willing to do the risky and arduous work of evading sanctions. Second,
the removal of sanctions became a sine qua non for any hope of Serbian
economic recovery. By sealing Serbia from access to investment capital
and international loans, the sanctions ensured that no economic recovery was possible.

Removal of Sanctions

The Bosnian case illustrates a basic lesson about sanctions: When they
are applied multilaterally, but without clarity about their purpose or
underlying causal theory, important differences will appear very
quickly about when and under what circumstances to lift them. Such
differences pose one of the biggest difficulties in creating a sense of
overriding sustained commitment to sanctions.

Trade sanctions had been in place less than six months when the Rus-
sians began to float the idea of reducing them as a means of influencing
the Yugoslav elections of December 1992. In March 1993 the French advocated their removal as a means of rewarding Milosevic for his support of
the Vance-Owen plan. Disagreements between the Americans and Europeans arose before Dayton over the timing of lifting sanctions: whether
they should be removed to induce Milosevic to sign or whether they
should be lifted only at the successful conclusion of the negotiations.

Throughout 1996, after the removal of most of the sanctions, disagreements occasionally arose over whether sanctions should be reimposed to punish Serbian lack of compliance with Dayton. Although the
Americans held out the possible return of sanctions to punish the Serbs,
there was nowhere near the early alliance consensus that had existed in
1992 about their value.

The "outer wall" of sanctions still remains against Serbia and Montenegro. A 1996 report of the South Balkans Working Group of the

Council on Foreign Relations Center for Preventive Action recommends that its removal should be clearly linked to "the normalization of relations among the successor states of the former Yugoslavia; full compliance with the Dayton agreement; cooperation with the International War Crimes Tribunal; and implementation of confidence-building and normalizing measures in Kosovo."[37] Although the Clinton administration began to repeal the remaining sanctions in March 1998 to reward Milosevic for supporting a new moderate government in Bosnia, renewed violence in Kosovo prompted it to back away from concessions and press its allies to reimpose trade and financial sanctions. The only European state that supported reimposition was Great Britain; in the end, the United States settled for a U.N. arms embargo on Serbia.

Recent assessments of Serbia's economy continue to paint a grim picture. Estimates put per capita income around $1,600, down from $3,000 in 1990; official unemployment is 26 percent, with unofficial estimates at double that. The official trade deficit in 1996 was $2.2 billion. In the words of one European diplomat, "There's nothing underpinning the economy—no liquidity, no realistic likelihood of foreign investment, no chance of raising taxes. . . . The economy is so close to chaos that at any moment it could spin out of control."[38] And while the economic free fall seemed to galvanize the Serbian opposition in the early winter of 1996–97, by the summer of 1997 Slobodan Milosevic seemed ensconced in power once again.[39]

Evaluation: Conflict Prevention

Analysts suggest several roles for sanctions in conflict prevention: to signal disapproval of a government's behavior toward other countries or its own citizens; to fulfill an obligatory step toward a tougher policy; to limit a state's freedom of action and motivate the state to stop bad behavior; and to punish or take a toll on the target state.[40]

As a tool of conflict prevention in the former Yugoslavia, the sanctions were obviously weak. The conflict itself already had become violent when the sanctions were imposed. Critics are probably correct that far from being an immediate deterrent to aggression, sanctions sent a signal of weakness to those committed to violent secession and to those committed to the use of force to maintain the Yugoslavian state. Susan Woodward's appraisal is on the mark: "Sanctions were an obvious solution to this dilemma of moral pressure without strategic interest—between the major powers' refusal to become militarily involved and the growing pressure for action from domestic publics outraged by their countries' apparent indifference to the particular immorality and injustice of the war."[41]

If sanctions are considered by the standards mentioned earlier, it is easy to see why they did little to prevent or dampen the conflict in the Balkans. The Nickles amendment had the potential to signal disapproval toward Serbian aggression in Kosovo, but it directed attention and punishment toward the Yugoslav government, not the Serbian one. Moreover, the amendment came much too late in the day and was too limited in its focus to serve as a useful tool of conflict prevention. Economic sanctions could have been tied to a strategy of conflict prevention, but those who would have applied them first would have had to recognize that there were several culprits in the Balkan drama deserving of international approbation. The war was not made solely by the Serbs; the Croats and Slovenes were also instigators of the war. Sanctions as a tool of prevention would have had to reflect the complexity of the conflict.

Second, while sanctions may be a necessary obligatory step toward a tougher policy—a box to check—they also can be applied without any reasoned connection to a theory of how they will prevent or mitigate conflict, or whether the mitigation of conflict should take precedence over other competing goods, such as justice. This was clearly the case with the arms embargo. Moreover, that case shows that while sanctions may be applied as a necessary step to gather support for tougher measures, policymakers can be held hostage by sanctions that take on a rationale of their own. This is especially the case when sanctions are locked in by U.N. Security Council vote.

The sanctions in 1991–92 also failed to meet the third and fourth goals of prevention: the limitation of a state's freedom of action and the punishment of the target state. Given the high stakes in the Yugoslav secession debate of 1991 and that organized violence already had taken place, thus raising fears and security concerns, and given that it always takes time for sanctions to work, it was unreasonable to believe that they could prevent or mitigate conflict in Yugoslavia.

Evalution: Conflict Resolution

Sanctions played a supporting role in the bargaining that ended the war in Bosnia in 1995. Their most important effect on the battlefield calculations of the warring parties was to separate Milosevic from the Bosnian Serbs and to deliver him to sign the Dayton agreement. The sanctions-induced split of the Serbs decreased the war-fighting capacity of the Bosnian Serbs; it also allowed large-scale military counteroffensives by the Croatians and Bosnians in summer 1995 to seize large swaths of territory without invoking Serbian military intervention on behalf of their Bosnian brethren.

Sanctions per se seemed to have little effect on the Bosnian Serb willingness to negotiate an end to the war. According to General Rupert Smith, commander of U.N. troops in Bosnia in 1995, the imposition of sanctions against the Bosnian Serbs and the willingness of Milosevic to enforce them dramatically weakened the Bosnian Serbs.[42] This weakness, however, had the unintended consequence of prompting the Bosnian Serbs to attempt to win the war outright in the summer of 1995 while they still held a decisive advantage in heavy weaponry. Smith therefore believed that the United Nations and NATO would have to use coercion to stop the Bosnian Serb summer offensive and convince them to negotiate. Subsequent events proved Smith correct; not until the Croatian army counteroffensive and subsequent ethnic cleansing of the Croatian Krajina and the protracted NATO air strikes of August and September 1995 did the Bosnian Serbs buckle to Milosevic's insistence on a negotiated settlement. The agreement at Dayton seemed to vindicate the strategy of using sanctions to punish Milosevic and to pressure him into pulling the plug on his former allies in Bosnia.

This evaluation is at odds with that of many experts on Yugoslavia who feel that the sanctions were counterproductive to the termination of the war. Scholars such as Susan Woodward and Steven Burg and journalists such as Misha Glenny ascribe various negative effects of the sanctions for resolving the conflict. According to these analysts, sanctions drove Serbians together by casting communal blame on all Serbians, thereby consolidating Serbian identity and paranoia. Sanctions were said to enable the Serbian state and Milosevic to seize greater economic power, by necessitating their more active role in managing the economy. They also were said to provide Milosevic with a scapegoat for Serbia's economic woes, to create a mafia class that benefited from sanctions, and to undercut the emergence of a democratic opposition and peace movement by cutting off external sources of information.

The negative evaluation of the effect of sanctions on war termination rests on questionable assumptions about Serbian elite calculations, economy, and society in the absence of sanctions. At heart, the negative critique rests on different assumptions about what strategy should have been substituted instead of sanctions.

Some of the criticisms seem niggling and either attribute too much effect to sanctions or confuse their effects with the effects of the war. For example, sanctions may have helped to consolidate a sense of Serbian nationalism and paranoia, but it is hard to imagine that in the absence of sanctions, Serbian nationalism and paranoia would have been reduced sufficiently that an effective peace movement would have quickly constrained its leadership. Likewise, to say that sanctions strengthened the Serbian state by giving it more economic decision-making power, by making it take a more assertive role in the economy, and by handing it the power to decide on allocation of scarce resources misses an obvious point. Given the formidable economic problems facing Serbia in the early 1990s, and given the proclivity of countries at war to become more statist in their economic decision-making, it was highly unlikely that private business and civil society would have increased its levers on power in the absence of sanctions. Again, while sanctions likely reduced the ability of Serbians to receive information through external, critical media and thus reinforced extreme Serbian nationalist interpretations of the conflict, the so-what question remains. How likely was outside information to bring forth the latent, unrecognized power of those Serbians who wanted peace? Given what we know about psychological distortions in human cognition—especially the biased assimilation of information—it seems highly unlikely that the presence of alternative information would have been sufficient to sway millions of Serb proto-nationalists.

Most important, the evaluation of sanctions comes down to judgments about Milosevic's decision-making. In the absence of economic isolation and in the face of the devastation of Serbia, would he have been likely to apply overwhelming pressure on the Bosnian Serbs and abandon the Croatian Krajina Serbs in 1995? Or to put it somewhat differently, if the effects of sanctions were so positive for the Serbian authorities, if their effects were so reinforcing of Serbian nationalism, and if their effects created a politically powerful mafia caste enriched by the sanctions, then why did Milosevic sign the Dayton accords?

On the issue of appropriateness of sanctions as a tool of strategy, critics see them as too soft or too harsh. Those who assert the latter argue that in 1991 the CSCE should have enunciated clearly specific norms that would guide their decisions about recognition, equally pressured all who sought to undermine CSCE norms (this would have included the leadership of Slovenia and Croatia), and assisted all those who wanted a peaceful, unified Yugoslavia. This begs the question of whether any amount of external incentives could have altered the strength and initiative of the nationalists and separatists. Those who argue that sanctions were too soft must acknowledge the fundamental calculations made by the states of Europe and the United States—that their national interests were not sufficiently engaged to warrant the risk of bolder military intervention. Finally, both alternatives require a degree of allied unity of analysis and prescription that was nowhere to be found in 1991. The governments of Europe and the United States disagreed about the content and practicality of various settlements to the crisis. The result was mixed messages, policy incoherence, and actions that seemed to fan the conflict instead of resolve it.

Conclusion

The most straightforward assessment of the sanctions against the former Yugoslavia is the most accurate. Although the sanctions failed miserably to prevent or mitigate the violence in the Balkans, they contributed to the war's termination by raising the costs to Serbian President Slobodan Milosevic of continuing to support the Bosnian Serbs. That such sanctions could not by themselves have delivered a negotiated settlement does not detract from their role in making peace. Sanctions proved a useful tool for bringing Milosovic to distance himself from his Bosnian Serb allies and to deliver them at the Dayton negotiations. The Bosnian case, like that of Zimbabwe in 1979, shows that after sanctions have been in place and taken a toll, the inducement of removing them provides useful leverage to a would-be mediator.[43]

To argue that sanctions contributed to bringing the war to an end does not imply that they were the optimal policy tool for war termination or that they were the normatively best tool. The critics of sanctions are right; there were more effective policy tools at the disposal of the United States and its European allies. But the effectiveness of those tools, whether the use of military force or hard-nosed insistence on established institutional rules of recognition, also required a degree of allied unity and commitment that did not exist. Sanctions then were a convenient tool not only for states concerned with appearing to be doing something for the benefit of domestic constituents appalled at the war but unwilling to risk blood and treasure to stop the killing. They were also convenient for states that felt compelled to act multilaterally but did not possess the unity and conviction to act forcefully.

Alas, American policymakers have not learned these lessons. When violence flared in Kosovo in March 1998, once again raising the specter of war in the region, American diplomacy reflexively turned to sanctions. In response to long-simmering political instability, an increasingly active and lethal armed independence movement in the province, and Serbian search-and-destroy tactics that kill both guerillas and civilians, the United States threatened renewed trade sanctions against Serbia. American diplomats failed, however, to explain how such sanctions would address ethnic Albanian demands for Kosovar independence, the security fears of the small minority Serbian population in the province, or the strategy of armed insurrection by Kosovar guerrillas. Although European governments resisted calls for renewed economic sanctions, no coherent strategy or conflict prevention emerged. Instead, the United States urged the reimposition of a U.N. arms embargo against Serbia, despite admissions by diplomats that both the Serbian army and the Kosovar guerrillas had ample weapons to engage in civil war. Once again the United States and its allies chose an irrelevant policy with little connection to the violence it sought to prevent. And once again American and European officials could engage in remarkable self-deception and verbal gymnastics and describe their policy as a powerful symbolic deterrent.

Notes

1. Elizabeth S. Rogers, "Economic Sanctions and Internal Conflicts," in Michael E. Brown (ed.), *The International Dimensions of Internal Conflicts* (Cambridge, MA: MIT Press, 1996), pp. 424–25; and John Stremlau, *Sharpening International Sanctions: Toward a Stronger Role for the United Nations*, A Report to the Carnegie Commission on Preventing Deadly Conflict (New York: Carnegie Corporation of New York, November 1996), pp. 25–30.

2. Susan L. Woodward, *Balkan Tragedy: Chaos and Dissolution After the Cold War* (Washington, DC: Brookings Institution, 1995), pp. 289–94 and 384–88; Misha Glenny, *The Fall of Yugoslavia: The Third Balkan War* (New York: Penguin, 1994), pp. 210–12; Steven L. Burg, "The International Community and the Yugoslav Crisis," in Milton J. Esman and Shibley Telhami (eds), *International Organizations and Ethnic Conflict* (Ithaca, NY: Cornell University Press, 1995), p. 245; Vojin Dimitrijevic and Vojin-Jelena Pejic, "U.N. Sanctions Against Yugoslavia: Two Years Later," in Dimitris Bourantonis and Jarrod Wiener (eds.), *The United Nations in the New World Order: The World Organization at Fifty* (London: Macmillan, 1995), pp. 124–53.

3. Thus Glenny, pp. 210–211, describes the effects of sanctions as "a waste of time" that strengthened Milosevic's political position, weakened the Serbian opposition, and accrued political capital for Milosevic within Serbia. Yet on p. 227 Glenny asserts that a public statement by the United States and other international actors in November 1992 that sanctions would be removed if Milosevic was defeated in forthcoming elections might have changed the election results in December 1992, thus implying sanctions were having an effect, that they were swaying opinion against Milosevic, and that the promise of removal was a potent weapon against him.

4. Thus Burg writes that "sanctions proved to have little effect"; similarly, Dimitrijevic and Pejic write that "sanctions are a total failure."

5. Ivo Daalder, "Fear and Loathing in the Former Yugoslavia," in Brown, *International Dimensions*, p. 42.

6. Woodward, *Balkan Tragedy*, pp. 58–67.

7. Ibid., pp. 67–74.

8. This dynamic is captured in Laura Silber and Allan Little, *Yugoslavia: Death of a Nation* (New York: Penguin, 1997).

9. James Gow, *Triumph of the Lack of Will: International Diplomacy and the Yugoslav War* (New York: Columbia University Press, 1997), pp. 46–66.

10. "U.S. Policy Toward Yugoslavia, May 24, 1991," *U.S. Department of State Bulletin*, June 3, 1991, pp. 395–96.

11. Warren Zimmerman, *Origins of a Catastrophe: Yugoslavia and Its Destroyers—America's Last Ambassador Tells What Happened and Why* (New York: Times Books, 1996), p. 131.

12. Susan L. Woodward, "Redrawing Borders in a Period of Systemic Transition," in Esman and Telhami, *International Organizations and Ethnic Conflict*, p. 209.

13. *Sanctions Legislation Relating to the Yugoslav Civil War, S.1793*, Hearing Before the Committee on Foreign Relations, United States Senate, 102nd Congress, First Session, October 16, 1991 (Washington, DC: Government Printing Office, 1992), p. 1.

14. Testimony of Ralph Johnson, Deputy Assistant Secretary of State for European and Canadian Affairs, ibid., pp. 4–17.

15. The text of the resolution is in Fred Tanner (ed), *Effects of International Sanctions* (Malta: Mediterranean Academy of Diplomatic Studies, January 1996), pp. 79–85.

16. "U.N. Bars Weapons Sales to Yugoslavia," *New York Times*, September 26, 1991, p. A3.

17. Ibid.

18. Ibid.

19. Woodward, *Balkan Tragedy*, p. 290.

20. Anthony Borden and Drago Hedl, "Twenty-One Days at Dayton: A Special Report," *War Report* (March 1996).

21. David Owen, *Balkan Odyssey* (New York: Harcourt Brace, 1995), pp. 57 and 125.

22. See especially Bob Woodward, *The Choice* (New York: Simon and Schuster, 1996), pp. 264–270.

23. Lori Fisler Damrosch, "The Collective Enforcement of International Norms Through Economic Sanctions," *Ethics and International Affairs* 8 (1994), p. 69.

24. Daniel Williams, "Bosnia Embargo Decision Puts U.S. Loyalty in Doubt," *Washington Post*, November 12, 1994, p. A21.

25. See, for example, the reporting of Timothy Garten Ash, "Bosnia in Our Future," *New York Review of Books*, December 21, 1995, pp. 27–31.

26. Blaine Harden, "Milosevic Viewed as U.N.'s Target," *Washington Post*, May 31, 1992, p. 1.

27. Zimmerman, *Origins*, pp. 213–14.

28. Ibid.

29. Owen, *Balkan Odyssey*, pp. 124–25.

30. Contrast, for example, statements by Clinton officials on November 26 that castigate European allies for their desire to lift sanctions against Milosevic with statements on November 28 that embrace rewarding Milosevic in order to get a settlement. For the former, see Daniel Williams, "U.S. at Odds

with Europe over Sanctions on Serbia," *Washington Post,* November 27, 1994, p. A22; for the latter, see Daniel Williams and Ruth Marcus, "U.S. Favors Making Concessions to Serbs," *Washington Post,* November 29, 1994, p. 1.

31. Both figures are in Julia Devin, Jaleh Dashti-Gibson, and George A. Lopez, "Sanctions in the Former Yugoslavia: Convoluted Goals and Complicated Consequences," in Thomas G. Weiss, David Cortright, George A. Lopez, and Larry Minear (eds), *Political Gain and Civilian Pain: Humanitarian Impacts of Economic Sanctions* (New York: Rowman and Littlefield, 1997). This article provides a thorough analysis of the deleterious effects of the sanctions on the Serbian population.

32. RAND Corporation, "American Policy Toward the Balkan Crisis: Economic Instruments and Options," mimeo., pp. 51–52. This is one of the best analyses of the effects of the sanctions and implications for American policy at the time.

33. Owen, *Balkan Odyssey,* p. 363, and Stremlau, *Sharpening International Sanctions,* pp. 29–30.

34. "Beating the Sanctions on Serbia," *The Economist,* July 2, 1994, p. 49.

35. For a description of NATO's role in sanctions enforcement, see Gow, *Triumph,* pp. 129–31.

36. Stremlau, *Sharpening International Sanctions,* p. 29; M. A. Napolitano, "Sanctions as a Preventive Diplomacy Instrument," in Fred Tanner (ed.), *Effects of International Sanctions,* pp. 23–28. Ambassador Napolitano was the EU/OSCE Sanctions Coordinator.

37. Barnett R. Rubin (ed.), *Toward Comprehensive Peace in Southeast Europe: Conflict Prevention in the South Balkans* (New York: Twentieth Century Fund Press, 1996), p. 13.

38. Jonathan C. Randal, "Weak Economy Restrains Milosevic," *Washington Post,* January 19, 1997, p. A37.

39. Tracy Wilkinson, "After Triumph in Streets, Serb Opposition Crumbles," *Los Angeles Times,* June 10, 1997, p. A1.

40. Stremlau, *Sharpening International Sanctions,* p. vi.

41. Woodward, *Balkan Tragedy,* p. 290.

42. Smith's views on the course of the war, the effects of sanctions against the Bosnian Serbs, and the implications for their strategy are described in Jan Willem Honig and Norbert Both, *Srebrenica: Record of a War Crime* (New York: Penguin, 1997), pp. 144–45, and David Rohde, *Endgame: The Betrayal and Fall of Srebrenica, Europe's Worst Massacre Since World War II* (New York: Harper/Collins, 1997), pp. 339–40, pp. 419–20.

43. See, for example, Stephen John Stedman, *Peacemaking in Civil War: International Mediation in Zimbabwe, 1974–1980* (Boulder, CO: Lynne Rienner 1991), pp. 165–204.

Conclusion: Lessons and Recommendations

Richard N. Haass

THIS FINAL chapter is divided into two parts. The first is analytical and addresses what is to be learned from the eight cases discussed in this volume and, more generally, from the use of economic sanctions as an instrument of American foreign policy in the post–Cold War era. Ten basic lessons are posited. The latter section sets forth 12 guidelines meant to inform future decisions to employ sanctions and goes on to suggest what the U.S. government, including both the executive branch and Congress, needs to do to translate these principles into effective policy.

Lessons

1. *Sanctions alone are unlikely to achieve desired results if the aims are large or time is short.* This lesson tends to all but rule out the use of sanctions to reshape the basic nature of another society or to alter policy in critical areas of another country's or entity's national security. The same realities preclude using sanctions to resolve crises or any "time-sensitive" situation. For these reasons, sanctions also are unlikely to be of much utility in moderating civil wars, which, by their nature, tend to be all-or-nothing struggles that develop quickly and are resistant to (if not impervious to) external influences.[1]

Evidence supporting these assertions is plentiful. Sanctions—even when they were comprehensive and enjoyed almost universal international backing for nearly six months—failed to get Saddam Hussein to withdraw from Kuwait. In the end, doing so took nothing less than Operation Desert Storm. Other sanctions also have fallen short of their stated goals. The Iranian regime remained defiant in its support of terrorism, its subversion of its neighbors, its opposition to the Middle East peace process, and in pressing ahead with its nuclear weapons program. Fidel Castro continued in place atop a largely authoritarian political system and a statist economic counterpart. Pakistan's nuclear program advanced significantly; it produced enough material for at least a dozen bombs. Libya refused to produce the two individuals accused of responsibility for the destruction of Pan Am Flight 103 over Lockerbie. Sanctions could not persuade Haiti's junta to honor the results of an election. Nor could they dissuade Serbia and others to call off their military aggression for several years. And, nearly a decade after Tiananmen Square, China continued to export sensitive, proliferation-related technologies to selected countries and remained a society where human rights were often violated.

2. *Under the right circumstances, sanctions nevertheless can achieve (or help to achieve) various foreign policy goals ranging from the modest to the fairly significant.* Sanctions introduced against Iraq in the aftermath of the Gulf War clearly have increased Iraqi compliance with resolutions calling for the complete elimination of its weapons of mass destruction. Such sanctions also have much diminished Iraq's ability to import weapons and weapons-related technology of any sort. The result is that Iraq today is considerably weaker militarily and economically than it would have been without these sanctions.

The other cases examined here show that sanctions have accomplished substantive ends even if they did not achieve the stated and often ambitious objective. In the former Yugoslavia, sanctions were one factor contributing to the Serbian decision to accept the Dayton agreement in August 1995. China appears to have shown some restraint in exporting nuclear and ballistic missile parts or technologies to countries other than Pakistan. Sanctions have constituted a drag on the economies of Iran, Cuba, and Libya and may, with the passage of more time, contribute to change in those societies or in their behavior. U.S. sanctions against Pakistan, while having little or no discernible effect on its nuclear weapons program, have hurt Pakistan both economically and militarily. Again, though, the difference in the apparent effect of the China and Pakistan sanctions is instructive. It is extremely difficult to alter the decisions of a would-be proliferating country such as Pakistan, which is likely to see nothing less than its national security or even survival at stake. Sanctions, no matter how draconian, are almost certain to fail. At the same time, limited sanctions might be more helpful against suppliers (such as China), for whom the interests at stake are partly or even mostly economic and in any event less than vital.

It is important to add that sanctions can be more effective when used in conjunction with other policy tools, especially the credible threat or use of military force. The former Yugoslavia is a case in point. Sanctions alone were unable to bring Serbia to the table, but sanctions along with North Atlantic Treaty Organization (NATO) air power and Croatia's successful ground offensive were enough to persuade the government in Belgrade that the time had come to settle. Military attacks along with sanctions may have dampened Libyan enthusiasm for sponsoring terrorism. Sanctions against Iraq, by limiting its ability to acquire military technology and equipment, rendered it a less capable foe once those sanctions gave way to Desert Storm; similarly, sanctions and periodic uses of military force appear to have persuaded Saddam for a time not to attempt any dramatic breakout from his predicament.

As noted at the outset of this volume, sanctions can be used for several sometimes overlapping purposes: to coerce, to deter, and/or to punish. The cases suggest that the ambitious and common use of sanctions—for coercive or "compellent" purposes—rarely succeeds, especially as the size of the objective grows. There is also another problem with using sanctions for the purpose of persuading the target to alter or cease a specified activity or behavior. By their nature, coercive sanctions leave the initiative in the hands of the target, which may decide that holding firm to its position or behavior is preferable to giving way. The United States, as the sending or sanctioning party, then has to decide among three options: giving up and dropping the sanctions, staying the course despite a lack of desired effect, or turning to military force.

By contrast, punitive sanctions almost always "succeed" in the limited sense that they impose some costs on the target. (Whether this cost is greater than the cost to the sender is another matter.) One advantage of any punitive action is that unlike sanctions meant to either coerce or deter, it keeps the initiative in the hands of the sender who decides "how much is enough." The disadvantage of punitive sanctions is that they tend not to alter the behavior much less the nature of the target, although it is almost always true that any sanction implemented for punitive purposes also is designed to coerce or even deter. The punitive dimension of sanctions thus becomes something of a fallback, the minimum purpose if more ambitious aims prove overly risky beyond reach. This appears to have been what happened in nearly every case studied in this volume.

The utility of threatening sanctions in order to deter unwanted behavior is the most difficult to assess, as one must endeavor to demonstrate the relationship between what was threatened and what did not happen. This said, threats of sanctions appear to have little effect on behavior, especially if the area of concern is of major importance to the target. Thus it is possible to claim that Pakistan would have tested nuclear weapons in the absence of a threat of additional sanctions, that China may have proceeded with additional exports of proliferation-related technologies, or that the Serbs might have done even more damage. But with the possible exception of China, where certain signs of some restraint suggest that the fear of additional sanctions may have had an impact, and Iran, where secondary U.S. sanctions appear to have discouraged European and Japanese firms from investing there, the cases examined here do not provide strong evidence that threatened sanctions carry a great deal of weight.[2] India's decision to test nuclear devices in 1998 in the face of threatened sanctions further reinforces this point.

3. *Unilateral sanctions are rarely effective.* All of the cases, with the exception of Iraq and the former Yugoslavia, involve sanctions that are in part or in whole unilateral. The critical issue here is a general lack of effectiveness. In a global economy, unilateral sanctions tend to impose greater costs on American firms than on the target, which usually can find substitute sources of supply and financing. Unilateral sanctions did, however, have more of an economic effect on Haiti and Cuba, which were heavily dependent on trade with the United States. They also hurt Pakistan, which was receiving substantial U.S. military and economic aid. Such impact is a far cry from realizing the desired aims of the sanctions, however. As a rule, unilateral sanctions will be little more than statements or expressions of opposition except in those instances in which the tie between the United States and the target is so extensive that the latter cannot adjust to an American cut-off.

The problem is that garnering international support for particular sanctions often is extremely difficult. Prospects for succeeding in bringing others on board tend to reflect a range of factors, including their commercial stakes, policy preferences, and the availability of funds to compensate lost revenues. Sanctions tend to work best when international political consensus exists as to their wisdom and when non-targeted countries that must bear an economic cost as a result of the sanctions are compensated. In most instances, other governments prefer no or minimal sanctions. Other countries tend to value commercial interaction higher than does the United States and are less willing to forfeit it voluntarily. In addition, the notion that economic interaction is desirable because it promotes more open political and economic systems is an argument that normally has more resonance in other capitals. (I say "normally" because this argument has been deployed successfully to defeat attempts in Congress to revoke China's most-favored-nation [MFN] status.) Such thinking makes achieving what is desirable, namely multilateral support for sanctions, less feasible than the United States tends to want. It usually takes something truly egregious—Saddam's invasion and occupation of Kuwait, incontrovertible support of terrorism such as in the Lockerbie case, the brazen rejection of Haiti's election results and associated widespread human rights abuses—to overcome this antisanctions bias. And even in the case of Iraq, generous compensation for affected states, such as Egypt and Turkey, was a prerequisite for these government's and others sustaining support for sanctions.

Trying to compel others to join a sanctions effort by threatening secondary sanctions against those third parties unwilling to sanction the target can cause serious harm to a variety of U.S. foreign policy interests. Congress, in large part because unilateral sanctions tend to be ineffective, is increasingly turning to secondary sanctions to bolster unilateral sanction regimes. This is what has happened with Cuba, Iran, and Libya; in all three instances, sanctions now apply to overseas firms that violate the terms of the U.S. legislation. This threat has had some deterrent effect on the willingness of certain individuals and firms to enter into proscribed business activities, but at a significant political price. It has increased anti-American sentiment, stimulated challenges that have the potential to jeopardize the future of the World Trade Organization, distracted attention away from the provocative behavior of the target governments, and made Europeans less likely to work with us in shaping policies to contend with post–Cold War challenges.

4. *Sanctions often produce unintended and undesirable consequences.* Several of the cases examined here underline this conclusion. Haiti is a prime example. Sanctions increased the economic distress on the island, which stimulated a massive exodus of people from Haiti to the United States—an exodus that proved life-threatening for Haitians and expensive and disruptive for Florida. In the former Yugoslavia case, the arms embargo had the effect of weakening the Bosnian (Muslim) side, given the fact that Bosnia's Serbs and Croats had larger stores of military supplies to begin with and greater access to additional supplies from outside sources. This military imbalance contributed to the fighting and to the disproportionate suffering of the Bosnian side. Military sanctions against Pakistan actually may have increased Pakistan's reliance on a nuclear option, both because the sanctions cut off Islamabad's access to U.S. weaponry and because they dramatically weakened Pakistani confidence in its traditional relationship with Washington.

What all this demonstrates is that sanctions can be blunt instruments. Traditionally, most sanctions do not discriminate within the target country. There is a rationale for this, one that reflects the reality that funds and goods can easily be moved around a society or that government often can command what is in the hands of others. The problem with such a broad-brush approach is that sanctions tend to affect those not necessarily responsible for making the policy—that is, the people—while those elites that are responsible—be they in the government, the dominant political organization, the military, or some similar entity—remain largely unaffected given their ability to skirt the sanctions.

This was clearly the case in Haiti, where the average Haitian suffered far more than the leaders of the junta. To some extent it is the reality in many of the other cases, where leaderships are able to insulate themselves. The danger (beyond missing the true target) is both moral, in that innocents are affected, as well as practical, in that sanctions that harm the population at large can bring about undesired effects that include strengthening the regime, triggering large-scale emigration, and retarding the emergence of a middle class and civil society. Mass hardship also can weaken domestic and international support for sanctions, such as is the case with Iraq, despite the fact that the sanctions have included from the outset a provision allowing the country to import humanitarian goods and services.[3]

Smart or "designer" sanctions are at best a partial solution. It is possible that Haiti's military leaders were bothered by the fact their families could no longer shop in Florida. And clearly executives who risk being denied access to the United States under the provision of Helms-Burton legislation think twice before entering into proscribed business deals. Sanctions aimed at firms similarly can affect their calculations. The problem is that the opportunities to employ sanctions effectively yet with great precision are rare. Gathering the necessary knowledge about assets and then moving quickly enough to freeze them often proves impossible. Leaders and governments have many ways to insulate themselves. Especially when the target is an authoritarian state run by a relatively few individuals, designing sanctions that can meaningfully penalize leaders but spare the general population is extraordinarily difficult.

It is important to note as well that the costs of sanctions transcend narrow calculations. Sanctions against Iraq tend to decrease world energy supply, thereby maintaining a higher price for oil than would otherwise be the case. The same holds for sanctions against Iran, especially because U.S. sanctions prevented the construction of gas pipelines in Central Asia that would need to cross Iran. Thus another cost of the Iran sanctions is that they add to the burden of the newly independent states of the former Soviet Union. The United States, as a result of sanctions against Iran, Libya, and Cuba, also incurs a political price in strained relations with its principal political and economic allies. Jeopardizing the future of the World Trade Organization—something that could result from the European Union's reaction to the Helms-Burton legislation—needs to be added in here, as well. The costs of sanctioning Haiti also need to include the cost of coping with refugees and, depending on one's view of events, the costs of the military intervention that came in the aftermath of sanctions and the refugee outflow.

5. *Sanctions can be expensive for American business, farmers, and workers.* There is a tendency to overlook or underestimate the direct cost of sanctions, perhaps because the costs of intervening with sanctions (unlike the costs of military intervention) do not show up in U.S. government budget tables. Sanctions do, however, affect the economy by reducing revenues of U.S. companies and individuals. Moreover, even this cost is difficult to measure because it needs to reflect not simply lost sales but also forfeited opportunities stemming from governments and overseas companies electing not to do business with the United States for fear that sanctions might be introduced and thereby interrupt the supply of spare parts or otherwise complicate or prohibit normal commercial relations.

Still, and although precise figures do not exist, it seems reasonable to estimate that sanctions cost U.S. companies billions of dollars a year in lost sales and returns on investment. One recent study concludes that in 1995 alone, sanctions cost U.S. companies between $15 billion and $19 billion, in the process affecting some 200,000 workers.[4] China has made a point of awarding lucrative contracts (e.g, aircraft purchases) to Europeans to signal displeasure with U.S. sanctions. U.S. individuals and firms also are forfeiting a chance to invest in Cuba, Iran, and Libya while Europeans and others do so. Iraq is a different case; the comprehensive, multilateral nature of the sanctions has meant that any opportunity cost has been borne by all members of the international community and not by Americans alone.

6. *Authoritarian, statist societies are often able to hunker down and withstand the effects of sanctions.* All eight of the case studies involve states that are, to one degree or another, authoritarian. Almost all are what can be termed statist in the economic sense. Sanctions appear not to have moved them noticeably and may have even increased governmental control over the population. The reasons for this phenomenon may be several: Sanctions sometimes trigger a rally-round-the-flag nationalist reaction; sanctions, by creating scarcity, enable governments to better control distribution of goods; and sanctions create a sense of siege that governments then exploit to maintain political control. This conclusion is consistent, too, with literature suggesting that market economic reform reinforces the development of civil society; sanctions, by reducing the scope for independent action, can work against forces promoting political pluralism.[5]

7. *Military enforcement can increase the economic and military impact (although not necessarily the political effect) of a given sanction.* The sanctions against Iraq, for example, were far tighter than they would have been had compliance been voluntary. Indeed, leakage was greatest along those routes such as Jordan where international presence and enforcement were relatively weak. Similarly, sanctions against Serbia were weakened by the absence of a strong, land-based military force to compel compliance and intercept contraband. Armed enforcement is not always an option, though. It applies primarily to trade sanctions, requires the full cooperation of neighboring states if it is to work, and risks a wider conflict with the target state, something that would, for example, preclude any such action against a country such as China.

8. *Sanctions can increase pressures to intervene with military force when they are unable to resolve the crisis at hand.* Such pressure was welcomed by the Bush administration in the aftermath of Iraq's invasion of Kuwait, a position that reflected concern over what the passage of time would mean for coalition cohesion (not to mention the survival of Kuwait and its people). In this instance, the imposition of sanctions and their inability to persuade Saddam Hussein to depart Kuwait had added benefits: They provided time for coalition military preparations to take place and then made it less difficult for the Bush administration to build domestic and international support for the use of military force.

In the case of Haiti, the inability of sanctions alone to persuade the military junta to step down and respect the results of the elections built political pressures in the United States to go ahead with a military invasion. Some of the pressures resulted from opposition to immigration, others from violations of human rights. Potentially considerable loss of life on all sides was averted only at the eleventh hour when the junta backed down and the "invasion" became consensual rather than resisted.

The former Yugoslavia is a third case in which the fact that sanctions alone could not achieve the desired end in a relatively short period of time increased pressures on the United States to take additional action. In this instance, action took the form of NATO air attacks on Bosnian Serb positions.

What all three of these cases have in common is that sanctions were introduced in response to a crisis rather than amid what might be described as an ongoing situation. Only when time is of the essence will the inability of sanctions alone to accomplish policy goals lead to demands for escalation to military force. Otherwise, and as the remaining cases show, the American public appears willing to tolerate sanctions even though they do not appear to be accomplishing their stated purpose.

9. *Sanctions tend to be easier to introduce than lift.* This is true no matter if the sanction is established through a U.N. Security Council resolution or a law passed by Congress and signed by the president. Such inertia is not unique to sanctions; it is always more difficult to change the status quo than continue with it when the burden of acting falls on those favoring change. Removal of a sanction is possible when a situation resolves or clearly reverses itself—such as was the case in Haiti following the invasion and occupation—but this is the exception. More often, the problems that led to sanctions in the first instance may linger or even diminish but not disappear. In such circumstances, it is often difficult or impossible to build a consensus for rescinding the sanctions, even if there has been some progress on the matter of concern, if the sanctions have been shown to be feckless or counterproductive, or if other interests can be shown to suffer as a result. This consequence may be seen as desirable, as it is in the case of Iraq, where the United States favors the continuation of U.N. sanctions. Or it may be judged unhelpful, a position held by critics of U.S. sanctions toward China, Iran, or others. The Bosnia case involves a powerful example of the danger of locking in sanctions, as the inability to amend or lift U.N. Security Council sanctions that prevented the provision of military support to all protagonists in the Bosnian war overwhelmingly worked to the disadvantage of the weaker Bosnian side.

10. *"Sanctions fatigue" tends to settle in over time, and as it does, international compliance tends to diminish.* In part this is because the issue that led to sanctions being introduced loses its emotional impact. International support for sustaining sanctions fades as the cumulative cost of maintaining the sanctions mounts. Concerns over the humanitarian impact of sanctions also weakens resolve. At the same time, the target of the sanctions has time to adjust. Working around sanctions, import substitution, and the gradual improvement of living standards due to adaptation all make sanctions bearable. All of these factors have eroded the impact of sanctions against Iraq, Libya, and Cuba. Interestingly, fatigue seems to be less of a factor in diluting American support for sanctions (be they unilateral or multilateral), perhaps because sanctions tend to get "locked in" and the domestic political costs of removing them become overwhelming.

Recommendations

1. *Economic sanctions are a serious instrument of foreign policy and should be employed only after consideration no less rigorous than what would precede any other form of intervention, including the use of military force.* The

likely benefits of a particular sanction to U.S. foreign policy should be greater than the anticipated costs to the U.S. government and the American economy. Moreover, how the sanction is likely to affect U.S. interests should compare favorably to the likely consequences of all other policies, including military intervention of various sorts, covert action, public and private diplomacy, or doing nothing. In particular, policymakers ought to consider carefully the pros and cons of a policy of economic engagement as opposed to one of broad penalization and isolation. If properly structured, an approach that would involve a mix of narrow sanctions and continuing political and economic interactions that were both limited and conditional might be preferable, especially if the goal is to weaken the near monopoly of an authoritarian leadership presiding over a country that does not pose a threat to U.S. interests.

A corollary to this injunction is no less important: *Broad sanctions should not be used as an expressive tool in a manner not justified by a careful accounting of likely costs and benefits.* Again, sanctions are serious business. There is a tendency to see them as "below" use of military force on some imagined ladder of foreign policy escalation. This tendency needs to be revised. Sanctions are a form of intervention. Depending on how they are used, they can cause great damage to innocent men, women, and children.[6] They also can cause great harm to U.S. business, workers, and foreign policy interests. I wrote in a previous book that foreign policy is not therapy and that the purpose of foreign policy is not to feel good but to do good. The same holds for sanctions.[7]

2. *Multilateral support for economic sanctions normally should constitute a prerequisite for their introduction by the United States.* Such support need not be simultaneous, but it should be all but certain and likely to follow with little delay. Unilateral sanctions should be avoided except in those circumstances that the United States is in a unique situation to derive leverage based on the economic relationship with the target. This is not so much a normative assertion as a pragmatic one, based on the overwhelming evidence that unilateral sanctions achieve little yet tend to cost the United States more than the target. Implementing this guideline will require intense, often high-level diplomatic effort and even then may not succeed. If this is so, then the task for policymakers is to compare what can be achieved by weaker sanctions as opposed to some alternative policy course.

One instrument that can increase compliance is the provision of assistance to third parties in order to offset the economic cost of implementing sanctions. Arrangements to compensate countries whose support for the sanctions is central thus can be critical. This was the case with the Iraq sanctions; it is possible that sanctions against Haiti might have proved stronger had the Dominican Republic been more cooperative. Greater use should be made of Article 50 of the U.N. Charter, which sets forth a means by which third-party states hurt by sanctions aimed at another state can approach the Security Council for redress. In addition, a fund for this purpose should be established within the U.S. foreign assistance budget. Given the current assistance budget, this money should be additional rather than come out of already underfunded aid accounts.

A call for greater multilateralism is not identical to a requirement to seek U.N. Security Council backing. Indeed, the United States should be careful about bringing sanctions to the Security Council. Although U.N. endorsement can buttress international compliance and complicate the task of any party seeking to ease sanctions—Iraq comes to mind here—it also can place the United States in the difficult position of having to choose between continued compliance with a policy judged to be no longer desirable or acting unilaterally in defiance of the Security Council, a step the United States is understandably reluctant to take, as it could create precedents easily abused by others. Bosnia is just such a case, forcing the United States to stand by a discredited arms embargo lest it set a precedent for unilateral abrogation that would be emulated by others to the detriment of U.S. interests elsewhere.

3. *Secondary sanctions or boycotts are not a desirable means of bringing about multilateral support for sanctions and should be avoided.* Instituting sanctions against those who do not comply with the sanctions at issue is an admission of a diplomatic failure to persuade. It is also an expensive response. The costs to U.S. foreign policy, including the state of relations with major partners and U.S. efforts to build an effective World Trade Organization, almost always outweigh the potential benefits of coercing friends to join sanctions in situations when the United States favors sanctions and they do not.

4. *Economic sanctions should focus to the extent possible on those responsible for the offending behavior or on penalizing countries in the realm that stimulated sanctions in the first place.* There are several reasons for a response that focuses on the unwanted behavior: It helps avoid jeopardizing other interests and the entire bilateral relationship with the target over one area of disagreement; it causes less collateral damage to innocents; and it makes garnering multinational support less difficult. Sanctions designed to stem the proliferation of weapons of mass destruction are a prime example. Where there are transgressions, the United States should direct any sanction against activity in this realm, for example, by cutting off technological cooperation or trade in this

area. Alternatively, political responses (event boycotts, visa denials, etc.) might be the best way to signal opposition to selected behavior when no appropriate economic or military sanction is available.[7] The Soviet Union was clearly stung by the U.S. decision not to go to the Moscow Olympics in the wake of the Soviet invasion of Afghanistan—just as the U.S. decision to oppose China's hosting the Olympic Games (to protest human rights performance) angered Beijing. China is clearly bothered, too, by being singled out in various international bodies over how it treats its own citizens. Political sanctions should not, however, extend to the breaking of diplomatic relations or the cancellation of high-level meetings. Such interactions help the United States as much as the targeted party and should not be taken away as if they benefited only the target.

5. *Sanctions should not be used to hold major or complex bilateral relationships hostage to a single issue or set of concerns.* This is especially the case with a country such as China, where the United States has to balance interests that include maintaining stability on the Korean Peninsula, discouraging any support for the weapons of mass destruction or ballistic missile programs of rogue states, managing the Taiwan-China situation, and promoting trade, market reform, and human rights. A nearly identical argument could be made about the wisdom (or lack thereof) of applying broad sanctions against Russia because of its transgressions in one or another realm. Similarly, the United States has a range of interests with Pakistan that go well beyond nuclear matters, including promoting democracy, economic development, and regional stability. The alternative to broad sanctions in such instances is to adopt sanctions that are narrow and germane to the issue at hand. In the case of Pakistan, this would have argued for focusing sanctions on specific defense articles and technologies but exempting all economic assistance and military education and training.

6. *Humanitarian exceptions should be included as part of any comprehensive sanctions.* In part this is a moral judgment, that innocents should not be made to suffer any more than is absolutely necessary. In part, including an exception that allows a target to import food and medicine should make generating and sustaining domestic and international support easier. A caveat requires mentioning in this regard, though. Sanctions should not necessarily be suspended if the humanitarian harm is the direct result of cynical government policy that creates shortages among the general population in order to create international sympathy.

7. *Any use of sanctions should be as swift and as purposeful as possible.* As is the case with other forms of intervention, including the military,

gradual escalation allows the target to adapt and adjust. Such an approach also tends to forfeit shock value. In the case of sanctions, it also allows asset shifting, hoarding, and the negotiation of arrangements to circumvent sanctions. This guidance is borne out by the Libya and Iran cases. Still, this recommendation is easier to suggest than to follow, as gaining international support for sanctions in many cases will require that the United States move in a slow and gradual manner. One result of this reality is to further limit the potential effectiveness of economic sanctions in today's world.

8. *Policymakers should prepare and send to Congress a policy statement not unlike the reports prepared and forwarded under the War Powers Act before or soon after a sanction is put in place.* Such statements should be clear as to the purpose of the sanction; the required legal and/or political authority; the expected impact on the target, including possible retaliatory steps; the probable humanitarian consequences and what is being done to minimize them; the expected costs to the United States; prospects for enforcing the sanction; the degree of international support or opposition that can be anticipated; and an exit strategy, that is, the criteria for lifting the sanction. In addition, policymakers should be able to explain why a particular sanction was selected as opposed to other sanctions or other policies altogether. If need be, portions of this report could be classified secret if necessary to avoid providing information that would be useful to the target. Any sanction initiated by Congress should be approved only after hearings in the relevant committees carefully considered the matter, thereby allowing voting members to refer to a report accompanying the proposed legislation that addresses these same questions.

9. *All sanctions embedded in legislation should provide for presidential discretion in the form of a waiver authority.* Such discretion would allow the president to suspend or terminate a sanction if he judged it was in the interests of national security to do so. Beyond being consistent with the Constitution's bias in favor of executive primacy in the exercise of the foreign affairs power, such latitude is needed if relationships are not to become hostage to one interest and if the executive is to have the flexibility needed to explore whether the introduction of limited incentives can bring about a desired policy end. The benefits of this latitude outweigh any diminution of the deterrent power inherent in automatic sanctions. Current legislation that mandates sanctions in specific circumstances should be repealed or modified.

10. *The federal government should challenge the right of states and municipalities to institute economic sanctions against companies and individuals operating in their jurisdiction.* The Constitution may not settle the strug-

gle between the executive and legislative branches over the foreign affairs power, but it limits the struggle to the federal branch of government. As a result, those states and municipalities that are adopting "selective purchasing laws" that prohibit public agencies from purchasing goods and services from companies "doing business" in or with particular target countries are overstepping their bounds.[9] To paraphrase Justice Louis Brandeis, states may be laboratories of democracy, but not of foreign policy.[10] In addition to foreign policy consequences, such local action creates difficult and expensive choices for U.S. businesses. If the courts will not decide this issue, then U.S. businesses would be wise to approach Congress for a remedy.

11. *U.S. intelligence capabilities must be reoriented to meet the demands created by sanctions policy.* The ability to design and implement so-called smart sanctions will require extraordinary collection requirements. Knowledge of where individuals and firms maintain financial assets will be critical. Improved collection of both signals (communications) and human intelligence is essential. But the demand for more and better intelligence support of sanctions policy involves analysis as well as collection. A sanctions analysis unit should be established within the intelligence community. Such a dedicated unit, to be located within the Central Intelligency Agency's Directorate of Intelligence, could prepare predictions of the likely impact of sanctions on the target state and others. Analysts could help identify particular vulnerabilities of target states or leaders. Predictions also could be extended to examine likely reactions or retaliation by the target as well as likely responses of third parties. It also could monitor the impact of a sanction over time. The results of such monitoring could be drawn on for the compilation of an annual sanctions impact statement (as suggested here just below).

12. *Any sanction should be the subject of an annual impact statement.* Such a statement, to be prepared by the executive branch and submitted in unclassified form to Congress, should provide far more in the way of information and analysis than the pro forma documents written to justify many current sanctions. It should include an assessment of the extent to which the sanction had served its purposes; the economic, political, and/or military impact on the target; the humanitarian effect on the population of the target country; the reactions of the target country; the degree of international compliance and noncompliance; the financial costs to U.S. businesses, workers, and the government; and any other perceived costs and benefits of any sort (including foreign policy costs) to the United States. Such a report also should judge whether the original aims continue to make sense and whether sanctions continue to be an appropriate policy tool. An annual report along these lines, much

as the report that would accompany any new sanctions, would introduce much-needed rigor into the sanctions decision-making process. A more careful calculation of economic costs also would furnish a basis for determining payments to workers and companies that are being asked to bear a disproportionate share of the sanctions burden.[11]

The fact that it is even necessary to suggest the need to mandate reports to accompany economic sanctions when they are being proposed or renewed represents an indictment of the way sanctions now are being introduced and maintained. Seriousness is not a hallmark of the American embrace of economic sanctions. To the contrary, sanctions often are employed and maintained with only cursory analysis of their likely or actual effects. This is bad policy, for all sanctions involve costs for the U.S. government, its citizens, or both. Again, it is essential that the likely benefits of a sanction outweigh the inevitable and potential costs, including that of retaliation, and appear more attractive than any other available policy instrument. If such rigorous assessment is undertaken, sanctions are likely to become less common. This will not be a bad thing; with sanctions as with many other things in life, less can be more.

Notes

1. Several of the lessons and recommendations put forward here, including calls for modesty in objectives and seriousness in analysis, are included in Gary Clyde Hufbauer, Jeffrey J. Schott, and Kimberly Ann Elliott, *Economic Sanctions Reconsidered: History and Current Policy*, 2nd ed. (Washington, DC: Institute for International Economics, 1990), pp. 94–105. Several of the recommendations are also included in draft legislation, the "Enhancement of Trade, Security, and Human Rights Through Sanctions Reform Act," introduced in both the House of Representatives and the Senate in late 1997.

2. The Clinton administration argues that the Iran-Libya Sanctions Act has discouraged European and Asian investment in Iran's oil and gas sector. See the testimony of Alan Larson and David Welch before the House International Relations Committee on July 23, 1997.

3. See Thomas G. Weiss, David Cortright, George A. Lopez, and Larry Minear (eds), *Political Gain and Civilian Pain: Humanitarian Impacts of Economic Sanctions* (Lanham, MD: Rowman and Littlefield, 1997).

4. See an unpublished paper by Gary Clyde Hufbauer, Kimberly Ann Elliott, Tess Cyrus, and Elizabeth Winston, "U.S. Economic Sanctions: Their Impact on Trade, Jobs, and Wages" (Washington, DC: Institute for International Economics, 1997).

5. See, for example, Seymour Martin Lipset, "Some Social Requisites of Democracy: Economic Development and Democracy," *American Political Science Review* 53 (March 1959); Stephan Haggard and Steven B. Webb (eds.), *Voting for Reform: Democracy, Political Liberalization and Economic Adjustment* (Oxford: Oxford University Press, 1994); and Larry Diamond and Marc C. Plattner (eds.), *Economic Reform and Democracy* (Baltimore, MD: Johns Hopkins University Press, 1995).

6. It is for this reason that those most concerned with the moral dimension of foreign policy are willing to support the use of broad economic sanctions only in narrow circumstances. America's Catholic bishops, for example, argue that comprehensive sanctions should be considered ". . . only in response to aggression or grave and ongoing injustice, after less coercive measures have been tried, and with clear and reasonable conditions set forth for their removal." The bishops also argue that sanctions should be targeted as much as possible to avoid harming innocents; that "the denial of basic human needs may not be used as a weapon"; and that consent to the sanctions by substantial portions of the affected population is morally relevant. See National Conference of Catholic Bishops, "The Harvest of Justice Is Sown in Peace: A Reflection of the National Conference of Bishops on the Tenth Anniversary of *The Challenge of Peace*" (Washington, DC: United States Catholic Conference, 1994), p. 15.

7. One recent article discussing the growing role of economic sanctions in American foreign policy was titled "Chicken Soup Diplomacy." See *National Journal*, January 4, 1997, pp. 13–17.

8. See Gary Clyde Hufbauer and Elizabeth Winston, "Smarter Sanctions: Updating the Economic Weapon," *National Strategy Reporter* 7, no. 2 (Summer 1997).

9. See David Schmahmann and James Finch, "The Unconstitutionality of State and Local Enactments in the United States Restricting Business Ties with Burma (Myanmar)," *Vanderbilt Journal of Transnational Law* 30, no. 2 (March 1997), pp. 175–207.

10. It is worth quoting from Brandeis's dissent. "It is one of the happy incidents of the federal system that a single courageous state may, if its citizens choose, serve as a laboratory; and try novel social and economic experiments without risk to the rest of the country." As is clear, Brandeis omits foreign policy from his position. *New States Ice Co. v. Liebmann*, 285 U.S. 262, 311 (1932).

11. See report of President's Export Council prepared with the assistance of Don Zarin and Meha Shah, *Unilateral Economic Sanctions: A Review of Existing Sanctions and Their Impacts on U.S. Economic Interests with Recommendations for Policy and Process Improvement* (Washington, DC: President's Export Council, June 1997), p. 19.

Index